T0237283

An Introduction to Design Science

Paul Johannesson • Erik Perjons

An Introduction to Design Science

Second Edition

 Springer

Paul Johannesson
Stockholm University
Kista, Sweden

Erik Perjons
Stockholm University
Kista, Sweden

ISBN 978-3-030-78134-7   ISBN 978-3-030-78132-3   (eBook)
https://doi.org/10.1007/978-3-030-78132-3

This Springer imprint is published by the registered company Springer Nature Switzerland AG.
The registered company address is: Gewerbestrasse 11, 6330 Cham, Switzerland

Preface to the Second Edition

We have been very grateful for the positive response to *An Introduction to Design Science* and were happy to undertake the writing of a second edition. Much research on design science has been carried out since the first edition, and an update on the literature was needed. Beyond updating the literature, we have introduced a number of changes and additions that will help to make the book even more useful to students of design science:

- Added a chapter (Chap. 14) with a new case study on digital health consultations, replacing the previous case.
- Added a number of sections on practical guidelines for carrying out basic design science tasks, for example, describing artefacts and formulating research questions.
- Modified the design science canvas for concise presentations of design science projects in order to make it easier to apply.
- Added a discussion on the notion of design principles as a kind of design science contribution.
- Added a discussion on design thinking and its relationship to design science.
- Extended the motivation and descriptions of artefact classifications.
- Made many minor updates in order to improve language, clarity, precision, and consistency.
- Updated and extended the companion web site at https://introtodesignscience. wordpress.com/.

We would like to add some acknowledgements to those made in the preface to the first edition. In particular, we are grateful for discussions with and comments from Ilia Bider, Alan Davidson, Andreas Paulsson, Anders W. Tell, Jakob Tholander, Thomas Westin, and Helena Zhemchugova.

Stockholm, Sweden   Paul Johannesson
Stockholm, Sweden   Erik Perjons
April 2021

Preface to the First Edition

This book is an introductory text on design science. It is intended to support both researchers and students in structuring, undertaking, and presenting design science work. The book does not presume any prior knowledge of design science.

Chapter 1 provides an overview of design science and outlines its relationships with empirical research. Chapter 2 discusses the various types and forms of knowledge that can be used and produced by design science research. Chapter 3 gives a brief overview of common empirical research strategies and methods. Chapter 4 introduces a method framework for supporting researchers in doing design science research as well as in presenting design science results. The framework includes five activities, which are described in detail in Chaps. 5–9. Chapter 10 discusses how to communicate design science results. Chapter 11 compares the proposed method framework with methods for systems development and shows how they can be combined. Chapter 12 discusses how design science relates to research paradigms, in particular to positivism and interpretivism. Finally, Chap. 13 discusses ethical issues and principles for design science research.

The book offers an introduction to design science, and almost all of the topics covered can be pursued to a much deeper level. In order to help readers to find their way through relevant works, the sections on further reading provide numerous pointers to the literature. Furthermore, complementary multi-media material can be found at the book's web site at http://introtodesignscience.wordpress.com/.

The book builds on established design science methods as well as recent work on presenting design science studies and ethical principles for design science. The book also offers novel instruments for visualising design science results, both in the form of process diagrams and through a canvas format.

The authors would like to thank Birger Andersson, Maria Bergholtz, Ilia Bider, Shengnan Han, Martin Henkel, Benkt Wangler, and Monica Winge for discussions and constructive feedback on earlier versions of this text. A special thanks to Göran Goldkuhl who has introduced us to new perspectives on design science and its role in work practices. Many thanks to Carol de Groot for her commitment to improving the language of the text and to Ralf Gerstner for supporting the entire book writing project.

Stockholm   Paul Johannesson
September 2014   Erik Perjons

Contents

Chapter 1
Introduction

Empirical research describes, explains, and predicts the world. For example, the Linnaean taxonomy describes the kingdoms of animals and plants and classifies them into classes, orders, families, genera, and species. Newton's laws are able to explain the motion of planets, the trajectories of missiles, and the reasons for tides. Meteorology can predict rainfall, storms, and other weather phenomena.

In contrast to empirical research, design research is not content simply to describe, explain, and predict. It also aims to change the world, to improve it, and to create new worlds. Design research does this by developing artefacts that can help people fulfil their needs, overcome their problems, and grasp new opportunities. In this endeavour, design research creates not only novel artefacts but also knowledge about them, their use, and their environment.

This book is about a strand of design research, called design science, which mainly has its origins in the fields of information systems and IT. Design science in these areas aims to create novel artefacts in the form of models, methods, and systems that support people in developing, using, and maintaining IT solutions. Although this book focuses on design science as applied to IT, it also includes examples from and perspectives of other fields of human practice. Since design science is used to create artefacts that address problems experienced by people, the rest of this chapter will introduce and relate the notions of people, practices, problems, and artefacts.

1.1 People, Practices, and Problems

Most of the activities that people carry out are structured in orderly and meaningful ways, i.e. they are not performed in isolation but are grouped together into coherent clusters called practices. A *practice* is a set of human activities that are performed regularly and are seen as meaningfully related to each other by the

© Springer Nature Switzerland AG 2021
P. Johannesson, E. Perjons, *An Introduction to Design Science*,
https://doi.org/10.1007/978-3-030-78132-3_1

people participating in them. One example is the practice of dentists, who engage in cleaning teeth, drilling teeth, taking X-rays, and many other activities. When people engage in practices, they typically need to handle both natural and man-made objects. For example, dentists and dental nurses repair teeth and therefore make use of pliers, drills, X-ray machines, and other tools. Another example of a practice is cooking, in which people cut fruit, fry meat, boil vegetables, and so on, while using stoves, refrigerators, pans, and other kitchen utensils.

Some practices are *purposive practices*, in the sense that they have goals that exist in the environment outside the practice itself; they produce something of value to people who are not participants in the practice. One example is a car manufacturing practice, which makes cars that are used by people who do not participate in the manufacturing. But there are also *self-contained practices* that provide value only to their participants, e.g. a game that is fun and interesting to its players but not to anyone else.

When people engage in practices, they may experience practical problems. A *practical problem* is an undesirable state of affairs, or more precisely a gap between the current state and a desirable state, as perceived by the participants in a practice. This desirable state is seen as better than the current one because it allows people to be more successful when engaging in the practice. An example of a practical problem in the practice of dentistry is that some patients find that their dental fillings fall out after a period of time; there is the current state in which some dental fillings tend to fall out, and there is a more desirable state in which dental fillings always stay put. The practical problem perceived by dentists is the gap between these two states.

Many practical problems are challenging to grasp and address because they are fuzzy, unclear, and complicated. These are often called *wicked problems*, meaning that they are difficult or impossible to solve due to incomplete knowledge and the complex interplay between related problems. There is no definitive formulation of a wicked problem. For example, the problem of poverty can be expressed and reframed in many different ways, such as in terms of absolute or relative deprivation, access to economic or cultural wealth, or social mobility. Furthermore, there is no "stopping rule" that tells us when a wicked problem has been solved; in principle, any additional effort may improve on a solution to a wicked problem. Thus, a problem solver stops working on a wicked problem not because it has been solved but due to external considerations, such as a lack of time or resources.

Wicked problems can be contrasted with *tame problems*, which are problems that can be stated with all the information required to understand and solve them, and for which there exist clear criteria for determining whether they have been solved. Many engineering problems are tame problems, e.g. designing an algorithm that sorts a list of letters alphabetically or constructing a bridge of a certain length and height. In contrast, social and practical problems are often wicked, and they need to be addressed with methods that can be quite different from those used to address tame problems. In particular, problem analysis and requirements definition are key concerns when handling wicked problems, as discussed in Chap. 5.

A problem is not always an obstacle to be overcome—it can also be a puzzling question or an unexpected circumstance that could provide an opportunity for improvement. Thus, there are two kinds of problems: firstly, there are those in which the current state is viewed as genuinely unsatisfying and the desirable state is seen as neutral, e.g. having a toothache or a flat tire; secondly, there are those where the current state is seen as neutral and the desirable state is regarded as a potentially huge and surprising improvement. Problems of the second kind are often not perceived until some innovation arises and captures people's imagination, and they realise that their current practice is inadequate and needs to be improved. An example is the invention of X-rays, which gave doctors the means to overcome the problem of not being able to view the inside of the human body. To summarise, the term "problem" is used here to denote troublesome situations as well as promising opportunities. It could be argued that "challenge" or "practical challenge" would be better choices of word than "problem" and "practical problem", but this book sticks with the latter terms, as these are well established.

1.2   Artefacts as Solutions to Problems in Practices

When faced with a practical problem, people may react to it in different ways. One option is to adopt a stoic attitude and just accept the problem as a fact of life without trying to do anything about it. The other extreme would be to view the problem as being so severe that the entire practice, or at least part of it, should be abandoned. One example is bloodletting, which was an established practice in medicine for centuries but ceased when evidence mounted regarding its adverse health effects. However, the most common reaction to a practical problem is to try to find some, often partial, solution to it.

In many cases, practical problems can be solved by means of artefacts. An *artefact* is defined here as an object made by humans with the intention that it be used to address a practical problem. Some artefacts are physical objects, such as hammers, cars, and hip replacements. Other artefacts take the form of drawings or blueprints, such as an architect's plan for a building. Methods and guidelines can also be artefacts, e.g. a method for designing databases. A common aspect of all these artefacts is that they support people when they encounter problems in some practice.

There are a plethora of artefacts in the IT area, ranging from algorithms, logic programs and formal systems over software architectures, information models and design guidelines to demonstrators, prototypes, and production systems. In the early years of IT, most artefacts were developed for military and business practices. However, in recent times, some of the most innovative IT artefacts have been designed for everyday practices, such as keeping in touch with friends, sharing and organising photos, or playing games.

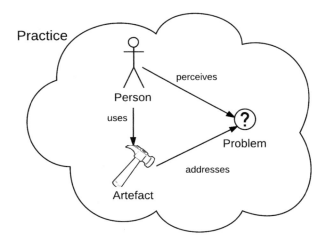

Fig. 1.1 People, practices, problems, and artefacts

The relationships between people, practices, problems, and artefacts are illustrated in Fig. 1.1. People engage in practices in which they may perceive problems that can be addressed by means of artefacts. Thus, artefacts do not exist in isolation but are always embedded in a larger context, a practice, in which people act to achieve their goals.

1.3   The Context and Anatomy of Artefacts

Every artefact has an inside, an outside, and an interface between the inside and outside. More precisely, each artefact has an inner structure that can produce certain behaviours, and these can offer functions for people in the *intended practice* of the artefact, i.e. the practice that encompasses the practical problem that the artefact addresses.

1.3.1 Functions

The *functions* of an artefact are what it can do for its users, what benefits it can bring to them in their practice, what role it can play for them, and how it can support them in their activities. For example, a function of a clock is to tell the time, a function of a lawn mower is to cut grass, and a function of a truck is to transport goods. The functions of an artefact can be seen as its raison d'être—the artefact has been created to offer its functions.

1.3.2 Behaviours

In order to be able to provide its functions, an artefact must be able to perform certain *behaviours*. A behaviour is typically an action that an artefact is able to carry out. For example, some of the behaviours of a truck are rolling, accelerating, braking, turning, and honking. However, in a broader sense, a behaviour is not necessarily about an action performed by the artefact—it may also be about a state of affairs that the artefact is able to bring about. For example, a painting can bring about feelings of joy or sadness in a person viewing it. In this case, the painting exhibits these behaviours although it does not actively carry out any action.

Some behaviours of an artefact are essential for its functions, e.g. the above behaviours of a truck are all required for its main function, which is to transport goods. However, an artefact may also exhibit behaviours that are not relevant to any of its functions, e.g. the truck may make engine sounds and emit fumes, which are behaviours that are not needed for its transport function. While a behaviour is simply something that an artefact can do or bring about, a function is something that the artefact can do to benefit its users in some practice. In this sense, a function is a relative concept that connects the behaviours of an artefact with the goals and activities of its users.

1.3.3 Structures

In order to produce its behaviours, the artefact has to be constructed and configured in a certain way. The *structure* of an artefact is about its inner workings, the components it consists of, how these are related, and how they interact with each other. Typically, an artefact is constructed from smaller parts that are assembled in such a way that they can interact with each other and produce the artefact's behaviours. One example is a clock, which is constructed from cogwheels, watch-hands, and other mechanical parts. Another example would be a truck, which is made of a chassis, an engine, wheels, and other parts that are all arranged in such a way that the truck is able to carry out its behaviours.

1.3.4 Environments and Effects

While the structure of an artefact is about its inside, its *environment* is about the outside, i.e. the external surroundings and conditions in which the artefact will operate. The environment of an artefact always encompasses its intended practice, including the people and other objects participating in this practice. The environment may also include other practices that are affected by the use of the artefact, as well as various other objects that are not related to any specific practice. For example, the environment of a truck includes the goods transportation practice, i.e. the intended practice. If the truck passes through areas in which kids are playing, the practice of children playing becomes a part of the truck's environment. Moreover, the environment includes the physical surroundings of the truck, including the streets and the air.

When an artefact is used in a practice, it will have certain *effects* on its environment, i.e. it will change it in intended as well as in unintended ways. The intended effects are related to the functions of the artefact, e.g. the intended effect of using a truck is that some goods are moved from one place to another. Using an artefact may also have unintended effects, often called *side effects*. These effects may concern not only the intended practice of the artefact but also other practices, sometimes with adverse consequences for them. For example, a truck passing through an area where children are playing may pose such a hazard to safety that the play has to stop. Side effects may also be harmful to other valuable resources even if these are not used directly in any specific practice. Emissions from trucks pollute the air, which may indirectly harm many practices.

Figure 1.2 illustrates how an artefact is situated within an environment, which may include several practices. The artefact offers its functions to the intended practice, but it may have side effects for this as well as for other practices. Thus, an artefact may have many *stakeholders*, i.e. people participating in practices that are affected by it.

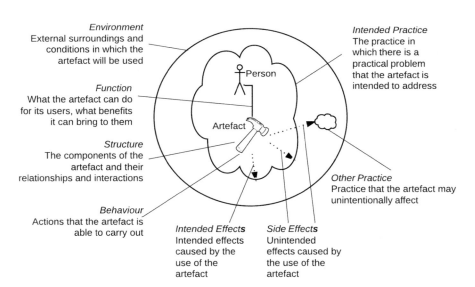

Fig. 1.2 Structure, function, and environment

1.3.5   *From Structure to Function*

A common guiding principle in the design of an artefact is to hide its structure from its future users and instead to focus on its functions. Users should not need to care about the internal structure of the artefact but only about its functions, i.e. how it can serve them. Ideally, users should not even be aware of the structure. One example is a clock, which someone can use without needing to know whether it is constructed using mechanical parts or electronic components. Throughout the history of IT, the idea of hiding the internals of an artefact has been repeatedly applied with labels such as encapsulation, object orientation, information hiding, and service-oriented architectures.

When designing an artefact, a designer often starts by creating a specification that defines its *functional requirements*, i.e. the functions that the artefact should offer. For example, two functional requirements for a watch might be that it should be usable both as a stopwatch and as an alarm clock. Typically, requirements are gathered from and validated by people within the intended practice. They can be expressed as a list of functions of the artefact, with no reference to its structure. Instead, the structure can be developed later on when the designer has a more thorough understanding of the requirements. However, in practice, function and structure are almost always elaborated in an iterative way. In addition to functional requirements, a designer can also specify *non-functional requirements* for an artefact, i.e. requirements that do not relate to functionality but instead general qualities such as security, usability, maintainability, and scalability.

The distinctions between structure, function, and environment are sometimes reflected in the professional roles of designers. For example, in the construction industry, a construction engineer will focus on the internal structure of buildings, including the selection of building materials, the layout of plumbing, the strength calculations, etc. An architect, on the other hand, will focus on the environment and functions of buildings in order to cater for external constraints as well as for the needs and requirements of users. Similarly, in the IT and information systems industry, enterprise architects address business requirements as well as legal, cultural, and other environmental factors, while programmers and software engineers focus on the construction of the software within the systems that are being built.

1.4   Use Plans

In some cases, a particular artefact can be used for very different purposes. One example is aspirin, which can be used both as a pain killer and as a preventive measure against blood clotting. Another example would be gun powder, which was originally used as a medical elixir and in fireworks but was later applied in firearms.

When an artefact is used for different purposes, it has to be used in different ways. For example, when aspirin is used as a pain killer, it should be taken in a medium dose, as and when pain occurs. However, when used as a preventive measure against blood clotting, it should be taken in small doses one or more times per day. In these two cases, the artefact (aspirin) is the same, but the ways of using it differ.

How to use an artefact can be described in a *use plan* that specifies when and under which circumstances an artefact should be used, the procedure for using it, and factors to take into account when using it. Some everyday examples of use plans are:

- *Cooking instructions.* Preparation, time, temperature.
- *Drug label instructions.* Frequency and dosage of a drug, how to take the drug (chew, swallow, dissolve in water, etc.), contraindications (something that serves as a reason not to take the drug), and side effects to look out for.
- *Dishwasher operating instructions.* How to place the dish in the dishwasher, how to add detergent, how to choose the right program, how to start the dishwasher, and how to cancel the dishwashing program.

In summary, the functions of an artefact do not depend only on the artefact itself; to achieve a desired function, an appropriate use plan must be applied.

1.5 Design Science: The Study of Artefacts

Artefacts, as well as their use and the effects of using them, are studied in different fields of science, including formal, behavioural, and social sciences. For example, a study in theoretical computer science (formal science) might be carried out to determine the complexity properties of a new algorithm for traversing a social graph. A study in psychology (behavioural science) might investigate how photo sharing on social networks influences stress levels. A study in business administration (social science) might examine how the adoption of Enterprise Resource Planning (ERP) systems in companies affects their internal communication.

Artefacts are also studied in design science, where they are investigated as solutions to practical problems that people experience in certain practices. In design science, researchers take an intentional stance in the sense that they view an artefact as something that should support practitioners, i.e. people in a practice. The researchers are not disinterested observers but take on the role of designers who strive to create objects that are useful for practitioners. Thus, design science can tentatively be defined in the following way:

- *Design science* is the scientific study and creation of artefacts as they are developed and used by people with the goal of solving practical problems of general interest.

The starting point for a design researcher is that something is not quite right with the world, and it should be changed. A new artefact should be introduced into the world to make it different, to make it better. Design science researchers do not only think and theorise about the existing world; they model, make, and build in order to create new worlds. They produce both a novel artefact and knowledge about it and its effects on the environment. In particular, they need to formulate problem statements, determine stakeholder goals and requirements, and evaluate proposed artefacts. In other words, artefacts as well as knowledge about these artefacts are research outcomes for design science.

In this book, design science is viewed mainly from an IT perspective. However, the principles underlying design science are applicable to many other areas, e.g. medical science, as discussed below.

1.6 Design and Design Science

Design science may appear to be very similar to design, as both focus on the development of artefacts to address problems experienced in practices. Both of them also aim to produce novelty, i.e. they are intended to produce or investigate original artefacts that differ from existing ones. However, their purposes are different with respect to generalisability and contributions to knowledge. While design is a process for developing a working solution to a problem that may only be relevant to a single actor or situation, design science is intended to produce and communicate knowledge that is of general interest. The results of design work are sometimes relevant only to a *local practice*, i.e. a practice in which just one single individual, group, or organisation engages. In contrast, design science produces results that are relevant both to a *global practice*, i.e. a community of local practices, and to the research community.

The different purposes of design and design science give rise to three additional requirements for design science research:

1. The purpose of creating new knowledge of general interest requires design science projects to make use of rigorous research methods.
2. The knowledge produced has to be related to an already existing knowledge base in order to ensure that proposed results are both well founded and original.
3. The new results should be communicated to both practitioners and researchers.

As an example of the specific requirements for design science, consider a project that involves designing a new Electronic Health Record (EHR) system. In order to count as design science, the project needs to fulfil three conditions.

Firstly, the project has to apply an overall research strategy to investigate the context of the problem and to elicit stakeholder requirements. This strategy includes research methods for data collection, e.g. questionnaires for large groups of healthcare professionals and in-depth interviews with selected physicians and healthcare managers. Moreover, the strategy includes methods for analysing the generated data. The project also needs to evaluate the artefact produced using

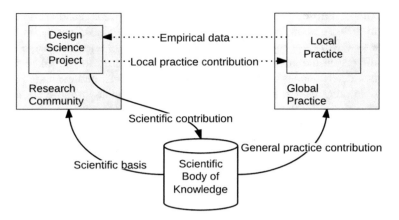

Fig. 1.3 Local and global practices in design science research (adapted from Goldkuhl 2012)

adequate research strategies and methods, which may be different from those used for problem analysis and requirements elicitation.

Secondly, the project has to relate the produced results to existing knowledge within various subareas of health informatics and information systems. This knowledge includes not only established theories and models but also relevant artefacts, in particular other EHR systems. Only by relating the project results to existing knowledge does it become possible to assess their originality and validity.

Thirdly, the project has to disseminate its results to both researchers and healthcare professionals through publications in academic journals and conferences as well as through presentations at healthcare fairs, professional conferences, and other similar events.

The relationships between a design science project and local and global practices are illustrated in Fig. 1.3. It can be seen from the figure that a design science project may, but does not need to, utilise empirical data from a local practice. The results may also provide a contribution to that practice. However, the project should always build on some scientific body of knowledge and contribute to it. And this body of knowledge should be of relevance not only to a research community but also to a global practice.

While a design science project always should contribute to a global practice as well as to a scientific body of knowledge, the project can still be carried out within a local practice. Iivari (2015) investigates two different strategies for doing design science research. In the first strategy, a researcher constructs or builds a generic artefact to address a problem in a global practice, while in the second strategy, a researcher attempts to solve a specific problem in a local practice by building a concrete artefact in that particular context. From that experience, the researcher distils prescriptive knowledge that can inform a general solution. Thus, the researcher remains situated within the local practice for almost the entire duration of the project, and generalisation to a global practice does not occur until the end of the project.

1.7 Medical Science and Design Science

The Encyclopaedia Britannica defines medicine as "the practice concerned with the maintenance of health and the prevention, alleviation, or cure of disease" (Encyclopaedia Britannica 2014).

Early medical practices incorporated plants, animal parts, and minerals as instruments for healing. They were often used in magical rituals overseen by priests or shamans. Medicine thereby became closely related to spiritual systems such as animism, shamanism, and divination. Today, these relationships have largely been broken, and instead, medical practices are usually supported by medical science.

Medical science is, in many ways, akin to design science. There is a practice, the medical practice, that aims to heal people. There are practical problems that have to do with the effectiveness, safety, and cost of engaging in this practice. There are artefacts that are used to address practical problems and support the practice, such as pharmaceutical drugs, medical devices, and therapies. A large part of medical science is devoted to studying, scientifically, how such artefacts can help solve practical problems in medical practice. Thus, many of the notions and principles underlying design science are also relevant to medical science.

1.8 Kinds of Design Science Contributions

A design science contribution can take several different forms. It may be based on a new artefact that is radical in the sense that it opens up entirely new avenues of human endeavour. However, a new artefact may also be an improvement upon an established solution to a well-known problem, or simply a marginal modification to an existing artefact. Another kind of design science contribution is the use of an existing artefact for a new purpose.

In order to classify the various kinds of design science contributions, Gregor and Hevner (2013) suggest that they be positioned along two dimensions: application domain maturity and solution maturity. Application domain maturity is about the maturity of the practice for which the contribution is intended, while solution maturity is about the maturity of the artefacts that could be used as a starting point for finding solutions. Based on these dimensions, Fig. 1.4 shows a matrix that identifies four kinds of design science contributions:

Invention—New solutions for new problems. This kind of contribution is a radical innovation that addresses an unexplored problem context and offers a novel and unexpected solution. Contributions of this kind can enable new practices and create the basis for new research fields. Some examples of inventions are the first X-ray machine, the first car, and the first data mining system. Inventions are rare and typically require broad knowledge and hard work, as well as ingenuity and a bit of luck to occur.

Fig. 1.4 Kinds of design
science contributions
(adapted from Gregor and
Hevner 2013)

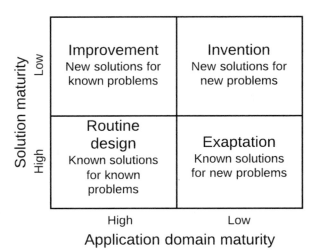

Improvement—New solutions for known problems. This kind of contribution
addresses a known problem and offers a new solution or a substantial enhancement
to an existing one. Improvements may concern efficiency, usability, safety, maintainability, or other qualities (see Sect. 6.5). Some examples of improvements are
the first sportbike, an X-ray machine with substantially reduced radiation, and a data
mining system able to handle very large data sets. Improvements are probably the
most common kind of design science contribution. They can be challenging because
a researcher needs to ensure that a proposed solution actually improves on the state
of the art.

Exaptation—Known solutions extended to new problems. This kind of contribution adapts an existing solution to a problem for which it was not originally
intended. In other words, an existing artefact is repurposed, or exapted, to a new
problem context. For example, the anticoagulant chemical Warfarin was introduced
as a rat poison but was later repurposed as a blood thinning medicine. Exaptations
occur frequently in design science research. One way of understanding the nature of
exaptations is to note that a designer usually produces not only an artefact but also
a use plan for it, as discussed in Sect. 1.4. Exaptation is indeed design, but it is the
design of a new use plan, not a new artefact.

Routine design—Known solutions for known problems. This kind of contribution
is an incremental innovation that addresses a well-known problem by making
minor modifications to an existing solution. Much of practical professional design
would fit into this category, e.g. the design of a new smartphone with slightly
better specifications than its predecessor. Routine designs typically do not count as
design science contributions because they do not produce new knowledge of general
interest, but they may still be valuable design contributions.

1.9 Technical Artefacts and Socio-Technical Systems

Some artefacts are purely material and have simple relationships with their practices and environments, such as knives or hammers. Other artefacts are deeply embedded in a complex environment that contains not only other artefacts but also humans and their social relationships, e.g. a reception desk at an airport. The desk is not there just to serve a few people in isolation, but instead is a part of a huge, interrelated system: the civil aviation system. This system includes buildings, aircraft, runways, luggage trolleys, and many other physical objects. It also includes humans, such as pilots, stewards, and passengers as well as the laws, rules, and norms that govern their behaviour. In this sense, the civil aviation system is a *hybrid system* consisting of physical, biological, and social objects.

A *socio-technical system* is a hybrid system that includes technical artefacts as well as humans and the laws, rules, and norms that govern their actions. In contrast, a *technical artefact* is a material artefact. Socio-technical systems are also artefacts, as they have been purposely designed to address a practical problem or enable some human endeavour. However, they are at the same time emergent phenomena that evolve due to spontaneous and unforeseen interactions among the humans participating in them.

The design of socio-technical systems poses a number of challenges due to their distinctive characteristics, in particular the roles and perspectives of the people in the systems, the need for rules and coordination mechanisms, the limits of systems controllability, and the vagueness of the system boundaries.

The roles and perspectives of people—Many people participate in a socio-technical system, and they play different roles. There are users who benefit from the services provided by the system, and operators who as professionals manipulate and manage the system, thereby ensuring its proper functioning. For example, in an aviation system, the users are the passengers who are transported, while the operators belong to several professional groups, including pilots, luggage personnel, and security guards. Due to their different roles, the participants in a socio-technical system have different interests and perspectives, which contributes to the complexity of the system. A recent trend in many socio-technical systems is to eliminate operators, or at least to substantially reduce their numbers. For example, autopilots and computerised air traffic control systems reduce the need for pilots and air traffic controllers. However, there will always be users in socio-technical systems, as they constitute the raison d'être for the systems.

The need for coordination and rules—The behaviour of technical artefacts is determined by the laws of physics and other natural sciences. However, the behaviour of socio-technical systems also depends on the actions and interactions of people. Thus, in order to manage and govern a socio-technical system, social mechanisms are needed that can coordinate the actions of its participants. Typically, these mechanisms take the form of laws, rules, norms, and traditions that tell people how to behave, and they often impose sanctions to deter inappropriate conduct.

The limits of controllability—Even if a socio-technical system includes adequate laws and rules, there is always a risk that people will choose not to follow them. In fact, designing laws and rules that people do accept and follow is one of the most challenging tasks when building socio-technical systems. As stated by Bennis (1999), managing people is like herding cats.

The vagueness of systems boundaries—Another challenge in designing socio-technical systems is to decide on their boundaries. In practice, every socio-technical system is embedded within another larger socio-technical system. For example, the baggage check-in system at an airport is embedded within the airport system, which, in turn, is embedded within the civil aviation system. There are no natural boundaries, where one system ends and another begins; instead, designers have to decide where to draw these boundaries. If they are drawn too narrowly, important aspects may be missed, resulting in a malfunctioning system. However, if they are drawn too widely, the design task easily becomes overwhelming.

In summary, the behaviour of socio-technical systems cannot easily be predicted or controlled. Different people in different roles with different backgrounds and perspectives give rise to conflicts and complexity. Social rules for controlling the behaviour of people may easily be disregarded or outright violated. Vague and changing system boundaries cause uncertainty and unclear divisions of responsibility. As a consequence, socio-technical systems are more difficult to manage and control than technical artefacts. This also means that problems occurring in socio-technical systems are often wicked, with vague formulations that only allow for partial and provisional solutions.

When carrying out design science research on socio-technical systems, or on technical artefacts to be used in such systems, social and organisational issues come to the fore. Analysing problems in social contexts, eliciting requirements from various stakeholders, and evaluating solutions in organisational settings become key activities for the researcher. For this purpose, research strategies and methods from the social sciences can be used to produce both practical and reliable results, as further discussed in Chap. 3.

1.10   How to Describe Artefacts

Describing an artefact is not only about describing its structure, functions, behaviours, side effects, and use plan; it is also about explaining how all of these are related. The following is a straightforward template for describing artefacts:

- *Structure.* Describe the components of the artefact, their main characteristics, and how they are related to each other. If possible, include a picture—it can be worth more than a thousand words. For a simple material artefact, a photo may be used, while for a complex material artefact, an exploded-view drawing may work better. For abstract artefacts, a picture could take the form of a drawing, a conceptual diagram, or a mindmap.

Fig. 1.5 A Santoku knife

- *Functions.* List the functions of the artefact. For each function, relate it to the relevant components or properties of the artefact. In other words, explain how the structure of the artefact enables each function.
- *Side Effects.* List the side effects of the artefact. In the same way as for the functions, explain how the structure of the artefact gives rise to these side effects.
- *Behaviours.* List the behaviours of the artefact and explain how they contribute to its functions and side effects. Explain also how the structure of the artefact gives rise to the behaviours. (This part is optional if the behaviours are evident from the description of the functions and side effects.)
- *Use Plan.* Describe the use plan, i.e. when and under which circumstances the artefact should be used, the procedure for using it, and factors to take into account when using it.

As an example, we consider the use of this template for a Santoku knife, which is a Japanese knife made for cutting, dicing, and mincing both vegetables and meat (see Fig. 1.5).

- *Structure.* A Santoku knife consists of a steel blade attached to a handle. The handle is often made of wood, but other materials may also be used. The blade is flat and very sharp and may have scallops hollowed out of the side of the blade. The knife is smaller and lighter than a typical Western chef knife.
- *Functions.* The functions of the knife include the following:

  - It offers a smooth and comfortable grip, thanks to the wooden handle.
  - It reduces fatigue, thanks to its low weight.
  - It offers fast and easy cutting, thanks to the sharp edge and the scallops.
  - It makes it possible to quickly cut, dice, and mince food, thanks to the sharp edge.

- *Side Effects.* There is one important side effect:

  - There is a risk for badly cutting the fingers due to the sharp edge.

- *Behaviours.* The scallops on the blade enable a behaviour:

  - The scallops create small pockets of air between the blade and the food being sliced, thereby improving separation and reducing cutting friction; this behaviour helps to make cutting fast and easy.

- *Use Plan.* Put the food on a cutting board that is completely flat and stable, so it will not move. Move the knife straight up and down but do not rock. Apply enough force that the blade makes a noise, but take care not to damage the blade or the cutting board in the process.

1.11   Summary of Chapter

- *Design science* is the scientific study and creation of artefacts as they are developed and used by people with the goal of solving practical problems of general interest.
- An *artefact* is an object made by humans with the intention of being used to address a practical problem.
- An artefact can be described by specifying:

  - The *structure* of the artefact, i.e. the inner workings of the artefact, the components it consists of, and how these are related.
  - The *behaviour* of the artefact, i.e. what the artefact can do or bring about.
  - The *function* of the artefact, i.e. what the artefact can do for its users.
  - The *environment* of the artefact, i.e. the external surroundings and conditions in which the artefact will operate.
  - The *effects* of the artefact, i.e. how the use of the artefact will change its environment. Effects can be divided into intended effects and side effects.

- An artefact is developed to address a *practical problem*, i.e. a gap between the current state and a desirable state, as perceived by some stakeholders of a practice.
- A *practice* is a set of human activities performed regularly and seen as meaningfully related to each other by the people participating in them.
- Design science can be contrasted with empirical science, such as the natural and social sciences. In empirical science, researchers describe, explain, and predict. In design science, researchers also design and develop artefacts to improve practices, thereby changing the world.
- The outcomes of design science research include not only artefacts but also contextual knowledge about these artefacts.

1.12   Review Questions

1. Can Internet surveillance be viewed as a practice? If so, give some examples of practical problems that arise in this practice.
2. A common practical problem that is encountered when introducing new digital systems or services is that many people prefer not to use them. Explain this problem in terms of a gap between two states.
3. Determine which of the following objects are artefacts: a stone, a stone axe, a coin, a tiger, a German shepherd, the planet Jupiter, the climate, a company.

4. Can two artefacts with different behaviours exhibit the same functions? If so, give an example.
5. Can two artefacts with different structures exhibit the same functions? If so, give an example.
6. Describe a tablet in terms of its structure, behaviour, function, and effects.
7. Are the side effects of using an artefact always harmful for its environment?
8. A photo-sharing service is an artefact. Give an example of a design science study and a social science study that can be carried out on this artefact.
9. In what ways can a design science project be more complex than a design project?
10. In what ways can a design project be more complex than a design science project?
11. Why is a function of an artefact a relative concept? Give some examples of other relative concepts presented in this chapter.
12. It is important to relate an artefact to a practice. Why?
13. Give an example of a wicked problem in a social-technical system and how a design science project can address this problem.

1.13   Answers to Selected Review Questions

2. The current state is that people do not want to use the new system, and the desirable state is that people do want to use the system.
3. A stone, a tiger, and the planet Jupiter are not man-made objects, so they are not artefacts. A stone axe and a coin are artefacts, as they are objects made by humans with the intention of solving practical problems relating to chopping and exchange, respectively. A German shepherd is a borderline case, as this race of dog was bred by people to solve the practical problem of herding sheep. A more extreme example is the Harvard oncomouse, which was genetically modified to make it suitable for cancer research. A company is also a borderline case, as it is partially an emergent phenomenon created through interactions among people, but also a socially designed and constituted entity. Possibly, the climate can also be seen as a borderline case, in particular if it is substantially modified in the future by humans for their own purposes. Hence, there is no sharp dividing line between artefacts and natural objects.
4. No. One example would be a broomstick and a vacuum cleaner, both of which have the function of cleaning floors but have very different behaviours. A behaviour is an action that an artefact can perform, while a function is a benefit that an artefact can offer to a user. Thus, a function is relative to a user, while a behaviour is not.
5. An electric car and a hybrid car have different structures, but they offer the same function of transporting people and goods. However, they have different behaviours, as only the hybrid car produces emissions.

7. No. An example is that using lamps in a cold room can help to make the room warmer.
8. A design science study could be to design and evaluate a novel mechanism for informing people about new photos that have been added. A social science study might investigate the ways in which people experience stress when using the photo-sharing service.
9. A design science project requires a rigorous application of research methods and a critical analysis of its results that relate them to a scientific body of knowledge. Still, a design project may also need to follow professionally recognised methods, and its results should typically be compared to the state of the art.
10. A design project requires that its results fulfil the demands and expectations of the customers, and it is typically carried out under strict time and budget constraints. Furthermore, a design project in an organisation needs to handle political issues. Still, a design science project may be subject to similar constraints and issues with regard to funding agencies and institutional politics.

1.14   Further Reading

One of the earliest and most influential texts on the relationship between design and science is *The Sciences of the Artificial* by Simon (1996). A starting point for Simon is that the world that people inhabit today is primarily human-made. He investigates the role of design in this context and asks how science can inform design.

An early paper on design science was written by March and Smith (1995), which presents a two-dimensional framework for research in information technology. The first dimension is based on common types of research activities in design and natural science: build, evaluate, theorise, and justify; these will be further discussed in Chaps. 4–9. The second dimension is based on the kinds of artefacts produced by design science research: representational constructs, models, methods, and instantiations; these will be introduced in more detail in Chap. 2. Another highly influential paper was written by Hevner et al. (2004), which contrasts two research paradigms in the information systems area: behavioural science and design science. The paper proposes a conceptual framework and guidelines for understanding, executing, and evaluating design science research. It also argues that within design science, knowledge and understanding of a problem and its potential solutions are achieved through building and applying artefacts. Österle et al. (2010) discuss the importance and relevance of design science. They argue that design science research is key to achieving results that are both rigorous in an academic sense and relevant to the information systems practice. Wieringa (2009) investigates the difference between, as well as the mutual nesting of, knowledge questions and practical problems in design science and argues that these need to be addressed using different methods. Design science has received much attention not only within the field of IT, but also in management science. Pandza and Thorpe (2010) argue that the design analogy is relevant in achieving an understanding of the different forms of management studies, but that it is applicable only in a fairly narrow sense.

Hevner and Chatterjee (2010) offer a comprehensive reference text on design science research that includes chapters by several authors. The chapters address the key principles of design science research, design for software-intensive systems, people and design, the past and present of software designs, evaluation methods, and design creativity. Vaishnavi and Kuechler (2004) have developed a web site on design science that includes an overview of design science research, discusses design science research methodologies, investigates the philosophical grounding of design science research, and offers a comprehensive bibliography of design science publications as well as other resources. New contributions to design science are regularly published, e.g. in the conference series Design Science Research in Information Systems and Technologies (DESRIST) and the SIG Prag workshop series on IT Artefact Design & Workpractice Improvement (ADWI).

Rittel and Webber (1973) investigate the notion of the wicked problem in the context of social policy. They identify a number of characteristics of wicked problems and conclude that they cannot be addressed using scientific methods, as science focuses on tame problems. In contrast, Farrell and Hooker (2013) argue that science also addresses wicked problems, and that there is a cognitive process that is common to both design and science. The discussion in Sect. 1.3 on the context and anatomy of artefacts builds on the framework proposed by Gero (1990) and Gero and Kannengiesser (2004). Similarly to the work by Gregor and Hevner (2013), Gero (1990) uses this framework to distinguish between routine design, innovative design, and creative design.

The notion of an artefact has been extensively investigated in various disciplines, including philosophy and psychology. Franssen et al. (2013) have edited a book on artefact ontology that addresses two key topics of metaphysics: the identity of entities and the foundations of classification. It discusses these topics not for natural entities but for human-made ones, i.e. artefacts. Vermaas et al. (2011) argue that artefacts are always associated with a use plan, as discussed in Sect. 1.8. A related notion is that of a treatment, introduced by Wieringa (2014), which can be seen as an aggregation of an artefact and a use plan. Weigand et al. (2021) propose an artefact ontology for design science research.

Gill and Hevner (2013) investigate the notion of usefulness in design science. A common view is that the usefulness of an artefact primarily concerns its immediate relevance within a practice, i.e. how well it addresses the problem for which it was designed. However, usefulness can also be viewed in a more dynamic way. This means that the usefulness of an artefact also depends on its ability to provide a basis for further evolution, i.e. an artefact that can be further refined and improved is more useful than one with no room for improvements. Based on these distinctions, Gill and Hevner (2013) propose a fitness-utility model that captures the evolutionary nature of design improvements. Their work also has a bearing on the difference between design and design science, where design often focuses on immediate relevance, whereas design science emphasises the evolution of a knowledge base.

The notion of practice has been hugely influential in modern social science through works such as those by Bourdieu and Nice (1977) and Giddens (1986). Cetina et al. (2005) have edited a text on the role of practice and practices in human activity. Practice research and its relationships to design science are investigated by Goldkuhl (2012). Several key concepts of practice research are introduced and contrasted, including local practice contribution vs. general practice contribution, theorising vs. situational inquiry, and abstract vs. situational knowledge.

Adler and Pouliot (2011) discuss the notion of practice and differentiate between behaviour, action, and practice, where actions are behaviour with meaning, and practice are actions repeated over time and space embedded in a particular context. Actions in a practice are socially developed through learning and training. Adler and Pouliot (2011) present five characteristics of a practice: (1) practice is performance, i.e. the process of doing something; (2) practice tends to be patterned, i.e. actions are repeated over time and space; (3) practice is more or less competent in the sense that it can be done correctly or incorrectly (in a socially recognizable way); (4) practice rests on background knowledge; and (5) practice weaves together the discursive and the material world, i.e. without written and spoken communication, people cannot differentiate between behaviour and practice, and the practice is mediated by material artefacts. Miller (1984) introduces the distinction between purposive and self-contained practices in order to analyse the notion of virtue.

Bider et al. (2013) propose a model that can be used to identify and conceptualise different strategies for carrying out design science projects. The model suggests that design science research can be viewed as movements in a space of specific situations, problems, and solutions, i.e. in a local practice, and generic situations, problems, and solutions. i.e. in a global practice.

The relationship between research and practice is sometimes viewed as a linear transfer of knowledge and technology from research laboratories to practice settings. Wieringa (2010) shows that this view is an oversimplification, noting that, historically, a great deal of technological development has occurred without research being involved, and that research has often investigated and systematized past innovations rather than prepared for new ones. Wieringa (2010) argues that these observations require an extended framework for design science that makes a distinction between practical problems and research questions. In a later book, Wieringa (2014) describes such a framework in detail.

Section 1.9 builds on the work by Vermaas et al. (2011), who offer a philosophical analysis and characterisation of the relationship between technical artefacts and socio-technical systems, including their ethical status and the possibilities for designers to influence this status.

References

Adler E, Pouliot V (2011) International practices: introduction and framework. In: Adler E, Pouliot V (eds) International practices. Cambridge Univ Press, Cambridge, pp 3–35

Bennis W (1999) Managing people is like herding cats. Executive Excellence Publishing, Provo

Bider I, Johannesson P, Perjons E (2013) Design science research as movement between individual and generic situation-problem–solution spaces. In: Baskerville R, De Marco M, Spagnoletti P (eds) Designing organizational systems. Lecture notes in information systems and organisation. Springer, Berlin, pp 35–61

Bourdieu P, Nice R (1977) Outline of a theory of practice, 1st edn. Cambridge University Press, Cambridge

Cetina KK, Schatzki TR, von Savigny E (2005) The practice turn in contemporary theory. Routledge, London

Encyclopaedia Britannica (2014) Medicine. http://global.britannica.com/EBchecked/topic/372431/medicine. Accessed 3 July 2014

Farrell R, Hooker C (2013) Design, science and wicked problems. Des Stud 34(6):681–705

Franssen M et al (2013) Artefact kinds: ontology and the human-made world. Springer, Berlin

Gero JS (1990) Design prototypes: a knowledge representation schema for design. AI Mag 11(4):26–36

Gero JS, Kannengiesser U (2004) The situated function–behaviour–structure framework. Des Stud 25(4):373–391

Giddens, A (1986) The Constitution of Society: outline of the theory of structuration. University of California Press, Berkeley

Gill TG, Hevner AR (2013) A fitness-utility model for design science research. ACM Trans Manage Inf Syst 4(2):5:1–5:24

Goldkuhl G (2012) From action research to practice research. Australas J Inf Syst 17(2):57–78

Gregor S, Hevner AR (2013) Positioning and presenting design science research for maximum impact. MISQ 37(2):337–355

Hevner A, Chatterjee S (2010) Design research in information systems: theory and practice. Springer, New York

Hevner AR et al. (2004) Design science in information systems research. MIS Q 28(1):75–105

Iivari J (2015) Distinguishing and contrasting two strategies for design science research. Eur J Inf Syst 24(1):107–115

March ST, Smith GF (1995) Design and natural science research on information technology. Decis Support Syst 15(4):251–266

Miller D (1984) Virtues and practices. Anal Krit 6(1):49–60

Österle H et al (2010) Memorandum on design-oriented information systems research. Eur J Inf Syst 20(1):7–10

Pandza K, Thorpe R (2010) Management as design, but what kind of design? An appraisal of the design science analogy for management. Br J Manag 21(1):171–186

Rittel HWJ, Webber MM (1973) Dilemmas in a general theory of planning. Policy Sci 4(2):155–169

Simon HA (1996) The sciences of the artificial, 3rd edn. The MIT Press, Cambridge

Vaishnavi V, Kuechler W (2004) Design research in information systems. http://www.desrist.org/desrist/. Accessed 26 June 2014

Vermaas P et al (2011) A philosophy of technology: from technical artefacts to sociotechnical systems. Synth Lect Eng Technol Soc 6(1):1–134

Weigand H, Johannesson P, Andersson B (2021) An artifact ontology for design science research. Data Knowl Eng 133:101878

Wieringa R (2009) Design science as nested problem solving. In: Proceedings of the 4th international conference on design science research in information systems and technology, DESRIST '09. ACM, New York, pp 8:1–8:12

Wieringa R (2014) Design science methodology for information systems and software engineering. Springer, Berlin

Wieringa R (2010) Relevance and problem choice in design science. In: Winter R, Zhao JL, Aier S (eds) Global perspectives on design science research. Lecture notes in computer science. Springer, Berlin, pp 61–76

Chapter 2
Knowledge Types and Forms

Scientific research produces different kinds of knowledge, and there have been numerous attempts to classify these; one of the earliest was Kant's distinctions between a priori vs. a posteriori and between analytic vs. synthetic knowledge. In this chapter, knowledge is classified into six types depending on its purpose. The classification builds on a broad view of knowledge as expressed in the following definition from Wikipedia: "Knowledge is a familiarity, awareness or understanding of someone or something, such as facts, information, descriptions, or skills, which is acquired through experience or education by perceiving, discovering, or learning. Knowledge can refer to a theoretical or practical understanding of a subject. It can be implicit (as with practical skill or expertise) or explicit (as with the theoretical understanding of a subject); it can be more or less formal or systematic" (Wikipedia Contributor 2014).

Another way of classifying knowledge is based on the form in which it can be materialised. This is particularly relevant to design science, as the knowledge it produces is not always explicit but is sometimes embedded in artefacts. After introducing knowledge types in Sect. 2.1 and knowledge forms in Sect. 2.2, we discuss different classifications of artefacts in Sect. 2.3. Finally, we introduce the notions of design principles and design theory.

2.1   Knowledge Types

Knowledge may be used for different purposes, such as describing, explaining, and predicting phenomena. Based on these purposes, a number of *knowledge types* can be identified. Being aware of these knowledge types can help design science researchers to articulate and communicate the meaning and value of their contributions. By explicitly stating the type of knowledge that they have produced, their audience will better understand the nature and relevance of their results.

© Springer Nature Switzerland AG 2021
P. Johannesson, E. Perjons, *An Introduction to Design Science*,
https://doi.org/10.1007/978-3-030-78132-3_2

2.1.1 Definitional Knowledge

Definitional knowledge consists of concepts, constructs, terminologies, definitions, vocabularies, classifications, taxonomies, and other kinds of conceptual knowledge. It may be formal and precise, such as the basic concepts of relational database theory, which includes relations, attributes, functional dependencies, and multi-valued dependencies. Definitional knowledge may also include vague and informal concepts such as the notions of usability, affordance, and situatedness used in the field of Human-Computer Interaction (HCI). Definitional knowledge does not include statements about the world that are claimed to be true. Instead, it is used as a basis for all other types of knowledge because it provides the basic concepts required to express that knowledge. Bennett (2018) succinctly phrased this as: "We do not know structures, but we know because of structures".

Examples of definitional knowledge:

- A *right triangle* is a triangle in which one angle is a right angle.
- A *unicorn* is a mythical creature depicted as a white horse with a large, pointed, spiralling horn projecting from its forehead.
- A *black hole* is a region of space from which nothing can escape.
- A *relation is in third normal form*, within relational database theory, if all of its attributes are dependent on the key, the whole key, and nothing but the key.

These statements only define certain concepts but do not claim that right triangles, unicorns, black holes, or third normal forms actually exist; such claims are made by descriptive knowledge.

2.1.2 Descriptive Knowledge

Descriptive knowledge describes and analyses an existing or past reality. This type of knowledge typically describes, summarises, generalises, and classifies observations of phenomena or events. For example, descriptive knowledge can claim that most users of a business intelligence system in a company are dissatisfied. It may also describe individual entities and events, e.g. that the company Ericsson has invested heavily in a new global business intelligence system. It may also describe relationships among entities, thereby providing an analysis of these, e.g. the modular composition of a pattern recognition system. Unlike definitional knowledge, descriptive knowledge does include statements that are claimed to be true. In other words, descriptive knowledge claims to describe the world "as is".

Examples of descriptive knowledge:

- The height of the Eiffel tower is 300 m.
- All swans are white.
- All large companies in Europe use ERP systems.

Descriptive knowledge does not claim to provide explanations or predictions; it only describes.

2.1.3 Explanatory Knowledge

Explanatory knowledge provides answers to questions of "how" and "why". It explains how objects behave and why events occur. Explanatory knowledge goes beyond descriptive knowledge, because it not only describes and analyses but also explains in order to offer understanding. Explanations often take the form of cause-effect chains, showing how events and outcomes are causally related to underlying mechanisms and factors. For example, the increased acceptance of Internet banking among the public can be partially explained by improvements in security infrastructures.

High-level explanatory knowledge aims to show how the world can be viewed in a certain way, sometimes with the intent to challenge conventional assumptions and bring about an altered understanding that is based on novel theoretical perspectives. Some theories that have been used for this purpose are structuration theory, action-network theory, and critical theory. For example, critical theory can be used to explain why information systems introduced to improve productivity sometimes evolve into instruments for monitoring and control.

Explanatory knowledge, on a lower level, provides explanations for particular situations, where it explains why and how specific events unfold. For example, the introduction of a reward system in an organisation can be a major cause for the employees' acceptance of a new information system.

Examples of explanatory knowledge:

- Humans are descended from other animals through a process of natural evolution.
- The earthquake in Japan in 2011 was a consequence of displacements of tectonic plates.
- The failure to introduce social software into the company was caused by its authoritarian organisational culture.

Explanatory knowledge can only explain events after they have happened and cannot be used for predicting future events.

2.1.4 Predictive Knowledge

Predictive knowledge offers black-box predictions, i.e. it predicts outcomes based on underlying factors but without explaining causal or other relationships between them. The goal of predictive knowledge is accurate prediction rather than understanding.

High-level predictive knowledge with a broad generality is not common in the field of IT; one of the few examples is the COCOMO model (Boehm 1981), which provides cost estimation for software development. In the same way as explanatory knowledge, predictive knowledge can exist on both higher and lower levels. In the latter case, it predicts outcomes in specific situations, e.g. that the risk of failure of a certain software development project is above average.

Examples of predictive knowledge:

- The treatment of patients by physicians with unwashed hands may result in diseases.
- Heavy exposure to sunlight may result in skin diseases.

These examples only predict certain outcomes and do not explain them. Today there are explanations for these predictions, but these were not known when this knowledge was discovered.

2.1.5 Explanatory and Predictive Knowledge

Explanatory and predictive knowledge offers both explanations and predictions. It predicts outcomes and explains how these are related to underlying mechanisms and factors, often through causal relationships. This kind of knowledge is considered the most common in natural science. It is much less common in the IT area, but there are some examples such as the Technology Acceptance Model (TAM) (Venkatesh and Davis 2000) and DeLone and McLean's model of information system success (Delone and McLean 2003). Explanatory and predictive knowledge can also be incorporated into more comprehensive theories, such as general systems theory and the soft systems methodology (Checkland and Scholes 1990).

Examples of explanatory and predictive knowledge:

- Microorganisms can survive in dirt and can infect people that come into contact with them.
- Exposure to the ultraviolet radiation of sunlight may cause burning of the skin, which may result in skin diseases.

These statements both predict possible outcomes and explain them by describing the underlying mechanisms that cause them.

2.1.6 Prescriptive Knowledge

Prescriptive knowledge consists of prescriptive models and methods that can help solve practical problems. Prescriptive models can be seen as blueprints for developing artefacts, while methods are guidelines and procedures that help people to work in systematic ways when solving problems. Prescriptive models and methods can be viewed as being composed of two parts. The first part is the model or method itself, while the second is a statement about some desirable effect of using it. This statement is not a subjective judgement that some effect is desirable in an absolute way. Instead, it is a predictive statement implying that if a prescriptive model or method is used in a certain practice, this will contribute to effects desired by some stakeholders. In this sense, prescription can be seen as a special case of prediction.

Typical examples of methods are systems and software development methods, such as the Rational Unified Process (RUP) (Kroll and Kruchten 2003), or agile methods, such as XP and SCRUM (Cohn 2009). Examples of prescriptive models are conceptual reference models, such as SCOR Bolstorff and Rosenbaum (2007), or architectural models, such as OSI (Day and Zimmermann 1983).

Examples of prescriptive knowledge:

- Wash your hands before carrying out surgery!
- Apply sun lotion before sun bathing!
- Develop your software system iteratively!

2.2 Knowledge Forms

While knowledge types describe the purposes for which knowledge can be used, *knowledge forms* specify how it can be materialised, i.e. where it exists and in what shape. Knowledge forms are important in design science research, as it creates not only knowledge that is explicitly codified in documents but also knowledge embedded in artefacts. The following subsections will introduce the three main knowledge forms and their roles in design science.

2.2.1 Explicit Knowledge

Explicit knowledge is articulated, expressed, and recorded in media, e.g. text, numbers, codes, formulas, musical notations, and video tracks. Typical containers of explicit knowledge are encyclopaedias, textbooks, and manuals. One of the main strengths of explicit knowledge is that it can be easily transferred between individuals, as it is stored in media that can be moved and decoded in a convenient way. However, not all knowledge can be articulated in an explicit way, e.g. practical skills, intuitions, and experiences—reading a manual on how to ride a bicycle will not help much in learning that skill.

2.2.2 Embodied Knowledge

Embodied knowledge, sometimes called *tacit knowledge*, resides in the minds of people and is often difficult to formulate explicitly. For example, although almost everyone is able to read facial expressions correctly and effortlessly, no one would be able to fully articulate how this is done. Other examples of embodied knowledge include tying a shoelace, speaking English, and using a video recorder.

Efforts are sometimes made to transform embodied knowledge into explicit knowledge, e.g. by companies who want to retain the knowledge of employees who are going to leave. The goal of such a transformation is that people without an expert background should be able to replicate the performance of those who possess relevant, embodied knowledge. However, the person using knowledge in an explicit form will typically lack the skilled practitioner's ability to innovate and adapt to new circumstances. In this sense, the extracted, explicit knowledge is inferior to the embodied knowledge.

2.2.3 Embedded Knowledge

Embedded knowledge resides not in humans but in entities, such as physical objects, processes, routines, or structures. As an example, consider a bread maker, i.e. a home appliance for making bread. When loaded with the right ingredients, such a machine is able to produce a loaf of bread by mixing those ingredients, kneading the resulting dough, and then baking it. Someone studying how the machine works can learn about bread making. Thus, the machine can be seen as embedding the prescriptive knowledge of how to make bread; it embeds a recipe, which is a method. Furthermore, by studying the structure of the machine, someone can learn about the architecture of bread making machines in general. It may even be possible to create a (prescriptive) model for building new bread makers. In this sense, the machine also embeds a model.

In general, an object can embed both models and methods. In the same way as for embodied knowledge, these embedded models and methods can sometimes be made explicit. However, this requires a transformation that typically loses some of the embedded knowledge, i.e. the extracted models or methods are poorer than the ones embedded in the object—something is lost in translation. The process of discovering the principles behind an artefact through an analysis of its functionality and structure is commonly known as reverse engineering, which has a long tradition within military as well as industrial practices.

2.2.4 Knowledge Forms in Craft and Science

In traditional crafts, representing and transferring design knowledge is most commonly achieved by embedding it within objects. This is not due to laziness on the part of the designer but because objects are able to embed design knowledge with all its richness and nuance. Apprentices who carefully study an artefact designed by a master will gain a deep and intuitive understanding of the principles used in creating it. In this way, the design knowledge embodied in the master becomes embodied in the apprentice, using the artefact with its embedded knowledge as an intermediary.

Representing and transferring knowledge by embedding it in artefacts can offer substantial benefits with respect to richness and intuition, but there are also several disadvantages. Firstly, acquiring knowledge by directly studying artefacts can be time consuming, as evidenced by the many years it usually takes a craft apprentice to become a master. Secondly, the knowledge someone actually acquires by studying an artefact is highly dependent on that person's background, interests, and capabilities. Some people may learn effectively from examining an artefact, while others may fail to do so. Thirdly, it is difficult to analyse, criticise, and evaluate knowledge embedded in an object—analysis, criticism, and evaluation are usually more effective and meaningful when the knowledge is explicit. In other words, explicit knowledge facilitates reflection and innovation.

One of the main purposes of design science is to support designers and researchers in making design knowledge explicit, thereby changing design from a craft to a science. Design science offers this support by clarifying the principles behind design and providing methods for creating artefacts as well as explicit knowledge about them. However, not all of the knowledge embedded in an artefact can be made explicit, and the artefact itself is therefore an essential outcome of any design science project.

2.2.5 Knowledge Forms in Organisations

Knowledge can be represented in different forms in an organisation, for example: embodied in individuals, explicit in documents, embedded in routines, and embedded in technology. Each of these knowledge forms has benefits and drawbacks in terms of the persistence and transfer of organisational knowledge.

Knowledge embodied in individuals—Individuals are a "key repository of organisational knowledge" (Argote 2012). One benefit of embodied knowledge is that knowledgeable individuals can easily be asked to describe their way of working and can explain why things are carried out in a certain way. They can also adapt their descriptions and explanations, depending on the listeners' prior knowledge, in order to facilitate understanding. Knowledgeable individuals can also be moved around within an organisation to support tacit-to-tacit knowledge transfer. However, there is a risk that these individuals may protect their knowledge assets in order to gain power or other benefits. Another risk is that these individuals may leave the organisation, which thereby loses access to essential knowledge assets.

Knowledge explicit in documents—An organisation can store information about organisational goals, plans, business processes, and business rules in different kinds of documents, such as business plans, budgets, and business process descriptions. This explicit knowledge is not dependent on access to individuals but can instead be accessed via different kinds of repositories. Explicit knowledge stored in documents is also easier to analyse, criticise, and evaluate than knowledge in other forms. However, documents can be hard to find and interpret, may be incomplete, and may not be updated with the latest changes.

Knowledge embedded in routines—The way of working in an organisation may emerge over time and transform into routines and standard operating procedures. These routines are often an effective way of storing and transferring knowledge within an organisation (Argote 2012). New employees can be introduced to the routines by colleagues, meaning that this knowledge will not be lost when individual employees leave the organisation. However, there is a risk that employees may forget the reason for a particular routine, or that certain routines become inappropriate when the external environment changes. There is also a risk that routines may prevent change, since "unlearning" routines and developing new ones can pose a considerable challenge to an organisation and its employees.

Knowledge embedded in technology—This is an effective way of storing and transferring knowledge within an organisation (Argote 2012). An example would be an IT system that would force employees to work in a standardised way. A major drawback of knowledge embedded in technology is that it can prevent change, since alterations can be time consuming and costly.

When developing an artefact in a socio-technical system, the designers of the artefact need to understand which knowledge exists in the system and how this knowledge is represented in individuals, documents, routines, and technology. Moreover, they need to decide which knowledge the artefact should represent, and they should understand how this will change the ways of working in the system, including knowledge transfer between people. There is always a risk that a new IT system, a new business process, or a new method introduced in an organisation will be contra-productive, as it may hinder existing practices, including those that are efficient, that promote innovation, and that result in high-quality products (Seely Brown and Duguid 2006).

2.3   Artefact Classifications

Artefacts can be classified in different ways, depending on the type of knowledge they express and whether that knowledge is explicit or embedded. Furthermore, artefacts can also be classified according to their function and use. When presenting design science results, it is always useful to state the type of the artefact created, since this information helps the audience to understand what they can expect from the artefact. Making explicit the artefact type also helps in identifying relevant requirements for the artefact, as discussed further in later chapters.

2.3.1 A Classic Artefact Classification

Within design science, it has become well established to identify four types of artefacts: constructs, models, methods, and instantiations.

Constructs—A construct is a term, a notation, a definition, or a concept that is needed when formulating problems and their possible solutions. Constructs do not make any statements about the world, but they make it possible to speak about it so that it can be understood and changed. Hence, constructs are definitional knowledge. They are the smallest conceptual atoms that can be used to analyse and communicate about phenomena in a practice. Examples include the concepts of a class in the Unified Modeling Language (UML), a method in Java, a functional dependency in relational database theory, and an affordance in HCI.

Models—A model is built up from constructs that are related to each other, and it represents a possible solution to a practical problem. Thus, a model can be used to support the construction of other artefacts. For example, a drawing can be used in building a house, and a database model can be used in developing a database system. Since models prescribe the structure of other artefacts, they express prescriptive knowledge.

Methods—A method expresses prescriptive knowledge by defining guidelines and processes for how to solve problems and achieve goals. In particular, they can prescribe how to create artefacts. Methods may be highly formalised, such as algorithms, or informal, such as rules of thumb or best practices. Examples include methods for database design, change management initiatives, and web service development.

Instantiations—An instantiation is a working system that can be used within a practice. Instantiations can always embed knowledge, e.g. a database can embed a database model. Some examples of instantiations are a Java program realising a search algorithm, a database for electronic medical records, or a new planet in the computer game Entropia.

The notion of a model in design science, as described above, is somewhat narrower than that which is common in many other areas. Generally, a distinction can be made between *descriptive models* that describe existing situations, *explanatory models* that offer explanations for observed situations and patterns, *predictive models* that can be used to forecast the behaviour of objects and systems, and *prescriptive models* that represent possible solutions to problems. These kinds of models express different types of knowledge, as discussed in Sect. 2.1. However, only prescriptive models count as artefacts.

An instantiation is defined above as a working system that can be used within a practice. However, the term "instantiation" indicates that the system should be an instantiation of another artefact, i.e. some other artefact should function as a template, form, or idea for a working system. Therefore, the question arises: what kinds of artefacts can be instantiated? The possible candidates are the three remaining types of design science artefacts: construct, model, and method. However, construct is not suitable because instantiating a construct would give rise to something that is too small to be a working system. In contrast, models, such as blueprints and architectures, can clearly be the basis of a working system, meaning that models can be instantiated. The remaining question is whether methods can also be instantiated. Applying a method for developing a system should result in a working system. However, this resulting system is not an instantiation of the method. Instead, the instantiation (or application) of the method consists of the actual actions and events that occurred during the system's development. Thus, a method instantiation would not count as an instantiation in the sense of a working system.

It could now be argued that the above definition of instantiation is too narrow and that method applications should also be included. One argument in favour of this view is that methods are so complex and situation dependent that they cannot be fully expressed as explicit knowledge. Instead, some of the knowledge can be embedded in a particular method application, i.e. in some actual use of a method in space and time. The knowledge embedded in the method application can then be communicated, for example, through video recordings or notes from participants. Although this argument has merit in principle, it is often difficult to transfer knowledge through method applications, especially when these span extended periods of time. For example, watching many hours of videos of meetings is not an attractive option. However, in some areas, such as physiotherapy, method applications could be useful design artefacts. Watching a one-minute application of an innovative physiotherapy exercise, recorded on video, could be a highly effective instrument for knowledge transfer.

2.3.2   A Function-Oriented Artefact Classification

Another way of classifying artefacts is to focus on their function. Iivari (2007) proposes the classification of IT applications (instantiations) into seven archetypes based on their functions, i.e. the roles they can play for their users, as shown in Table 2.1.

Table 2.1 Archetypes of IT applications (adapted from (Iivari 2007))

Archetype	Function	Examples
Processor	To automate	Transaction processing systems, embedded control systems
Tool	To augment	Computer-aided design systems, word processors, spreadsheets
Medium	To mediate	Email, blogs, social software
Information source	To inform	Information systems
Game	To entertain	Computer games, edutainment
Piece of art	To create art	Computer art
Pet	To accompany	Digital, virtual, and robotic pets

As these archetypes are ideal types, a single IT application may be classified under two or more archetypes. For example, an email system is primarily meant to mediate, but someone may also use it as a personal storage of information, thereby employing it as an information source.

2.3.3 A Pragmatic Artefact Classification

Another classification of artefacts was proposed by Offermann et al. (2010), who introduced eight artefact types based on a literature review within the area of IT:

- *System design.* A structure or behaviour related description of a system, typically using text and some formal language.
- *Method.* A definition of activities used to create or interact with a system.
- *Language/notation.* A (formalised) system to formulate statements about some domain.
- *Algorithm.* An executable description of system behaviour.
- *Guideline.* A suggestion regarding behaviour in a particular situation.
- *Requirement.* A statement about required behaviours and functions of a system.
- *Pattern.* A definition of reusable design elements with their benefits and application context.
- *Metric.* A mathematical model that is able to measure aspects of systems or methods.

It can be argued that this classification faithfully mirrors what practitioners in IT would recognise as the key types of artefacts. Therefore, for this area, the classification can be viewed as more practical and more easily applicable than the more abstract classification of constructs, models, methods, and instantiations.

2.4 Theory Types

Theories are key instruments for structuring and organising large bodies of scientific knowledge. According to the Encyclopaedia Britannica, a scientific theory is a "systematic ideational structure of broad scope, conceived by the human imagination, that encompasses a family of empirical (experiential) laws regarding regularities existing in objects and events, both observed and posited. A scientific theory is a structure suggested by these laws and is devised to explain them in a scientifically rational manner" (Encyclopaedia Britannica 2014).

A theory consists of a set of statements about objects and their relationships and behaviours. It aims to explain these, typically through cause-and-effect relationships. Sometimes, a theory can also be used to predict future events.

One example of a theory is Agency Theory, which is concerned with conflicts between people with different interests in the same assets (Eisenhardt 1989). For example, the owners of a company (principals) may have different interests from those of the managers (agents of the principals). Basic constructs in Agency Theory include principal, agent, risk, goal, contract, and monitoring. These constructs are used in formulating descriptive statements, such as "Often agents do not act in the interest of their principals". The theory also includes explanatory statements, such as "As the principal and the agent have different goals, the agent does not always act in the interest of the principal", and predictive statements, such as "Monitoring may improve the efficacy of behaviour-based contracts". Thus, Agency Theory describes, explains, and predicts phenomena and events that occur in agency relationships.

Theories can vary widely in scope, from addressing narrowly defined phenomena to covering entire disciplines.

Grand theories—A grand theory is comprehensive in scope, highly abstract, and aims at providing grand theoretical schemes for explaining a wide variety of phenomena. Although a grand theory is typically not testable, it can inform and provide a basis for theories at a lower level. Within the social and behavioural sciences, some examples of grand theories are Marxism, functionalism, psychoanalysis, and structuration theory.

Middle-range theories—A middle-range theory explains a phenomenon on an intermediate level across different contexts. One example is Agency Theory as discussed above. Another example is the Technology Acceptance Model (Venkatesh and Davis 2000), an information systems theory that explains and predicts how users come to accept and use a technology.

Micro-range theories—A micro-range theory deals with a specific phenomenon in a particular setting, e.g. patient care in urban hospitals. The distinction between middle-range and micro-range theories is more one of degree than of kind, where middle-range theories address more general phenomena and wider contexts.

Within design science, many contributions are akin to micro-range theories, in which specific artefacts are developed and evaluated in particular practices. More abstract and mature design knowledge in the middle range may be organised in the form of design principles or design theories, as discussed in the next section.

2.5 Design Principles and Design Theory

Design science research does not only aim to produce artefacts but also to generate knowledge about them. For example, when having developed an artefact, it is often possible to generalise some of its features or structure into prescriptive statements that can be used across different contexts. Such statements are called *design principles* and express prescriptive knowledge that is not tied to a particular artefact or context but can help in designing different artefacts in many situations. Examples of design principles are architectural patterns and principles of HCI design. Norman (2013) has proposed a number of well-established principles for user interface design, including the following ones:

- *Visibility.* Users should know, just by looking at the interface, which options are available and how to access them.
- *Feedback.* Users should receive feedback whenever they have performed an action so they know whether or not it has been successful.
- *Affordance.* It should be easy for a user to figure out what to do by just looking at the components of the interface.
- *Consistency.* Similar-looking items in the interface should produce similar results when activated.

When design knowledge is mature and comprehensive, it can be systematised into a *design theory*. The purpose of expressing design knowledge as a theory is to make it explicit and systematic so that it can be used and extended in a process of cumulative knowledge development. Gregor and Jones (2007) have proposed an anatomy for design theories in the information systems area. Its components are described below and exemplified using Codd's relational database theory (Codd 1970):

- *Purpose and scope.* The set of requirements or goals that specifies the type of artefact to which the theory applies and in conjunction also defines its scope and boundaries. (Improved database technology is needed for increasing productivity as existing approaches of managing data persistence are failing.)
- *Constructs.* Representations of the entities of interest in the theory. These entities may be physical as well as abstract. (Attribute, tuple, n-ary relation, domain of values.)
- *Principle of form and function.* The abstract blueprint or architecture that describes an artefact. For a model, its components and their relationships and functions would be described. For a method, its activities and their order and purpose would be given. (A relation is defined over a domain of values and includes attributes and tuples.)
- *Artefact mutability.* The changes in the state of the artefact anticipated in the theory, i.e. the degree of artefact change encompassed by the theory. (The relational model allows for easy adaptation and change to base tables, while user views appear unchanged.)
- *Testable propositions.* Testable propositions about instantiations of the artefact under consideration. Typically, these propositions state that if a model or method is instantiated, then it will work, or it will have certain characteristics. (A relational database can perform as well as a non-relational database.)
- *Justificatory knowledge.* The underlying knowledge or theories that provide a basis and justification for the design. (Set theory and behavioural science about human cognitive processes.)
- *Principles of implementation.* Processes for implementing, i.e. instantiating, the artefact to which the theory applies (model or method) in specific situations. (Guidelines on how to create a relational database through normalisation procedures.)

- *Expository instantiation.* An implementation of the artefact that can assist in representing the theory both as an expository device and for purposes of testing. An instantiation can support communication about the artefact of a design theory. (A working relational database with tables filled with data.)

A design theory structures the knowledge about an artefact. A related question is how to organise the research activities through which an artefact is designed and evaluated; this question is the focus of the following chapters.

2.6   Summary of Chapter

- Knowledge can be classified in different ways, e.g. based on its purposes and the different ways of materialising the knowledge.
- *Knowledge types* classify knowledge based on its different purposes. The main knowledge types are:

  – *Definitional knowledge*, which includes concepts, constructs, terminologies, definitions, vocabularies, classifications, and taxonomies.
  – *Descriptive knowledge*, which describes and analyses an existing or past reality.
  – *Explanatory knowledge*, which provides answers to "how" and "why" questions and thus explains how objects behave and why events occur, often through causal relationships.
  – *Predictive knowledge*, which offers black-box predictions, i.e. it predicts outcomes based on underlying factors but without explaining causal or other relationships between them.
  – *Explanatory and predictive knowledge*, which offers both explanations and predictions.
  – *Prescriptive knowledge*, which consists of prescriptive models and methods that help to solve practical problems.

- *Knowledge forms* classify knowledge based on its materialisation, i.e. where it exists and in what shape. Example of knowledge forms are:

  – *Explicit knowledge*, i.e. knowledge that is articulated, expressed, and recorded in media, e.g. text, numbers, codes, formulas, musical notations, and video tracks.
  – *Embodied knowledge*, i.e. knowledge that resides in the minds of people and is often difficult to express in an explicit way.
  – *Embedded knowledge*, i.e. knowledge that resides not in humans but in entities, such as physical objects, processes, routines, or structures.

- There are four types of artefacts, according to a well-established classification within design science: *constructs, models, methods, and instantiations.*

- A *theory* aims to explain objects and their relationships, typically through cause-and-effect relationships. A theory can sometimes also be used to predict future events.
- A *design theory* is a theory that systematises the knowledge about an artefact, including purpose and scope, constructs, principle of form and function, artefact mutability, testable propositions, justificatory knowledge, principles of implementation, and expository instantiations.

2.7 Review Questions

1. For each of the following, determine the type of knowledge expressed (definitional, descriptive, explanatory, predictive, explanatory and predictive, or prescriptive):

   (a) Programming code should always be carefully commented.
   (b) Humans have 32 teeth.
   (c) The primary cause of global warming is the emission of carbon dioxide into the atmosphere.
   (d) Every rectangle has four sides.
   (e) The atomic number of gold is 79.

2. Some knowledge can be both explanatory and predictive. Can some knowledge be both definitional and descriptive?
3. Why are cause-and-effect relationships important in explanatory knowledge?
4. Explain the role of predictive knowledge for prescriptive knowledge.
5. Below are three cases of embodied knowledge. Which one of these would be most difficult to transform into explicit knowledge?

   (a) How to diagnose a disease
   (b) How to console a patient
   (c) How to transplant a kidney

6. Is it more difficult to transform embedded knowledge into explicit knowledge for novel artefacts than for established ones?
7. For each of the following artefacts, determine whether it is a construct, a model, a method, or an instantiation:

   (a) A mobile currency converter app
   (b) An HTML tag
   (c) A framework for decision support systems
   (d) A business intelligence system
   (e) Guidelines for change management
   (f) A privacy architecture

8. How are constructs related to models?
9. Can a model be both descriptive and prescriptive?

2.8   Answers to Selected Review Questions

1. (a) prescriptive (b) descriptive (c) explanatory (d) definitional (e) descriptive.
2. No. Definitional knowledge does not say anything about the world as it exists or has existed.
6. It is typically more difficult to make knowledge about novel artefacts explicit, since such artefacts may be less well understood, and there is not much information available about their use.
7. (a) instantiation (b) construct (c) model (d) instantiation (e) method (f) model.
8. Constructs are the building blocks of models.
9. As an example, consider an architecture for an Electronic Health Record (EHR) system. If this architecture faithfully describes the structure of existing EHR systems, it is a descriptive model. At the same time, someone can claim that the architecture should be used for building new EHR systems, thereby turning it into a prescriptive model. Thus, the answer is yes, as the same model can play different roles in different contexts.

2.9   Further Reading

The discussion on knowledge types in this chapter is informed by the work by Gregor (2006), who investigates the structural nature of theory in the area of information systems. She proposes a taxonomy of information systems theories based on the goals they address: analysis, explanation, prediction, and prescription. She then distinguishes among five types of theories: theory for analysing, for explaining, for predicting, for explaining and predicting, and for design and action. She also discusses how the theory under development relates to the choice of epistemological and methodological approach. While the knowledge types of this chapter are close to Gregor's theory types, they differ in that they are applicable not only to entire theories but also to smaller pieces of knowledge. Furthermore, we also consider an additional type, definitional knowledge, which offers solely conceptual and terminological structure without analysing, explaining, predicting, or prescribing. Definitional knowledge (conceptual knowledge) is also included among the types of knowledge proposed by Iivari (2007).

Knowledge forms are discussed by Madhavan and Grover (1998) in the context of new product development with the notions of tacit knowledge and distributed cognition as a basis. Blackler (1995) investigates forms, or images, of knowledge as they have been viewed within the area of organisational learning, and he identifies five images of knowledge: embodied, embedded, embrained, encultured, and encoded. He also criticises this static way of viewing knowledge and argues that knowledge, or knowing, can better be viewed as an active process that is mediated, situated, provisional, pragmatic, and contested. Lam (2000) offers a classification of knowledge forms by combining ontological and epistemological dimensions, which is then used for relating knowledge forms, organisational forms, and societal institutions. Curley et al. (2013) discuss how results from design science research can be encoded as design patterns that are similar to the architectural patterns proposed by Alexander et al. (1997). Design principles are investigated by Sein et al. (2011).

The four types of artefacts discussed in Sect. 2.3.1 were originally introduced as kinds of research outputs by March and Smith (1995) and have been further investigated by Hevner et al. (2004).

References

Alexander C et al (1997) A pattern language: towns, buildings, construction. Oxford University Press, New York

Argote L (2012) Organizational learning: creating, retaining and transfer ring knowledge, 2nd edn. 2013 edition.Springer, New York

Bennett JG (2018) The dramatic universe: volume 1: the foundations of natural philosophy (The collected works of J.G. Bennett), vol. 4, 3rd edn. CreateSpace Independent Publishing, Scotts Valley

Blackler F (1995) Knowledge, knowledge work and organizations: an overview and interpretation. Org Stud (16)(6):1021–1046

Boehm BW (1981) Software engineering economics. 1st edn. Prentice Hall, Englewood Cliffs

Bolstorff P, Rosenbaum R (2007) Supply chain excellence: a hand-book for dramatic improvement using the SCOR model: 4, 2nd edn. AMACOM, New York

Checkland P, Scholes J (1990) Soft systems methodology in practice. Wiley, Chichester

Codd EF (1970) A relational model of data for large shared data banks. Commun ACM 13(6):377–387

Cohn M (2009) Succeeding with agile: software development using scrum, 1st edn. Addison-Wesley, Boston

Curley M, Kenneally J, Ashurst C (2013) Design science and design patterns: a rationale for the application of design-patterns within design science research to accelerate knowledge discovery and innovation adoption. In: Helfert M, Donnellan B (eds) Design science: perspectives from Europe. Communications in computer and information science. Springer, Berlin, pp 29–37

Day JD, Zimmermann H (1983) The OSI reference model. Proc IEEE 71(12), 1334–1340

Delone WH, McLean ER (2003) The DeLone and McLean model of information systems success: a ten-year update. J Manag Inf Syst 19(4):9–30

Eisenhardt, KM, Agency theory: an assessment and review. Acad Manage Rev 14(1), 57–74

Encyclopaedia Britannica (2014) medicine. http://global.britannica.com/EBchecked/topic/372431/medicine. Accessed July 3 2014

Gregor S (2006) The nature of theory in information systems. MIS Quarterly 30(3), 611–642

Gregor S, Jones D (2007) The anatomy of a design science theory. J Assoc Inf Syst 8(5), 312–335

Hevner AR et al (2004) Design science in information systems research. MIS Quarterly 28(1), 75–105

Iivari J (2007) A paradigmatic analysis of information systems as a design science. Scand J Inf Syst 19(2):39–64

Kroll P, Kruchten P (2003) The rational unified process made easy: a practitioner's guide to the RUP. Addison-Wesley, Boston

Lam A (2000) Tacit knowledge, organizational learning and societal institutions: an integrated framework. Organ Stud 21(3):487–513

Madhavan R, Grover R (1998) From embedded knowledge to embodied knowledge: new product development as knowledge management. J Mark 62(4):1–12

March ST, Smith GF (1995) Design and natural science research on information technology. Decis Supp Syst 15(4):251–266

Norman D (2013) The design of everyday things: revised and expanded edition, 2nd edn. Basic Books, New York

Offermann P et al (2010) Artifact types in information systems design science – a literature review. In: Winter R, Zhao JL, Aier S Global perspectives on design science research. Lecture notes in computer science. Springer, Berlin, pp 77–92

Seely Brown J, Duguid P (2006) Balancing act: how to capture knowledge without killing it. In: Prusak L, Matson E (eds) Knowledge management and organizational learning: a reader. Oxford University Press, Oxford

Sein M et al (2011) Action design research. Manage Inf Syst Quart 35(1), 37–56

Venkatesh V, Davis FD (2000) A theoretical extension of the technology acceptance model: four longitudinal field studies. Manage Sci 46(2):186–204

Wikipedia Contributor (2014) Knowledge. http://en.wikipedia.org/wiki/Knowledge. Accessed June 26 2014

Chapter 3
Research Strategies and Methods

Design science is not a research strategy, nor is it a research method. But design science projects make use of both research strategies and research methods.

The purpose of research is to create reliable and useful knowledge based on empirical evidence and logical arguments. Evidence and arguments need to be presented clearly to other researchers, so that they can review them and determine whether they hold up to the standards of academic research. In order to support researchers in creating, structuring, and presenting their results, many scientific communities have developed and established a number of research strategies and methods. This chapter offers an overview of a number of well-established research strategies and methods for empirical research, specifically within the social sciences. These strategies and methods are also useful for design science research, in particular when investigating practical problems, defining requirements, and evaluating artefacts.

3.1 Research Strategies

A *research strategy* is an overall plan for conducting a research study. A research strategy guides a researcher in planning, executing, and monitoring the study. While the research strategy provides useful support at a high level, it needs to be complemented with research methods that can guide the research work at a more detailed level. Research methods tell the researcher how to collect and analyse data, e.g. through interviews, questionnaires, or statistical methods. Thus, a research strategy offers high-level guidance, while a research method can be seen as a technique or tool for performing a specific task.

© Springer Nature Switzerland AG 2021
P. Johannesson, E. Perjons, *An Introduction to Design Science*,
https://doi.org/10.1007/978-3-030-78132-3_3

Since there are numerous different research strategies, a researcher needs to determine which one of these to choose and apply to embark on a study. This choice depends on the goals and characteristics of the study being undertaken, and three main questions should be considered when choosing an appropriate strategy:

- Is it suitable for the research question?
- Is it feasible, taking into account the resources of the research project?
- Is it ethical, considering its possible effects on people, animals, and the environment?

A research strategy should be suitable for its purpose, i.e. it should help the researcher to find an answer to the research question under consideration. For example, an experiment may help identify the cause of some event, but it is probably less suitable for exploring an unknown topic. It may be the other way around for grounded theory. Similarly, a case study can be the right choice for investigating complex social relationships in a specific setting, while it is probably inappropriate for measuring attitudes in a large population.

The research strategy should also be feasible from a practical standpoint. The researcher needs to have access to data sources, such as people and documents, which may be difficult to obtain when people are busy or documents are confidential. The researcher may also need special resources, such as laboratory equipment or computer software. The need for various resources depends on the choice of research strategy; therefore, some strategies may not be feasible in certain situations. Furthermore, some research strategies, such as action research, are highly time consuming, which can make them inappropriate for small-scale research projects.

The researcher should ensure that the chosen research strategy can be followed in an ethically responsible way. On a general level, this means that no one should suffer harm as a consequence of the research study, neither humans, nor animals, nor the environment. In social research, it is common to require that the participants in a study be allowed to remain anonymous, that they should have the possibility to withdraw from the study whenever they so desire, that they should be informed about their role and rights in the research study, and that data collected will be confidential and not used for purposes other than those of the study.

In the rest of this section, a number of empirical research strategies are discussed, followed by a brief summary of the role of simulation and mathematical proof in research.

3.1.1 Experiments

An *experiment* is an empirical study that investigates cause-and-effect relationships. The purpose of an experiment is to prove or disprove a causal relationship between a factor and an observed outcome. Such a relationship can be formulated as a *hypothesis*, often in the form "Factor X causes outcome Y". Some examples of hypotheses are:

- Solar radiation causes skin diseases.
- Introducing workflow systems causes an increase in productivity.
- The high usability of an IT system has a positive effect on its actual use.

A hypothesis can be expressed more precisely by using the notions of *dependent variables* and *independent variables*. An independent variable corresponds to the cause in a hypothesis, while the dependent variable corresponds to the outcome. An independent variable affects one or more dependent variables, e.g. the amount of solar radiation positively affects the frequency of skin diseases. In other words, the independent variable has a causal effect on the dependent variable, meaning that the latter is dependent upon the former.

A researcher carrying out an experiment for testing a hypothesis will manipulate an independent variable and then observe whether this has any effect on the dependent variables. The researcher can do so by introducing, removing, or changing the value of an independent variable. For example, a researcher may distribute a new medication (the independent variable) to a group of people with diabetes and observe whether this reduces their symptoms (the dependent variables). If the people actually get better, this fact supports the hypothesis that the medication eases the symptoms of diabetes patients. However, the experiment cannot definitively prove that the medication has had this effect, as other factors may have influenced the result, such as other diseases of the patients, their social situations, or their expectations. This observation holds true for all experiments. No experiment can definitively prove or disprove a hypothesis; an experiment can only increase or decrease the support for it.

The purpose of an experiment is to show that one single factor has a certain effect on another factor. Still, there is always a risk that other factors may come into play and invalidate the results of the experiment. Therefore, a researcher needs to control these other factors, and several techniques have been designed to allow for this. One technique is to eliminate a factor from the experiment, e.g. people suffering from a cold would not be allowed to participate in the experiment described above. Another technique is to hold a factor constant, e.g. by only allowing people of the same age to participate in an experiment. A third technique is to randomly select the subjects in an experiment, as this would cancel out the effects of factors that could interfere with the results. Yet another technique is to use control groups, in which two groups with similar compositions are identified. One of these groups forms the treatment group, and the other forms the control group. The independent variable is manipulated for the treatment group (e.g. a medication is distributed) but not for the control group. The researcher then measures the values of the dependent variables for the two groups, and any differences between them can be attributed to the manipulation of the independent variable.

To fully control the various factors influencing experiments, researchers typically prefer to carry them out in an artificial environment, such as in a laboratory. Such *laboratory experiments* not only allow for close control of factors but also for precise measurements. However, laboratory experiments have the drawback that the settings in which they are carried out may be so artificial that the conclusions drawn from them are not valid outside the laboratory. In order to overcome this challenge, field experiments can be conducted. A *field experiment* starts from a naturally occurring situation and tries to study it in the form of an experiment. The researcher still manipulates the independent variable but does so in a real-life setting, meaning that the experiment can be influenced by many factors that are difficult to control. An example is an experiment for investigating whether physical exercise influences weight in which the treatment group is asked to exercise more often in their day-to-day life, while the control group does not change their daily habits. Clearly, many factors can confound the results, e.g. people in the treatment group disregarding the instructions. A *natural experiment* is also carried out in the everyday environment of the participants, but unlike a field experiment, the researcher has no influence over the independent variable. Instead, changes in the independent variable occur due to natural causes. For example, a natural experiment could compare the incidence of skin diseases in regions with many sun hours and few sun hours.

The advantages and disadvantages of laboratory and field experiments can be explained in terms of internal and external validity. *Internal validity* depends on whether the observed change in a dependent variable is indeed caused by a corresponding change in an independent variable rather than by other factors. *External validity* depends on the generalisability of the results of an experiment, i.e. whether the same results can be expected for other occasions and situations. Laboratory experiments are typically strong on internal validity, as potentially interfering factors can be closely controlled. But they can be weak on external validity, as their artificial characteristics may not apply to real-world situations. For example, even if a medical treatment has beneficial effects when given in a controlled hospital environment, the same effects may not be observed when patients receive the treatment in their ordinary, day-to-day, living environment. The situation is reversed for field experiments, in which internal validity is low because many factors cannot be controlled, while external validity may be high.

3.1.2 Surveys

The word "survey" means to look upon or oversee something. This is also the purpose of a *survey* as a research strategy, which aims to map out some world, be it physical or social. A survey usually has a broad coverage and provides a helicopter view of some area of interest. In the social sciences, surveys are frequently used to gather basic data about large groups of people, including their activities, beliefs, and attitudes. This is also done in non-academic surveys, such as opinion polls and market surveys. The breadth of surveys means that they work best for collecting data on narrow and well-defined topics, while they are less suitable for studying complex phenomena in greater depth. For example, a survey is a good strategy for identifying the attitudes held by people in different income groups about the value of various diets. In contrast, a survey is less appropriate for investigating the feelings that people experience when they fail to comply with a new diet.

Surveys can take many different forms. A traditional form is the *postal survey*, in which a questionnaire is mailed to a number of people. *Telephone surveys* have also been used in the social sciences for a long time, and they enable a researcher to interact with a respondent during a telephone call. Another survey form that is becoming more popular is the *Internet survey*, for which the Internet is used as a medium for delivering the survey. This can be done via email, a web site, or through social media such as Facebook or LinkedIn. A common disadvantage of postal as well as telephone and Internet surveys is that they tend to get low response rates because people are often too busy to participate in them. One form of survey that is able to, at least partially, overcome this problem is the *face-to-face survey*, in which the researcher directly interacts with the respondents. An example of a face-to-face survey is when a researcher interviews people who are waiting at a bus stop. While all of the above forms of surveys aim to obtain responses from people through interviews or questionnaires, there are also surveys that rely on observations or documents.

An *observational survey* does not view people as respondents but instead as actors whose behaviour can be studied. One example of an observational survey is a study that measures how much people actually consume of various food categories, i.e. the real intake is recorded, and not what people state that they eat. A *document survey* uses documents for gathering data. Such documents include newspaper articles, legal documents, annual reports, medical records, computer logs, web pages, or photographs. The wealth of data that is continuously produced by social media nowadays provides a rich source for document surveys, e.g. a survey based on retweets of Twitter posts by European politicians.

A main concern of any survey study is that of sampling. *Sampling* is about the selection of individuals within a population, e.g. selecting 500 people to interview from a city population of 1,000,000. Sampling is almost always required for surveys, as studying an entire population is usually prohibitively expensive. A major challenge in sampling is to determine whether results that hold for a particular sample can be generalised to the population from which it was drawn. A useful distinction is made between representative and exploratory samples. A *representative sample* is intended to offer a true mirror image of the entire population in the sense that it has the same distribution of relevant characteristics. For example, a representative sample of a national population should include roughly as many men as women and have an age distribution similar to that of the population. An *exploratory sample*, on the other hand, is not required to be representative of its population but instead is used as a means of gathering information in order to explore a new area. For example, an exploratory sample taken in order to elicit requirements for a new tech gadget would include people with a particular interest in that type of gadget, as they are most likely to provide the best ideas; it is not important that they faithfully mirror the population from which they come.

In order to generate a representative sample, various sampling techniques can be used. Common to all of them is that they ensure that the researcher cannot influence the inclusion of particular individuals in the sample. *Random sampling* means that each individual has an equal chance of being selected and is seen as the gold standard for creating representative samples. However, in some cases, random sampling can become expensive, and other techniques have been designed that offer a balance between cost-effectiveness and random selection, e.g. cluster sampling and stratified sampling.

Purposive sampling is a useful technique for generating an exploratory sample. The goal here is to identify a limited number of individuals who can provide especially valuable information to the researcher. The individuals may have some privileged knowledge or experiences about the topic being explored, e.g. through their professional roles. Therefore, the researcher may personally invite them to be part of the sample. One example would be a study of electronic health records, where experienced physicians and nurses could be handpicked to form an exploratory sample. Purposive sampling is sometimes combined with *snowball sampling*, in which the initial participants are selected and they, themselves, suggest further individuals to add to the sample. When using purposive sampling, the sample size is typically small, as the goal is not to ensure representativity but to identify individuals who can offer insights on the research question addressed.

A strength of surveys is that they allow researchers to collect large amounts of data inexpensively and over a short time span. They also enable the collection of quantitative as well as qualitative data. One disadvantage is that the collected data may be superficial when individuals do not have the time or inclination to provide detailed answers to the researcher's questions. For the same reason, some individuals may choose not to participate at all, resulting in a low response rate.

3.1.3 Case Studies

A *case study* focuses on one instance of the phenomenon to be investigated, and it offers a rich, in-depth description and insight into that instance. With its focus on depth and context, a case study differs from a survey or a laboratory experiment. While a survey can provide a broad but shallow view of an area, a case study can paint a pregnant and detailed picture of its subject. A laboratory experiment reduces complexity by controlling, even eliminating, factors that can interfere with the experimental results. In contrast, complexity is essential to a successful case study, as it investigates multiple factors, events, and relationships that occur in a real-world case.

The case study research strategy can be characterised as follows:

- *Focus on one instance.* The idea is "To see a World in a Grain of Sand, And a Heaven in a Wild Flower, Hold Infinity in the palm of your hand, And Eternity in an hour" as expressed by Blake (2012).
- *Focus on depth.* As much information as possible about the instance studied should be obtained, without shying away from any details.

- *Natural setting.* The instance exists before and independently of the research project, and it should be studied in its ordinary context; it should not be moved to, or created in, a laboratory.
- *Relationships and processes.* The instance should be studied in a holistic way, taking into account all the relationships and processes within the instance as well as in its environment.
- *Multiple sources and methods.* Multiple information sources should be consulted in order to obtain rich, multi-faceted knowledge about the instance; when doing this, different data collection methods could be used, such as interviews and observation.

A case study often addresses only a single instance, but it can also address a small number of instances. Each instance should be self-contained and have a clear boundary so that it can be distinguished from its environment. In social sciences, a typical instance may be a person, a company, a department in an organisation, a project, an IT system, or a regulation. An instance can be studied at a single point in time by investigating the present situation, but it can also be studied over time in a *longitudinal study*.

Case studies can be used for different purposes, including exploratory, descriptive, and explanatory ones. An *exploratory case study* is used to generate research questions or hypotheses that can be used in other studies. It is particularly valuable when a researcher enters a new area in which little is known, and the literature is scarce. A *descriptive case study* aims to produce a rich and detailed description of an instance and its environment. An *explanatory case study* not only offers a description but also tries to identify cause and effect relationships that can explain why certain events occurred.

A key decision in any case study is the choice of the instance to be studied. The first step is to determine the kind of phenomenon to investigate, which depends on the research question to be answered. For example, in the context of workflow systems for companies, there are at least three kinds of phenomena that can be investigated: people, companies, and workflow systems. If the research question is about the effect of workflow systems on profitability, the instance could be a company. On the other hand, it could be a person, if the research question is about the psychological effects of workflow technology. When the kind of phenomenon has been determined, the next step is to choose the actual instance. This choice can be based on several different considerations. One option is to choose a typical, representative instance so that the findings from it can be generalised to an entire class. Another option is to choose an extreme instance in order to investigate special and unusual features of a phenomenon. Yet another reason for choosing an instance is that it can work as a test bed for a theory, i.e. it can be used for investigating whether predictions and explanations offered by a theory actually conform to the instance. A complementary reason for choosing a certain instance is convenience, i.e. that it is easily accessible.

A common criticism of case studies is that their results only apply to the instance being studied, i.e. that the results cannot be generalised. To address such criticism, a case study researcher needs to clarify the extent to which an instance is representative of a class of similar instances. For example, if the use of workflow systems has been studied in a small company in the retail sector, it would be reasonable to claim that the results from the study can be generalised to other small companies in the same sector. However, the results may neither generalise to large companies in the retail sector nor to companies in other industry sectors.

3.1.4 Ethnography

Ethnography is about describing peoples or cultures. Ethnography has its roots in anthropology, in which researchers visited far-off exotic places and studied the people living there. The researchers did so by staying at one place for a long time and trying to live in the same way as its inhabitants, thereby learning how the people perceived their world, interacted with each other, and formed beliefs about themselves and their environment. While anthropology has focused on people in foreign lands, ethnography has turned to study groups and sub-cultures in modern society. Some work in ethnography has targeted people who can be seen as living outside mainstream society, such as drug users, religious sects, criminal gangs, and homeless people. Other ethnographic work has investigated more mundane settings, such as schoolyards and workplaces. Within the IT area, ethnographers have studied topics, such as the work practices of programmers and the use of social media services. Regardless of the area studied, ethnographic works have a number of common characteristics:

- Ethnographers spend a large amount of time in the field, living together with the people they are studying; they are active participants rather than passive observers.
- Ethnographers do not set up any laboratory experiments but take part in the existing practices of the people they are studying.
- Ethnographers try to understand the culture they are studying from the perspective of its members, i.e. how they perceive and understand their world and how they attach meaning to it.
- Ethnographers not only study special events and ceremonies in a culture but also the activities and thoughts of ordinary people in their everyday lives.
- Ethnographers take a holistic stance incorporating a multitude of perspectives in their work, including social, cultural, religious, political, and economic ones.
- Ethnographers use multiple data collection methods, including interviews, observations, and documents, and record their experiences and interpretations in extensive field notes.

There are different approaches, or schools, of how ethnographic work is to be carried out. The *holistic school* emphasises empathy and argues that the ethnographer needs to live among the people being studied; only then can they fully understand and absorb the culture of those people. Critics argue that this is an unrealistic goal—the preconceptions and previous experiences of ethnographers will limit their empathetic capabilities so much that a deep understanding of unknown cultures is out of reach. The *semiotic school* does not focus on identification and empathy but instead argues that the ethnographer should primarily investigate signs, symbols, and signification. Key research objects are then words, expressions, sayings, rules, institutions, and rituals. The ethnographer studies the relationships between these symbolic forms and how they relate to each other and to the culture at large. The *critical school*, in contrast, suggests that the ethnographer needs to go beyond the symbolic forms and investigate the power relationships and structures of subordination that lie beneath them. The researcher should take a critical attitude and reveal unstated assumptions that are taken for granted in a culture, e.g. about the role of women or the authority of political leaders.

A main concern in ethnography is that of *reflexivity*, i.e. the relationship between the ethnographer, the people being studied, and the research process. It is purported that the researchers can never be objective and disinterested observers of a culture but will always perceive and interpret based on their own culture and background. Thus, an ethnographic work may not reflect the lives and beliefs of the people being studied, but rather its author's preconceptions and prejudices. In other words, the researchers themselves may obstruct the study of the people and culture. In order to meet this challenge, researchers need to reflect on, and in their writings report upon, their own background, including their age, gender, education, personal beliefs, and interests. Other related issues are how researchers may influence, and be perceived by, the people they study.

One of the main difficulties in ethnographic work is the tension between the desire to provide a descriptive account of a culture and the insight that any such description is inevitably coloured by the background of the researcher. Another difficulty is that ethnographic studies easily become stories, which may be vivid and interesting reads in themselves but do not contribute to analytical insights or theory development. Ethnographical work also often gives rise to ethical challenges, in particular concerning privacy and consent.

3.1.5 Grounded Theory

Grounded theory is a research strategy that strives to develop theories through the analysis of empirical data. In contrast to experiments, grounded theory does not start with a hypothesis to be tested but instead with data from which a theory can be generated. Grounded theory also differs from research strategies, such as ethnography, which are content to provide rich descriptions of particular situations but no theories. Grounded theory challenges a top-down theorising approach, in which the researcher first develops a theory and then checks whether it conforms to empirical data. Instead, grounded theory insists that empirical data is the starting point upon which theories are to be built—theory emerges through analysis and is grounded in the data.

Grounded theory is particularly useful for exploratory research studies. When a researcher addresses an area for which established theories do not exist, grounded theory offers an approach for developing a new theory. Grounded theory is also well suited for small-scale projects, as it does not require the collection of massive amounts of quantitative data.

Open-mindedness is essential to the research process of grounded theory. Researchers should not start with a theory or preconceptions through which they view the field and the empirical data. No theory should determine what the researchers focus upon. Instead, the analysis of empirical data should guide the researchers in their investigation. In other words, researchers should come with an open mind to the field and be prepared to discover new data, concepts, and insights as they go along. This does not mean that they must be ignorant about existing theories that might be relevant but that they should not allow themselves to be limited by these.

In most research strategies, the sample to be used in a study should be determined at the beginning of the research process. However, in grounded theory, the sample emerges gradually during the entire process. The researchers start by collecting and analysing data on one or a few objects (a person, site, event, document, etc.). Based on the outcome of this analysis, they select additional objects to investigate. When selecting these objects, the researchers do not try to identify typical or representative objects but instead look for objects that can help illuminate or extend concepts and categories built in the previous analysis. The researchers select objects that they can compare and contrast to other objects already analysed, thereby helping them to further develop the partial theory that they have built so far. Thus, the sampling is informed by the analysis of the empirical data, and sampling, data collection, and data analysis proceed in an iterative manner. This form of sampling is called *theoretical sampling*.

The researchers collect data continuously, i.e. they add objects to their sample as long as these provide new insights. In grounded theory, this idea is expressed by saying that researchers continue sampling until they reach the point of *theoretical saturation*. At this point, new empirical data does not help researchers to further develop the theory, i.e. no new concepts, categories, or relationships between these are discovered. When theoretical saturation has been reached, additional data do not extend or refine the theory but only confirm it. Reaching theoretical saturation can be seen as a "stop condition" for data collection.

In grounded theory, researchers typically collect qualitative data, e.g. from interviews. The data are analysed through coding and categorisation, meaning that researchers identify small pieces of raw data and label them by assigning codes to them. For example, if researchers have interviewed people about their experiences of a new IT system that has been introduced in their organisation, they will first transcribe the interviews and then start coding. They will identify perceptions, attitudes, emotions, and other factors expressed in the material. For example, they may identify that the respondents have talked about things like increased control, short response times, and training needs. They will make these into codes and highlight portions in the transcription, thereby producing so-called excerpts. They will then assign one or more codes to each excerpt. In this way, researchers label pieces of data based on their content. This activity is often called *open coding*.

In open coding, researchers describe empirical data by chopping them up and labelling the resulting pieces with codes. But this is not sufficient for arriving at a deep understanding of the data; there is also a need to categorise the codes and relate them to each other. In *axial coding*, researchers identify the most important codes and suggest categories under which the codes can be grouped. For example, they may introduce categories, such as *success factor* (and make it to include the codes: *short response time* and *positive attitude*). Finally, researchers move on to *selective coding*, in which they focus on the main codes and categories and identify relationships between these. Based on the results from the open, axial, and selective coding, researchers can suggest and identify core concepts and their interrelationships in the domain under investigation. From these, they can then build a theory for explaining events and other phenomena in the domain.

A major challenge for any study using grounded theory is to maintain the ideal of an open mind. Every researcher will have a background of previous experiences and knowledge, and the extent to which these really can be set aside when collecting and analysing data in the field is an open question. Another question is whether researchers should refrain from acquiring knowledge on a domain before embarking on a study based on grounded theory. The advantage of doing so would be that they can avoid preconceptions that could bias their work, but at the same time, they might forgo valuable knowledge that could help to build a relevant theory.

3.1.6 Action Research

Action research is a research strategy that is used to address practical problems that appear in real-world settings. An action researcher does not only strive to generate new scientific knowledge but also to solve important problems that people experience in their practices. Action research has become particularly popular in areas where the practitioners themselves can contribute to the improvement of their own practices, such as in education, health care, and organisational change. The main characteristics of action research are as follows:

- *Focus on practice.* Whereas a laboratory experiment takes place in an artificial environment, an action research study is carried out in a local practice, in the real world where people live, breathe, and act.
- *Change in practice.* The local practice should be changed and this change should be evaluated; researchers need to move beyond observing, describing, and theorising and become change agents.
- *Active practitioner participation.* Practitioners are not passive subjects to be studied by the researcher; instead, they are active participants who contribute with their own knowledge to help solve practical problems, and they may even initiate and govern an action research study.

- *Cyclical process.* Research is carried out within a feedback loop in which the researcher plans changes to be introduced in a practice, carries out these changes, and then evaluates and reflects on them; this cycle can then be repeated several times.
- *Action outcomes and research outcomes.* An action research project should ideally produce results that are valuable for the local practice in which the project was carried out as well as results that contribute to the academic knowledge base.

The cyclical action research process consists of five phases:

1. *Diagnosis.* Investigate and analyse the problem situation in order to understand how it can be changed.
2. *Planning.* Plan actions that can change and improve the current situation.
3. *Intervention.* Carry out actions in order to change the current situation in accordance with the plan.
4. *Evaluation.* Evaluate the effects of the intervention, in particular whether the situation has improved.
5. *Reflection.* Reflect on the research carried out, in particular the results for the local practice and the new knowledge generated; decide whether or not to carry out a new action research cycle.

Action research differs significantly from other research strategies with respect to active practitioner participation. The typical situation for most work within other strategies is that a researcher asks a research question and designs a study to answer it. Without the active participation of practitioners, the researcher then carries out the study and arrives at results that answer the research question. The results may be shared with the practitioners involved in the study, and they may decide to use the results later on to improve their practice if they so desire. Thus, carrying out research is separate from making changes in a practice. In contrast, doing research and introducing changes is intertwined in action research studies, and practitioners take a leading role in both these activities. Practitioners may even initiate and sponsor an action research study, and their knowledge and actions are essential resources for the research process.

Action research studies may have different purposes, and a distinction can be made between technical, practical, and emancipatory studies. *Technical action research* aims at functional improvements, i.e. improving effectiveness and efficiency in a practice, often from a managerial perspective. *Practical action research* also aims to improve the practitioners' understanding of themselves and their work. The purpose is not only practice improvement but also self-education, including self-reflection, which can help people to change themselves. *Emancipatory action research* includes the purposes of both technical and practical action research, but it also aims to help people to critically evaluate and reflect upon their practice as well as its organisational and social context. Practitioners are equipped with the means to question the goals of their practice and organisation. Instead of accepting the goals uncritically as they have been handed down through tradition, or have been defined by management, practitioners are empowered to reject or revise the goals on rational grounds.

One challenge for action research studies is to generalise their results, as they are often closely tied to a single local practice. Another challenge is that the participants in an action research study, both practitioners and researchers, may not be able to remain impartial, as they are deeply involved in the study personally. From a project management point of view, another challenge is that practitioners may be so busy with their ordinary work that they cannot contribute as much as desired to the action research study.

3.1.7 Phenomenology

Phenomenology is a research strategy that focuses on the perceptions and experiences of people as well as their feelings and emotions. A phenomenological study does not aim to establish cause-and-effect relationships or to describe a population through statistical means. Instead, it aims to describe and understand the lived experiences of people and thereby provide insight into the topic being studied. For example, a phenomenological study of drug addicts does not seek to identify the causes of drug abuse or survey the frequency of drug addiction in a certain population. Instead, the goal is to gain understanding of what it means to be a drug addict, what it feels like, and what kinds of experiences the drug addicts have in their daily lives.

A key notion in phenomenology is that of *lived experiences*, i.e. how people experience the world in an immediate sense, pre-reflectively, without objectifying, classifying, or abstracting it. Based on these lived experiences, phenomenology investigates how social life is constructed by the people who participate in it. This means that social structures are not imposed from above and neither are people just automatons that follow a basic script. Instead, they create the social world together by giving meaning to their lived experiences. The goal of the phenomenological researcher is to understand this meaning.

In order to understand the lived experiences and sense-making of other people, phenomenological researchers need to step back from their own preconceptions and common sense. They need to suspend, as far as possible, their everyday beliefs as well as theoretical assumptions, so they become able to approach other people with an open mind. Only then can they get a clear understanding of the perceptions and experiences of other people.

The primary form of data collection in a phenomenological study is the long, unstructured interview. In such an interview, respondents are able to really tell their own story without being unduly influenced by researchers. They can also choose to bring up now topics that are important to them but which were not foreseen by the researchers. Researchers can also use the interview to check that they have understood the respondent correctly.

Phenomenological work often generates results that are highly readable and interesting for a broad audience, as they concern ordinary people in their everyday lives. Phenomenology can also enable novel insights into complex social phenomena, as it frees the researcher from specific theories. However, phenomenology has been criticised for lacking scientific rigour and for being too focused on description rather than on analysis and explanation. Thus, phenomenology has many similarities with ethnography, but it is more focused on the creation of individual meaning and identity.

3.1.8 Simulation

While the above empirical research strategies investigate a naturally occurring or contrived reality, a simulation studies an imitation of reality. More precisely, a *simulation* is an imitation of the behaviour of a real-world process or system over time. Simulations are useful for training people, when the real-world process can be hazardous or expensive, e.g. flight simulations. Simulations can also be used for analysing and making predictions about complex systems, e.g. weather simulations. Today, simulations are used in a wide variety of contexts, including safety engineering, education, finance, production, and games.

A *computer simulation* is a simulation that runs on computers and reproduces or predicts the behaviour of a system. Underlying the computer simulation, there is an abstract model of the system being simulated. As the power and sophistication of computers increase, ever more complex computer simulations can be carried out in areas such as traffic engineering, weather forecasting, climate change, and strategic management.

Simulations can also be carried out by humans, e.g. in role-playing. A *role-play simulation* is a simulation in which human participants take on different roles or profiles in the enactment of a process in a contrived setting. An example is a war game in which no actual military engagement occurs; instead, the participants use maps, computers, and other devices to simulate combat. Role-play simulation has also become popular in learning, as it allows for more creative and engaging learning experiences than language-based learning.

3.1.9 Mathematical and Logical Proof

A *mathematical proof* is a rigorous deductive argument that demonstrates the truth of a certain proposition. In a proof, other previously proven propositions can be used as parts of the argument. In the end, a proof should rest on self-evident or assumed propositions, often called axioms. A proven proposition is called a theorem, while a still unproven proposition that is believed to be true is called a conjecture. Mathematical proofs typically employ logical reasoning but may also make use of more informal reasoning through natural language. A proof that is written in a symbolic language instead of a natural language is called a *logical proof* or *formal proof*.

Mathematical proofs differ from the empirical research strategies discussed above in terms of certainty. A proof demonstrates unequivocally that a proposition is always true, while an empirical study only can provide additional support for a proposition. Even if a large number of empirical studies support a certain proposition, future studies may always invalidate it.

The empirical research strategies discussed above are summarised in Table 3.1.

3.2 Data Collection Methods

A key activity in any empirical research study is to collect data about the phenomenon under investigation. For this purpose, *data collection methods* are used. The data collected may be numeric (often called *quantitative data*), e.g. number of lines of code or number of search results. Other kinds of data include text, sound, images, and video (often called *qualitative data*). Regardless of the kind of data, five of the most widely used data collection methods are: questionnaires, interviews, focus groups, observation studies, and document studies. Some of these data collection methods have become closely associated with certain research strategies, e.g. surveys typically use questionnaires, and ethnographic studies almost always involve observation. However, in principle, any data collection method can be useful for a given research strategy, and the traditional associations should not restrain a researcher in choosing an appropriate data collection method.

Within a research project, it is common to use only a single data collection method. However, it can be helpful to employ several methods to improve accuracy and broaden the picture. For example, researchers can be more confident in the results of a questionnaire if they carry out a number of interviews and these produce confirmatory results. Likewise, a questionnaire can be used to collect a large amount of basic, quantitative information, which can be complemented with more qualitative information from interviews, thereby providing a more complete picture. A researcher may also carry out a number of interviews to better understand what questions to ask in a questionnaire. The approach of combining research strategies and methods (not only data collection methods) is called the *mixed methods* approach.

The mixed methods approach is related to the principle of *triangulation*, which is about viewing the same phenomenon from different perspectives. One way of doing this is to use different research strategies and methods but also different sources of data or even different researchers.

Table 3.1 Overview of research strategies

Strategy	Purposes	Key concepts	Key activities	Forms	Concerns
Experiment	Investigate cause-and-effect relationships	• Hypothesis • Dependent variable • Independent variable	Control factors that may influence the dependent variable	• Laboratory experiments • Field experiments • Natural experiments	• Weak internal validity for laboratory experiments • Weak external validity for field experiments
Survey	Investigate some aspects of a phenomenon to get an overview	• Sample • Representative sample • Exploratory sample	Sampling (random, purposive, and convenience)	• Interview survey • Observational survey • Document survey	• Lack of depth • Limitation to measurable aspects • Lack of theoretical grounding
Case study	Investigate in depth a phenomenon with a well-defined boundary	• Case/instance • Natural setting • Holistic view	• Multi-source data collection • Triangulation	• Exploratory case study • Descriptive case study • Explanatory case study	Weak generalizability
Ethnography	Investigate cultural practices and social interaction	• Culture • Empathy • Researcher as active participant	• Field work • Capture social meanings	• Holistic study • Semiotic study • Critical study	• Reflexivity • A-theoretical storytelling • Ethical dilemmas

(continued)

Table 3.1 (continued)

Strategy	Purposes	Key concepts	Key activities	Forms	Concerns
Grounded theory	Develop concepts and theories through analysing empirical data	• Categories and codes • Openmindedness • Theory and concept generation • Theoretical saturation	• Theoretical sampling • Coding (open, axial, and selective)	• Positivist • Interpretivist • Constructivist	• Reflexivity • Lack of context
Action research	Produce useful knowledge by addressing practical problems in real-world settings	• Active practitioner participation • Change in practice • Action and research outcomes	• Cyclical process • Diagnosis • Planning • Intervention • Evaluation • Reflection	• Technical action research • Practical action research • Emancipatory action research	• Weak generalizability • Lack of impartiality
Phenomenology	Describe and understand the lived experience of people	• Lived experience • Reflectivity	Unstructured interviews		Lack of rigour

3.2.1 Questionnaires

A *questionnaire* is a written document including a list of questions to be distributed to a number of respondents. When the respondents answer the questions, they provide the researcher with data that can be interpreted and analysed. Questionnaires are typically used to gather straightforward information that is brief and unambiguous. The information collected may be about simple facts, such as the age, gender, or income of the respondent. The information may also pertain to opinions, e.g. consumer preferences or political views. As questionnaires are inexpensive to distribute, they are particularly appropriate for gathering information from a large number of people. A questionnaire often consists of three parts:

- *Background*. Information about the researchers and their sponsors, including contact information, the purpose of the questionnaire, ethical concerns including confidentiality and voluntary participation, and a thank you statement.
- *Instructions*. Detailed instructions on how to answer the questions, preferably with an example.
- *Questions*. A list of numbered questions.

The questions in a questionnaire may be open or closed. A *closed question* is a question for which the researcher has determined a set of permissible answers in advance. For example, "What is your marital status?" is a closed question with "single" and "married" as permissible answers. An *open question* is a question that has no predefined answers, and the respondents answer in their own words. An example is "What is your opinion on the EU's response to the climate question?". The respondents answer this question using their own formulations. Closed questions have the advantage of being easy and quick to answer for the respondent, and they are also easy to analyse with statistical methods. On the other hand, closed questions do not allow for nuances in the answers, as the respondent only can answer by choosing from a set of predefined alternatives. Open questions have the opposite characteristics. They are more difficult and time consuming to answer and require more effort to analyse, but they allow for more elaborated and creative answers. Many questionnaires include both closed questions for collecting basic information and open questions to gather more subtle and complex information.

The questions of a questionnaire need to be carefully chosen and formulated, in particular, as suggested by Peterson (2000, pp. 50–59), they should be:

- *Brief*. The question should preferably be no longer than 20 words.
- *Relevant*. The question should be relevant to the questionnaire and its purpose.
- *Unambiguous*. The question should have only one possible interpretation; ambiguous and unfamiliar words should be avoided.
- *Specific*. The question should not be vague, e.g. "Do you often read email on your tablet?"
- *Objective*. The formulation of the question should not suggest an answer, e.g. "Do you agree that our country needs a new government?"

The questions should be ordered in such a way that earlier questions do not affect the answers given later in the questionnaire. The number of questions should also be limited so that respondents do not feel overwhelmed and deterred from completing the questionnaire.

As questionnaires can be challenging to design, it is often useful to carry out a pilot study before distributing the real questionnaire. In such a pilot, a small number of test subjects answer the questionnaire as if they were actual respondents. The pilot will help to determine whether the instructions given are sufficient, whether there are unclear or ambiguous questions, whether the predefined answers are exhaustive, and whether the questionnaire can be completed in a reasonable amount of time.

Questionnaires can be distributed in different ways. Traditionally, postal questionnaires have been the most popular ones. The questionnaires were sent by post to the respondents, who then had to send them back. Today, however, the Internet has become the most common medium for administering questionnaires, and there are many web-based tools that support the design as well as the distribution and analysis of questionnaires.

A main advantage of questionnaires, compared to other data collection methods, is that they are inexpensive, as many respondents can be reached at a low cost. Another advantage is that questionnaires offer standardised data when closed questions are used, which eliminates the need for interpretation of answers and thereby simplifies data analysis. However, closed questions carry the risk that the respondents' answers will be biased towards the views of the researchers, as they decide which answer-options are available. Another disadvantage of questionnaires is that it can be difficult to achieve a high response rate, as respondents easily can ignore a request to answer a questionnaire.

3.2.2   Interviews

An *interview* is a communication session between a researcher and a respondent, in which the researcher controls the agenda by asking questions to the respondent. While questionnaires are appropriate for collecting simple and straightforward information, interviews are more effective for gathering complex and sensitive information. Thus, interviews are often used for eliciting emotions, attitudes, opinions, and experiences from the respondents. Interviews are also suitable for getting into contact with people who have access to privileged information, i.e. people possessing deep and unique information and knowledge about some domain.

Interviews allow for a more or less structured interaction between the researcher and the respondent. A *structured interview* follows a predefined protocol and is similar to a questionnaire in that it builds on a fixed list of questions that can be answered by choosing from a predetermined set of allowed responses. A *semi-structured interview* is also based on a set of questions, but these can be discussed in a flexible order and they are open, i.e. the respondents are allowed to formulate the answers in their own words. In an *unstructured interview*, the researcher is as unobtrusive as possible and lets the respondent talk freely about a topic without being restricted to specific questions. Structured interviews have the advantage that they can be carried out relatively fast and that the researcher does not need to interpret the answers. However, semi-structured and unstructured interviews are better when it comes to investigating complex issues, as the respondents can express their ideas and feelings in a more unrestricted way.

When conducting an interview, researchers need to be aware of the possible effects of their personal attributes as well as the venue for the interview. Respondents may be less willing to fully disclose information to someone who is very different to them, e.g. in terms of age, gender, and occupational status, especially when sensitive issues are discussed. Furthermore, the venue for an interview may affect what a respondent is prepared to disclose, e.g. if the interview is carried out in an office or in the respondent's home.

A researcher should seize the opportunities for interaction in an interview. The researcher can do so by mixing closed and open questions and by prompting, probing, or checking. Prompting is about nudging the respondent to start speaking. Probing means asking for more details. Checking is to make sure that the researcher has correctly understood what the respondent stated. Through these techniques, the researcher can guide the interview so that the respondent provides answers that are as informative as possible.

The answers provided by a respondent need to be recorded and transcribed so that the researcher can further interpret and analyse them. An interview is often documented through both an audio (or video) recording and field notes, i.e. written notes taken by the researcher. While the audio recording captures all of the speech, the field notes complement with non-verbal communication. Sometimes, a respondent may refuse to record the interview, and the researcher will then have to rely only on the field notes.

A main advantage of interviews is that they allow a researcher to go into depth in order to gather detailed and complex information. Another advantage is that interviews typically have a high response rate. However, there are also disadvantages. One is that interviews are time consuming, in particular the transcription and analysis processes after an interview. Furthermore, the researcher's personal attributes can affect the outcome of an interview.

3.2.3   Focus Groups

A *focus group* can be seen as an interview in which a group of respondents participate and discuss a specific topic. The aim of a focus group is to understand and interpret the topic from the participants' perspective. Focus groups allow for interaction between the participants, which can enable them to be more creative and pursue the topic addressed in greater depth than in one-to-one interviews. The participants can surprise, inspire, and encourage each other to come up with novel ideas.

Focus groups need to be designed and executed so that they support free and fruitful discussions. For this purpose, researchers have two roles to play, as moderator and as note-taker. The main task of the moderator is to encourage the participants to contribute actively to the discussion. The moderator also guides the focus group, ensures that the discussion stays focused, and handles any conflicts that may arise. While the moderator is highly active in running a focus group, the note-taker has more of a back-office role, taking field notes of the discussion, including activities or movements that an audio recording cannot capture.

Focus groups have become popular in the social and health sciences, as they allow researchers to study the conversation and thought patterns of people in a more natural way than in one-to-one interviews. Focus groups are also cost effective, as many respondents can participate in the same session. However, a drawback of focus groups is observer dependency, i.e. the results obtained are often highly dependent on the researcher's interpretation and analysis, which can make them quite subjective. Strong participants in the group can also influence the rest of the participants during the focus group sessions and drive the discussion in a certain direction. A focus group may, therefore, not be useful for understanding the views of all of the participants.

3.2.4   Observations

Observation is a data collection method, in which a researcher directly observes a phenomenon. Observation is often an alternative to questionnaires or interviews and offers the advantage that the researcher can observe what people actually do, not what they say they do or think. The researcher is in immediate contact with the observed phenomenon, as she watches or listens to people as they act in a situation in which the phenomenon appears. Observation can be used within any research strategy, both in the field and in the laboratory as part of an experiment.

There are different kinds of observations, and two of the main ones are systematic observation and participant observation. *Systematic observation* addresses the reliability issue, which is one of the most challenging problems for observation. When two researchers observe the same situation, their accounts of it may differ widely due to differences in competence, experiences, interests, perception, etc. People do not passively record information from the environment like a camera, but they inevitably interpret it, which can result in large discrepancies in their accounts of it. In order to overcome these difficulties, systematic observation suggests a number of techniques that can help make observation more objective. The primary technique is the *observation schedule*, which consists of a predefined system for classifying and recording events and interactions as they occur. It tells the researchers explicitly what they should look out for and how they are to record their observations, often by means of a checklist. An observation schedule also includes rules for the timing of observations, e.g. a schedule might state that they are to take place during one hour, three times a day for one week. By following an observation schedule, data collection becomes structured and systematic, thereby improving its reliability.

The main advantage of systematic observation is that it is structured and rigorous, which helps to produce reliable and objective results. It can also be efficient, as it allows researchers to collect large amounts of data in a short period of time. A disadvantage of systematic observation is that the data collected may be superficial, as observation schedules can bias researchers to focus on easily observable events in isolation, meaning that they miss the context around the events.

Participant observation is a data collection method in which a researcher builds a deep and close familiarity with a group of people by observing them in their daily life, often for an extended period of time. Participant observation is a key method within ethnography, since it enables the researcher to gain an understanding of a culture from the perspective of its members. In participant observation, researchers often remain covert, i.e. they do not disclose their identity and purpose to those being studied. In this way, they are able to preserve the naturalness of the setting, as people will continue to behave naturally if they do not know that an outsider is observing them. Furthermore, participant observation allows researchers to arrive at a holistic understanding, as they are able to study the context in which people act and interact.

Participant observation can produce valid and context-sensitive results, as it enables researchers to study a phenomenon in depth and without the restrictions of observation schedules or other protocols that can limit the scope of the observations. However, the method is highly dependent on the individual researcher's competence and experiences, which may jeopardise reliability and objectivity. Another issue is that there are ethical problems when researchers act undercover, as they cannot obtain informed consent from the research subjects.

3.2.5 Documents

Documents constitute an alternative source of data in addition to those of questionnaires, interviews, and observations. Documents often contain textual data, but they may also consist of photographs, images, audio or video files, etc. Some common types of documents are the following:

- *Government publications.* These include official statistics, laws and regulations, political documents, official reports, and public records, such as electoral registers.
- *Organisational records.* These include annual reports, personnel records, sales figures, company memos, and minutes of meetings.
- *Academic publications.* These include publications in journals, conferences, and workshops as well as monographs and doctoral dissertations.
- *Newspapers and magazines.* These include daily newspapers, trade press, and illustrated magazines.

- *Personal communications.* These include diaries, letters, emails, SMS messages, movie tickets, and to do lists.
- *Social media streams.* These consist of posts on social networks, including blog posts and tweets.

A main issue when using documents for data collection is to assess their credibility, i.e. to determine whether they are authentic, correct, and free from bias and errors. How this is determined depends on the kind of document being used. Government publications are generally seen as trustworthy, as they have been produced by the state, often by experts. However, political purposes may bias some official reports. Academic publications in well-established journals and conferences are also generally viewed as credible, as they have been carefully peer reviewed. For any document, a researcher needs to consider the goal of its authors and how this may affect its credibility. For example, an opinion piece in a newspaper may deliberately omit inconvenient facts in order to make its point more convincing.

Using documents as a data source means that a great deal of data can be collected in a shorter period of time and more inexpensively than with questionnaires or interviews. Furthermore, when documents are in the public domain, there are almost no ethical problems to address. A disadvantage of documents is that it is often difficult to judge their credibility. A case in point is Wikipedia, where anyone can edit its pages, which may result in low credibility.

3.3 Data Analysis

Data analysis derives valuable information from data in order to describe or explain some phenomenon under investigation. Raw data do not speak for themselves; they need to be prepared, interpreted, analysed, and presented before any conclusions can be drawn from them. Thus, a researcher needs to transform large volumes of data into manageable and meaningful pieces of information.

Two main kinds of data analysis are quantitative and qualitative analysis. These terms are used in a variety of senses in the social sciences. In a narrow sense, the meaning is that quantitative data analysis works on quantitative data (numbers), while qualitative data analysis works on qualitative data (words, images, video clips, etc.). In a broader sense, quantitative and qualitative research are two research paradigms, approximately corresponding to positivism and interpretivism, respectively, as discussed in Chap. 12. In this chapter, the terms are used in the narrow sense.

3.3.1 Quantitative Data Analysis

Questionnaires and observations tend to produce large amounts of quantitative data. However, any data collection method can generate quantitative data. Even if the raw data generated take the form of text or images, they can be categorised and coded so as to produce numbers, which can then be analysed quantitatively.

3.3.1.1 Kinds of Quantitative Data

There are different kinds of quantitative data, which differ in terms of how they can be manipulated mathematically:

- *Nominal data*. Nominal data (also called *categorical data*) denote categories and have no numeric value on which arithmetical operations can be carried out. For example, to represent marital status, "1" can denote single, "2" married, and "3" cohabiting. It is not meaningful to carry out computations such as mean or median on these data, nor can they be ordered. They can only be used for representing frequencies.
- *Ordinal data*. Ordinal data (also called *ranked data*) also denote categories, but these categories can be ranked, i.e. there is an order between them. An example would be the following values that can be used to categorise answers about the attractiveness of a product ($1 =$ completely dislikes, $2 =$ dislikes, $3 =$ neither likes nor dislikes, $4 =$ likes, $5 =$ completely likes). These values can be ranked, and it is meaningful to say that 5 is higher than 4, which in turn is higher than 3. However, it is not meaningful to say that 4 is twice as high as 2.
- *Interval data*. Interval data are ordered, just as ordinal data, and the distance between two adjacent points on the scale is always the same. This makes it meaningful to apply addition and subtraction to this kind of data. One example of interval data are calendar years, where the difference between 2030 and 2025 is the same as the difference between 2025 and 2020.
- *Ratio data*. Ratio data are similar to interval data, and in addition, there is a zero to the scale. Typical examples are age, height, and income. For ratio data, all kinds of arithmetic operations are meaningful. For example, it is meaningful to say that a person earning 6000€ makes twice as much as someone earning 3000€.

3.3.1.2 Descriptive Statistics

Descriptive statistics is used for quantitatively describing a sample of data. Descriptive statistics is different from inferential statistics, as it only intends to describe a given sample of data, while inferential statistics is used to draw conclusions about a population that the sample represents.

A basic form of descriptive statistics is to display parts of a data sample through tables or charts. Tables make it possible to display highly detailed data, but they can be taxing for the reader, while charts can be made more visually attractive. Some common types of charts are: bar charts, which often are used to display frequencies;

pie charts, which are useful for showing proportions; and line graphs, which can show trends in data.

Data samples can also be described through various aggregate measures:

- *Mean*. For a data sample, the mean (or average) is the sum of the values divided by the number of values. For example, the mean of 2, 4, 8, 15, 16, 16, 100 is 23. As can be seen from this example, the mean can be heavily influenced by outlier values.
- *Median*. The median is the value that separates the higher half of a data sample from the lower half. In the example above, the median is 15. The median is less strongly influenced by outlier values than the mean.
- *Mode*. The mode is the value that appears most often in a data sample. For the example above, the mode is 16.
- *Range*. The range of a data sample is the difference between its highest and lowest value. In the example above, the range is 98. As for the mean, the range is very sensitive to outlier values.
- *Standard deviation*. The standard deviation of a data sample specifies the average amount of variability. It is computed by taking the square root of the mean of the squared differences of the values from their mean. The standard deviation of the example sample is 31.9.

Tables, charts, and aggregate measures are all valuable for describing a data sample, and they are typically used in combination.

3.3.1.3 Inferential Statistics

Inferential statistics aims to reach conclusions that extend beyond a single data sample, e.g. whether there is a relationship between two variables or whether a difference exists between two populations. Thus, inferential statistics is used for making inferences from collected data to more general conditions.

It is often interesting to investigate whether a relationship exists between two variables, e.g. whether income and education level are related to each other. A common technique for determining the strength of a link between two variables is to compute the *correlation coefficient*. A correlation coefficient is a value between −1 and +1, in which a positive (negative) value means that there is a positive (negative) relationship between the two variables, and a value close to +1 or −1 means that there is a strong correlation, while 0 means there is no correlation. However, even if there is a strong correlation between two variables in a data sample, this does not mean that there is a correlation between the variables in the population from which the sample was taken; maybe the sample was unrepresentative, so the apparent relationship was just down to chance. In order to determine whether two variables are associated to a significant level, various statistical techniques have been developed, one of these being the chi-square test.

Another question that often arises is whether there is any significant difference between two populations, e.g. whether people on a certain diet are healthier than others. When comparing samples from the two populations, there is a risk that a difference between them is due to chance. In order to find out if identified differences in the samples can be generalised to the populations, there are tests, such as the t-test.

3.3.2   Qualitative Data Analysis

Qualitative data analysis works on qualitative data, including text, sound, photos, images, and video clips. While quantitative data measure phenomena, qualitative data characterise them. Large amounts of qualitative data can be generated by unstructured interviews, but any data collection method can be used for producing qualitative data. For example, a questionnaire with open questions will give rise to text that needs to be analysed. Some general characteristics of qualitative data analysis, as suggested by Denscombe (2017), are the following:

- *Iterative*. Data collection and data analysis typically occur in parallel and iteratively, where results from data analysis influence how data collection proceeds.
- *Inductive*. The analysis moves from the particular to the general, i.e. based on analysis of specific cases and situations, more general statements are proposed.
- *Researcher-centered*. The background, values, and experiences of the researcher are important factors that influence the data analysis.

There are different approaches to qualitative data analysis; three of the main ones are content analysis, grounded theory, and discourse analysis.

3.3.2.1   Content Analysis

Content analysis is used to quantify the contents of a text or other qualitative data. The idea is to classify elements of the text into categories and then calculate the frequencies of the elements in each category. Content analysis is carried out in six activities:

1. *Choose a sample of texts.* The criterion for including texts in the sample should be made explicit.
2. *Break the texts down into units.* The units may be individual words, sentences, or even entire paragraphs.
3. *Develop categories for analysis.* The categories should be selected so that they are relevant to the research question being addressed. For example, if the research question is about investigating the main themes in the speeches by American politicians, possible categories include healthcare reform, Russia, terrorism, polarisation, and unemployment.
4. *Code the units according to the categories.* The units identified in activity 2 are coded using the categories from activity 3, i.e. each unit is assigned to one or more of the categories.

5. *Count the frequency of the units for each category.* For each category, the number
   of units is calculated.
6. *Analyse the texts in terms of the frequencies.* Study and compare the frequencies
   from activity 5 in order to further analyse the texts. For example, the trends in
   interest for various political themes may be investigated.

One of the strengths of content analysis is that the process is clear and simple,
which means that reliability will be high, i.e. different researchers will come to
essentially the same results. A weakness of the approach is that it is quite insensitive
to context, as only individual units are analysed. The relationships between the units
and the intentions of the writer are not taken into account. Thus, content analysis is
primarily useful for studying fairly uncomplicated aspects of a text.

3.3.2.2 Grounded Theory

Grounded theory can be applied not only as a research strategy as described in
Sect. 3.1.5 but also as a method for qualitative data analysis. The principles for
coding will be the same when grounded theory is used for data analysis. During
open coding, the researcher categorises the units of the text, which may be words,
sentences, or paragraphs. The codes are then categorised and related to each other
in axial coding. During selective coding, the most important codes and categories
are identified, as well as the relationships between them.

A key difference to content analysis is that in grounded theory, the codes are
not set in advance but emerge gradually from the researcher's work with the text.
The codes are not based on some pre-existing theory; instead, the researcher keeps
an open mind and allows the text to provide the basis for deciding which codes to
include.

3.3.2.3 Discourse Analysis

While content analysis focuses on what is explicitly stated in a text, *discourse
analysis* digs into its implicit and hidden meanings. The starting point of discourse
analysis is that the meaning of a text does not lie on the surface. The words in the text
cannot be taken at face value. Instead, they can only be understood within a larger
context, which includes the author, her intentions, and the underlying assumptions
that are taken for granted. Researchers need to take this context into account when
they analyse a text, and in particular, they have to understand the purpose of the
author, i.e. what effects she wanted to achieve.

In discourse analysis, a text is never solely an objective representation of an
existing world. Instead, the text contributes to creating and sustaining the world.
The researcher's task is to deconstruct the text, reveal its hidden meanings, explain
how it creates the world, and show which cultural messages it communicates and
reinforces.

While grounded theory requires the researcher to approach data with an open mind and without any theoretical assumptions, discourse analysis encourages the researcher to make use of concepts and theories that can help to "fill in the blanks" in a text. As discourse analysis aims to find out what is implicit in a text, there is a need for theory that can function as a pair of glasses to support the researcher in discovering the hidden meanings of the text. For example, a seemingly innocent nursery rhyme can be seen as reinforcing gender stereotypes when viewed through the lens of feminist theory.

Discourse analysis is often criticised for being highly subjective, i.e. dependent on the individual researcher's competence, insights, and theoretical stance. This subjectivity may be accepted or even embraced, but it can also be mitigated if the researcher makes her reasoning traceable by making explicit her background and theoretical assumptions.

3.4 Relating Research Strategies and Research Methods

The relationships between research strategies, data collection methods, and data analysis methods are illustrated in Fig. 3.1. The figure can be read from top to bottom as a simple guide to the initial decisions that need to be made in a research

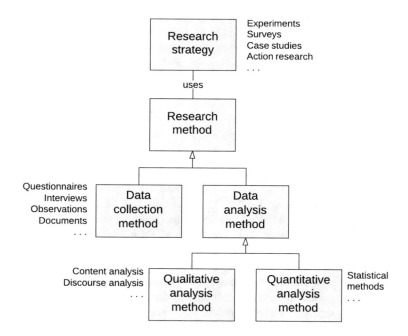

Fig. 3.1 Research strategies and research methods

project. First, the researcher will select one or more research strategies to be applied. For each research strategy, she will select one or more data collection methods to use as well as one or more data analysis methods. In practice, these decisions may not be as serial as suggested here but instead will develop in iterations over the entire research project.

Within a single design science project, several different research strategies and methods can be used in the different activities. A concrete example would be a researcher who intends to develop a method for designing business process models. The purpose here is to develop an artefact (a method). In order to gather requirements for the method, the researcher chooses a survey as one of the research strategies in the project and tries to get suggestions for requirements from experts in business process management. To gather information from the experts, she chooses to use interviews (a data collection method), and to analyse the gathered interview data, she uses content analysis (a qualitative method). In addition to the requirements elicitation, she also decides to evaluate the method. For this purpose, an experiment as the research strategy is chosen and a situation is set up in which students, as well as experienced process designers, are asked to use the method. The researcher observes (a data collection method) the behaviour of these people when they use the method and logs their results (another data collection method), which are later analysed using statistical (quantitative) methods.

As illustrated by the above example, design science is not yet another research strategy or method; instead, different research strategies and methods can be used within the same design science project.

3.5 Summary of Chapter

- The purpose of research is to create reliable and useful knowledge based on empirical evidence as well as on logical arguments. To support researchers in this endeavour, established research strategies and methods have proven to be useful.
- A *research strategy* is an overall plan for conducting a research study, guiding a researcher in planning, executing, and monitoring the study. A research strategy needs to be complemented with research methods that can guide the research work on a more detailed level.
- A *research method* tells the researcher how to collect and analyse data.
- Some established empirical research strategies are:

  - *Experiment*, which investigates cause-and-effect relationships.
  - *Survey*, which maps out some physical or social world.
  - *Case study*, which investigates an instance of a phenomenon in depth.
  - *Ethnography*, which aims to understand groups and cultures.
  - *Grounded theory*, which develops theories through the analysis of empirical data.

- *Action research*, which addresses problems that people experience in their practices through active collaboration between researchers and practitioners.
- *Phenomenology*, which aims to describe and understand the lived experiences of people.

- A non-empirical research strategy is:

  - *Simulation*, which imitates the behaviour of a real-world process or system over time.

- Some established data collection methods are:

  - *Questionnaire*, which gathers facts and opinions from respondents by using a written document including a list of questions distributed to the respondents.
  - *Interview*, which is a communication session between a researcher and a respondent, in which the researcher controls the agenda by asking questions to the respondent.
  - *Focus group*, which is a form of interview in which a group of respondents participate and discuss a specific topic.
  - *Observation*, which is a method where a researcher directly observes phenomena.
  - *Documents*, which is a method where documents are the data source.

- Data analysis can be classified into:

  - *Quantitative data analysis*, which analyses quantitative data (numbers).
  - *Qualitative data analysis*, which analyses qualitative data (words, images, video clips, etc.).

- Quantitative data analysis can be classified into:

  - *Descriptive statistics*, which is used for describing a given sample of data.
  - *Inferential statistics*, which is used for making inferences from a data sample to an entire population and more general conditions.

- Some qualitative data analysis method are:

  - *Content analysis*, which is used to quantify the contents of a text or other qualitative data.
  - *Grounded theory*, which is similar to content analysis, but the codes are not given in advance; instead, they emerge gradually from the researcher's work.
  - *Discourse analysis*, which focuses on deconstructing the (hidden) meaning of a text, explaining how it creates the world, and showing what cultural messages it communicates and reinforces.

3.6   Review Questions

1. When documenting a research project, can it be sufficient to describe only the data collection methods but not the research strategy chosen?
2. Given a research question, can more than one research strategy be appropriate for addressing the question?
3. Experiments can be used to investigate cause-and-effect relationships. Can any other research strategy be used for this purpose?
4. Why is it often difficult to achieve high external validity in experiments?
5. Is random sampling always the best sampling technique for surveys?
6. Would a representative sample be preferable to an exploratory sample for eliciting novel ideas on e-democracy?
7. Why is it important to make use of multiple information sources in a case study?
8. Why is it difficult to generalise findings from a case study?
9. How can an ethnographer address the challenges caused by reflexivity?
10. Can grounded theory be used for testing hypotheses?
11. Why is grounded theory especially useful for exploratory research studies?
12. Grounded theory uses theoretical saturation as a stop condition for data collection. Would this approach be useful for representative samples in surveys?
13. Can action research be carried out in laboratories?
14. Is it easier to obtain active practitioner participation in the healthcare sector than in the retail sector?
15. The cyclical action research process consists of five phases: diagnosis, planning, intervention, evaluation, and reflection. Why is it important to carry out these phases iteratively?
16. An important concept in phenomenology is that of lived experiences. How do they differ from experiences in general?
17. How can role-play simulations and computer simulations be combined?
18. What is the difference between quantitative data and qualitative data?
19. Why are questionnaires frequently used for surveys? Can questionnaires be used also in other research strategies?
20. What advantages do questionnaires have over interviews?
21. Would an open or a closed question be most useful for obtaining information about:
    (a) The age of a person
    (b) The food allergies of a person
    (c) The food preferences of a person
    (d) The nationality of a person
    (e) The political opinions of a person
22. Why is it helpful to carry out a pilot study before distributing a questionnaire to a large population?

23. The questions in a questionnaire should be brief, relevant, unambiguous, specific, and objective. Use these criteria to evaluate the following questions:

    (a) Do you stay up late in the night?
    (b) Why do you think it is necessary to raise the taxes?
    (c) Is the distribution between capital income and labour income satisfactory?

24. What are the main advantages and disadvantages of structured interviews?
25. How can a researcher ensure that a respondent provides informative answers in an interview?
26. The personal attributes of the researcher can influence the respondent in an interview. How can this challenge be addressed?
27. What advantages do focus groups have over one-to-one interviews?
28. Why should the same person not act as both moderator and note-taker in a focus group?
29. Consider researchers who work covertly in participant observation and do not obtain informed consent from the people they study. How could they make sure that they still work in an ethically acceptable way?
30. Which factors can influence the credibility of a book?
31. What is the difference between descriptive statistics and inferential statistics?
32. Why is it helpful to describe a data sample by means of aggregate measures?
33. For which purposes is content analysis preferable to discourse analysis?
34. Why is theory needed for discourse analysis?
35. It is often argued that qualitative data analysis is subjective. But is not quantitative data analysis also subjective?
36. What is the difference between internal validity, external validity, and reliability?

3.7 Answers to Selected Review Questions

1. No. The chosen research strategy and its application are just as important as the data collection method for assessing the validity of the research results.
2. Yes. For example, an artefact can be evaluated using a case study or an experiment.
5. No. Which sampling technique to choose depends upon the purpose of the study.
6. Probably not. An exploratory sample of knowledgeable and committed participants would probably come up with better ideas than a representative sample.
7. A case study aims to paint a rich and complex picture of a case, and, therefore, several data sources need to be consulted.
10. Grounded theory is used for generating new theories, not for testing existing ones.
12. No. A representative sample should mirror the population from which it is drawn.

13. No. An action research study should be carried out in the real world.
15. Researchers and practitioners need to test and refine the knowledge they produce in several iterations in order to learn from practical application and arrive at high-quality results.
19. Questionnaires are frequently used in surveys as they are inexpensive. They can be used also in other research strategies, e.g. in experiments to collect data from participants.
21. Open questions are preferable for (c) and (e) as it is difficult to determine all possible answer alternatives for these questions in advance.
23. (a) is not specific; (b) is not objective; (c) is not unambiguous.
26. One approach is that the venue is neutral and the researcher acts in a neutral manner.
28. Acting as a moderator in a focus group is a full-time job, leaving no room for taking notes.
31. Descriptive statistics describes a specific sample, while inferential statistics draws conclusions about an entire population based on a sample.

3.8 Further Reading

There are many introductory books on research methodology for both natural and social sciences. This chapter, to a large extent, follows the structure of research strategies and methods proposed by Denscombe (2017); this book is a practical and comprehensive introduction to research methodology in the social sciences, with a focus on small-scale research projects. The book by Oates (2006) also offers an easy-to-read and comprehensive introduction to research methodology, which focuses on computer and information sciences. Bryman (2016) provides a broad and deep introduction to social research methodology, covering a wide range of qualitative and quantitative methods. A more advanced text is the one by Bhattacherjee (2012) that is intended for doctoral and graduate students in the social sciences, business, education, public health, and related disciplines. Creswell and Creswell (2017) gives an introduction to approaches using mixed methods, showing how they can combine quantitative and qualitative research.

Field and Hole (2003) offer a map of the experimental design process, beginning with how to get ideas about research, how to refine the research question, and the actual design of the experiment and continuing with statistical analysis and assistance with the writing up of results. Fowler (2013) provides an introduction to survey research and investigates how each aspect of a survey can affect its precision, accuracy, and credibility; the book also covers recent developments that influence survey research, such as the use of the Internet and mobile devices for data collection. Yin (2017) offers comprehensive coverage of the design and use of case studies as a research strategy. The book provides a clear definition of the case study strategy, as well as a discussion of relevant data collection and analysis methods; it also offers a number of exemplary case studies. LeCompte and Schensul

(2010) provide a highly accessible introduction to ethnographic research and applied anthropology with a large number of examples, as well as discussions on various research paradigms and epistemologies. Glaser and Strauss (1999) offer a classical introduction to grounded theory, discussing how theory can be discovered from data. Another well-known text on grounded theory is the one offered by Charmaz (2014), which shows how grounded theory is related to a variety of qualitative data analysis methods. Kemmis et al. (2016) provide a detailed guide to conducting critical participatory action research, including research ethics, principles of procedure for action researchers, protocols for collaborative work, keeping a journal, gathering evidence, writing up results, and selecting academic partners. Another text on action research is the one by McNiff (2013), which targets both practitioners and researchers.

Seidman (2019) gives an introduction to interviewing as part of the qualitative research process and describes principles and techniques that can be used in a range of interviewing approaches and situations. Bradburn et al. (2004) offer a classical text on questionnaire design, covering the entire design process from start to finish, with examples from actual surveys. Coghlan (2019) provide practical advice on participant observation within the context of action research in your own organisation. Prior (2008) surveys the use of documents in social research and argues that by focusing on the functioning of documents instead of content, social science can make use of a broad range of methods of both data collection and analysis.

There are a large number of introductory books on statistics and quantitative data analysis. Urdan (2016) provides a brief and easy-to-read overview of statistics. A more advanced, but still accessible, treatment of statistics is given by Stephens (2004). Silverman (2018) offers a comprehensive introduction to qualitative research, including topics such as case studies and focus groups, and illustrates the qualitative research process by means of several examples and common pitfalls. Dey (2003) also provides an introduction to qualitative research and discusses the use of computer-based qualitative data analysis. Krippendorff (2018) provides a classical treatment of the content analysis method, which ranges from the history of content analysis to a review of computer-aided content analysis tools. Fairclough (2013) collects a number of papers on socially oriented and emancipatory discourse analysis, investigating language in relation to ideology and power.

References

Bhattacherjee A (2012) Social science research: principles, methods, and practices, 2 edn. CreateSpace Independent Publishing Platform, Tampa, FL

Blake W (2012) Delphi complete works of William Blake, 2nd edn. Delphi Classics

Bradburn NM, Sudman S, Wansink B (2004) Asking questions: the definitive guide to questionnaire design – for market research, political polls, and social and health questionnaires, revised edition. Jossey-Bass, San Francisco

Bryman A (2016) Social research methods, 5th edn. Oxford University Press, Oxford

Charmaz K (2014) Constructing grounded theory, 2nd edn. SAGE Publications, Thousand Oaks, CA

Coghlan D (2019) Doing action research in your own organization, 5th edn. SAGE Publications, Thousand Oaks, CA

Creswell JW, Creswell JD (2017) Research design: qualitative, quantitative, and mixed methods approaches, 5th edn. SAGE Publications, Thousand Oaks, CA

Denscombe M (2017) The good research guide, 6th edn. Open University Press, London

Dey I (2003) Qualitative data analysis: a user friendly guide for social scientists. Routledge, London

Fairclough N (2013) Critical discourse analysis: the critical study of language, 2 edn. Routledge, London

Field A, Hole GJ (2003) How to design and report experiments, 1st edn. Sage Publications, Thousand Oaks, CA

Fowler FJ (2013) Survey research methods, 5th edn. SAGE Publications, Thousand Oaks, CA

Glaser B, Strauss A (1999) The discovery of grounded theory: strategies for qualitative research. Routledge, London

Kemmis S, McTaggart R, Nixon R (2016) The action research planner: doing critical participatory action research, 1st edn. Springer, Berlin

Krippendorff K (2018) Content analysis: an introduction to its methodology, 4th edn. SAGE Publications, Thousand Oaks, CA

LeCompte MD, Schensul JJ (2010) Designing and conducting ethnographic research: an introduction, 2nd edn. AltaMira Press, Lanham, MD

McNiff J (2013) Action research: principles and practice, 3rd edn. Routledge, London

Oates BJ (2006) Researching information systems and computing. SAGE Publications, Thousand Oaks, CA

Peterson RA (2000) Constructing effective questionnaires. Sage Publications, Thousand Oaks

Prior L (2008) Repositioning documents in social research. Sociology 42(5):821–836

Seidman I (2019) Interviewing as qualitative research: a guide for researchers in education and the social sciences, 5th edn. Teachers College Press, New York

Silverman D (2018) Doing qualitative research, 5th edn. SAGE Publications, Thousand Oaks, CA

Stephens L (2004) Advanced statistics demystified, 1st edn. McGraw-Hill Professional, New York

Urdan TC (2016) Statistics in plain English, 4th ed. Routledge, London

Yin RK (2017) Case study research and applications: design and methods, 6th edn. SAGE Publications, Thousand Oaks, CA

Chapter 4
A Method Framework for Design Science Research

Design science projects may be large undertakings, involving many people and being carried out over an extended period of time, or they may be small-scale projects with only a single researcher. In either case, researchers can benefit from methodological support that helps them to structure their work and ensure the quality of their results. Such support can also help design researchers to present their work in a logical and easily understandable way. This chapter introduces a method framework for design science research that any design science project can use. The framework consists of four components:

- A number of logically related activities, with well-defined input and output
- Guidelines for carrying out the activities
- Guidelines for selecting research strategies and methods to be used in the activities
- Guidelines for relating the research to an existing knowledge base

The activities of the framework inform researchers about what they need to do in a design science project, in particular what questions they need to answer and what results they should produce. The guidelines for carrying out these activities offer practical advice that can support and facilitate the research work. In order to ensure scientific rigour, the framework also gives guidelines for selecting research strategies and methods that can be used for designing and enacting the activities. Finally, the framework provides guidelines for relating the research to an existing knowledge base, thereby facilitating cumulative knowledge development. The remainder of this chapter gives an overview of the activities of the method framework by means of a process model, while Chaps. 5–9 offer more details on both the guidelines and the activities.

© Springer Nature Switzerland AG 2021
P. Johannesson, E. Perjons, *An Introduction to Design Science*,
https://doi.org/10.1007/978-3-030-78132-3_4

4.1   Activities in Design Science Research

The method framework introduced here includes five main activities that range from problem investigation and requirements definition, through artefact design and development, and finally, to demonstration and evaluation.

4.1.1   From Problem Explication to Evaluation

Explicate Problem—This activity is about investigating and analysing a practical problem. The problem needs to be precisely formulated and justified by showing that it is significant for some practice. The problem should be of general interest, i.e. significant not only for one local practice but also for some global practice. Furthermore, underlying causes to the problem may be identified and analysed. As discussed in Sect. 1.8, some design science contributions are radical innovations in which no specific problem is explicitly addressed. Such research is driven by curiosity rather than by a perceived problem, and this activity may then be less prominent than for other types of design science contributions.

Define Requirements—This activity outlines a solution to the explicated problem in the form of an artefact and elicits requirements, which can be seen as a transformation of the problem into demands for the proposed artefact. The requirements will be defined not only for functionality but also for structure and environment.

Design and Develop Artefact—This activity creates an artefact that addresses the explicated problem and fulfils the defined requirements. Designing an artefact includes determining its functionality as well as its structure.

Demonstrate Artefact—This activity uses the developed artefact in an illustrative or real-life case, sometimes called a "proof of concept", thereby proving the feasibility of the artefact. The demonstration will show that the artefact can actually solve an instance of the problem.

Evaluate Artefact—This activity determines how well the artefact fulfils the requirements and the extent to which it can solve, or alleviate, the practical problem that motivated the research.

4.1.2   Temporal and Logical Ordering

An overview of the proposed method framework is shown in Fig. 4.1, which also indicates the results of each activity. The framework, as described here, may look highly sequential. However, a design science project is always carried out in an iterative way, moving back and forth between all the activities of problem explication, requirements definition, development, demonstration, and evaluation. This way of working is fully in line with the method framework, which does

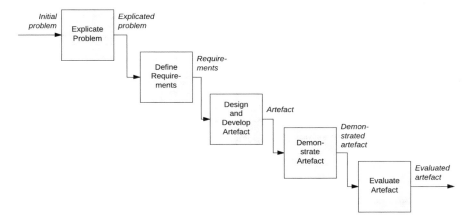

Fig. 4.1 Overview of the method framework for design science research

not prescribe a sequential work ordering. The arrows in Fig. 4.1 should not be interpreted as temporal orderings but as input-output relationships. In other words, the activities should not be seen as temporally ordered but instead as logically related via these relationships. In principle, each activity can receive input from, and produce output for, any other activity; Fig. 4.1 indicates only the most important of these input-output relationships. These issues are elaborated further in Chap. 11.

4.2 Research Strategies and Research Methods in Design Science

The purpose of design science research is not solely to create artefacts but also to answer questions about them and their environments. In order to ensure that the answers express valid and reliable knowledge, the use of research strategies and methods is vital. Any research strategy or method can be used in design science research to answer questions about artefacts. In other words, no research strategies or methods can be excluded in advance from a design science project, as each of them may be valuable, depending on the project's characteristics and goals.

In large design science projects, it is common to use several research strategies and methods, because different design science activities may require different approaches. For example, a survey may be an appropriate instrument for eliciting requirements, while an experiment may be the best choice for evaluation. Figure 4.2 shows research strategies that are commonly used for design science activities—this should be seen as merely indicative, as any research strategy can be used in any activity.

For problem explication, surveys are effective instruments, as they can be used to gather opinions and perceptions about a problem quickly from a large number of

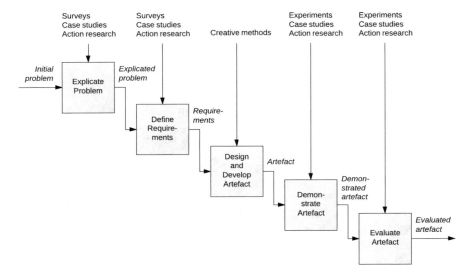

Fig. 4.2 Examples of the use of research strategies in the method framework

stakeholders. However, the results from surveys are often superficial, as stakeholders may not be prepared to spend much time and effort on describing and analysing the problem under consideration. Researchers can achieve a deeper understanding of a problem and its context through a case study, in which they investigate the problem for an extended period of time, using interviews, observation, and document studies. However, results from case studies may be difficult to generalise if they are based on only one local practice.

For requirements definition, surveys are also effective instruments. However, it may be hard for stakeholders to suggest relevant requirements when the artefact to be designed is highly innovative or complex. In such cases, action research and case studies may be better alternatives, as they allow practitioners to participate and learn in an iterative design process.

For design and development, research strategies are often less important, as the primary goal of this activity is typically to produce an artefact and, to a lesser extent, knowledge about it. Instead, creative methods are more useful, e.g. brainstorming, participative modelling, empathetic thinking, and lateral thinking. However, the use of research methods during problem explication and requirements definition has provided a solid foundation of knowledge, which will help researchers to come up with relevant ideas for artefact design. Furthermore, research methods will be used for the evaluation of these design ideas.

Demonstration is about using an artefact in a specific case in order to prove its feasibility. Thus, the most obvious research strategies to apply are action research and case studies, which may include interviews and observations of people using the artefact.

For evaluating an artefact, experiments are widely used instruments, as they allow a researcher to achieve high internal validity by carefully controlling the conditions under which an experiment is undertaken. On the other hand, external validity can suffer because the artificial setting of the experiment may be markedly different from the practice in which the artefact is to be used. One alternative is to use case studies or action research, in which the artefact is used and evaluated in a local practice. Simulations can also be effective for evaluating certain aspects of an artefact.

4.3   Relating to a Knowledge Base

The results from a design science project should be original and well founded. Therefore, it is required to relate both the design science activities and their results to an existing knowledge base. Such a knowledge base may include models and theories from several fields of science, often called kernel theories. In other words, a kernel theory is a theory that informs artefact design. In the IT area, kernel theories from the natural, social, and behavioural sciences are relevant, as are models from the formal sciences. For example, theories of human perception can support the development of methods for user interface design, and cryptography can inform the design of security architectures.

In addition to scientific theories, a knowledge base usually includes information about existing artefacts that are similar, in function or structure, to the one under consideration. These artefacts may originate from academia as well as industrial practice. A design science study should always clarify in what ways the new artefact differs from the already existing artefacts and what additional benefits it can provide.

Relevant knowledge may be found in academic publications, including textbooks and research papers in journals and conferences. A good starting point for identifying these kinds of publications is a search engine for academic papers, such as Web of Science or Google Scholar. Other sources of knowledge include magazine articles, white papers, fair trade presentations, and artefact manuals.

4.4   Focus in Design Science Research

Many design science projects do not undertake all of the five activities of the method framework in depth. Instead, they may focus on one or two of the activities, while the others are treated more lightly. Based on their focus, it is possible to distinguish between at least five typical cases of design science research.

Problem-focused Design Science Research—Some design science projects focus on problem explication. They carefully investigate a problem and carry out a root cause analysis. For this, they employ research strategies and methods in a rigorous way and typically include comprehensive empirical studies. These projects also define requirements for an artefact based on more or less detailed investigations. The design of the artefact is only outlined, and neither demonstration nor evaluation is carried out. Projects of this kind often have a strong social science flavour and the design element is downplayed. However, they can provide an essential understanding of a problem, upon which subsequent design science projects can build.

Requirements-focused Design Science Research—Other design science projects focus on requirements definition. These projects start with an existing problem that is simply accepted as is, or is slightly explicated. Careful and rigorous investigations are carried out in order to collect requirements, which will involve literature studies as well as interaction with relevant stakeholders. The design of the artefact is only outlined, and neither demonstration nor evaluation is carried out.

Requirements- and development-focused Design Science Research—Many design science projects focus on a combination of requirements definition and artefact development. Such projects do not involve any problem explication but move directly to requirements definition§. The artefact is then developed using research as well as creative methods. The viability of the artefact is demonstrated or a lightweight evaluation is performed.

Development- and evaluation-focused Design Science Research—It is also common for design science projects to focus on development and evaluation. Such projects will neither perform problem explication nor requirements definition but instead start from an existing requirements specification. The focus will be the design and development of an artefact using both research and creative methods. There will also be a demonstration and a thorough evaluation by means of experiments, case studies, or other research strategies.

Evaluation-focused Design Science Research—Some design science projects focus on the evaluation activity. Thus, no artefact is developed nor even outlined, and, therefore, it could be questioned whether such a project should count as design science. It may seem that it should not, as design science is typically concerned with the development of novel artefacts. However, an evaluation study may form part of a larger design science undertaking, which may extend over a long time and involve a number of research groups and individuals. One study may explicate a problem and suggest an artefact that can help to solve it; another study may define requirements for the artefact; a third study may develop the artefact; and yet another study may evaluate it. All of the studies are part of the same design science undertaking, although the same people do not necessarily carry them out. In this sense, the studies can all be viewed as design science contributions. Furthermore, an evaluation produces knowledge about an artefact, which is also a design science contribution.

4.5   Visualising the Method Framework

The proposed method framework can be visualised using IDEF0, which is a technique for describing systems as a number of interrelated activities, graphically represented as boxes (Fips 1993), see Fig. 4.3. Each activity can be decomposed into sub-activities, which themselves can be decomposed into further sub-activities, and so on. Furthermore, channels conveying data or objects are related to each activity.

There are four kinds of channels in IDEF0: input, output, controls, and resources. Inputs are transformed or consumed by an activity to produce outputs. Controls (e.g. blueprints, rules, guidelines, methods, and instruments) govern an activity to produce the correct outputs, while resources are the means (e.g. generic and domain knowledge) that support an activity. Channels are represented graphically as arrows: input arrows point to the left side of a box; output arrows leave the right side of a box; control arrows point to the top side of a box; and resource arrows point to the bottom of a box.

In the method framework, the channels can be defined as follows:

Input (arrow from left)—The input channel describes what knowledge or object is the input to an activity.

Output (arrow to right)—The output channel describes what knowledge or object is the output from an activity.

Controls (arrow from above)—The controls channel describes what knowledge is used for governing an activity, including research strategies, research methods, and creative methods.

Resources (arrow from below)—The resources channel describes what knowledge is used as the basis of an activity, i.e. the knowledge base including models and theories.

Figure 4.4 presents the method framework by means of an IDEF0 diagram. When applying the framework in a design science project, the diagram can be used as a

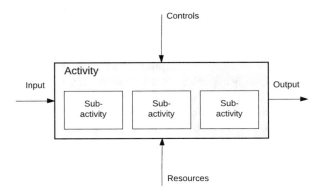

Fig. 4.3 An IDEF0 diagram

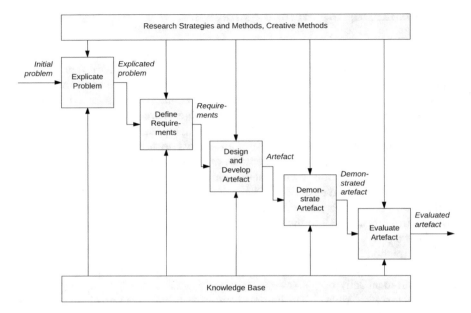

Fig. 4.4 The method framework for design science research with research strategies and knowledge base

template and filled in with the specifics of the project. This will result in a convenient overview of the project, which can be used for documentation and communication.

4.6   The Design Science Canvas

Through the IDEF0 representation of the method framework, it is possible to obtain a comprehensive yet compact overview of a design science project. However, it is sometimes desirable to provide an even more compact description, and the Design Science Canvas can be used for this purpose. The Canvas offers a concise, easily understandable, and visually appealing overview of the key components of a design science project. The Canvas consists of a rectangle divided into a number of boxes that describe the practice and the problem that the project addresses, the artefact being designed, the requirements for this artefact, the quality of the artefact and the effects of using it, the research process followed, and the knowledge base used as a foundation for the project.

A template for the Design Science Canvas with descriptions of the fields is presented in Fig. 4.5. The parts of the Canvas are as follows:

• The top part of the canvas describes the practice that provides the context for the problem to be addressed.

Practice
Describe the practice in which the problem exists, in particular its purpose, main activities and participants.

Problem
Describe the practical problem to be addressed. Formulate it in a precise and concise way. Explain why the problem is important and of general interest. Specify the stakeholders of the problem and how they are affected by it.

Research Process
Describe the research process of the project. State and justify the selection of research strategies and research methods. Possibly discuss which alternative research strategies and methods that were considered and why they were discarded. Clarify which of the main activities in design science (problem explication, requirements definition, design and development, and evaluation) that were included in the project. Describe how the research was carried out in the project. Discuss design rationale when applicable. Describe ethical issues encountered and how they were addressed.

Artefact
Specify the type of artefact. Describe the artefact, in particular, its structure, behaviour and functions. Describe how the artefact is to be used in the practice. Explain why and how the artefact can address the problem.

Requirements
Describe requirements on the artefact in a precise and concise way. Include functional as well as non-functional requirements. Justify the requirements by relating them to both the problem and the stakeholders.

Quality and Effects
Describe how well the artefact fulfils the requirements and to what extent it solves the practical problem. Describe the effects of using the artefact, including the side-effects. Discuss ethical and societal consequences of using the artefact.

Knowledge Base
Describe the knowledge base that was used as a foundation for the project. The knowledge base may include theories and models as well as existing artefacts. Explain how the knowledge base was utilized in the research process.

Fig. 4.5 The Design Science Canvas

- The leftmost middle part describes the problem as well as the requirements on the artefact being designed.
- The rightmost middle part describes the artefact in terms of structure, behaviour, and function, as well as the results of evaluating the artefact.
- The inner box within the middle part describes the research process.
- The bottom part describes the knowledge base used.

The Design Science Canvas can be used in several different situations. It can be used as a first sketch in order to improve communication and create a common understanding between members of a new design science project. It can also be used as a monitoring tool for continuously recording changes to the plans for a project. Furthermore, the Canvas can help to present the overall setup of a project to stakeholders and other interested parties. A similar use would be to include the Canvas in the final project report as part of an executive summary. In general, the Canvas is useful whenever there is a need to provide a compact, easily understandable overview of a design science project.

4.7   Action Research and Design Science

The purpose and activities of design science are similar to those of action research. Both aim to change and improve human practices and thus can be viewed as practice research, as pointed out by Goldkuhl and Sjöström (2018). Furthermore, both include problem solving and evaluation. However, there are also differences. Design science addresses practical problems through the design and positioning of artefacts, while action research does not require an artefact to be part of the solution addressing the practical problems. Instead, action research often addresses problems through psychological, social, and organisational change. Furthermore, design science does not require a practical problem from a local practice as the starting point for the research, while this is required in action research. Action research also requires active practitioner participation, which is common but not necessary for design science. Finally, action research is a single research strategy, while design science can make use of several complementary research strategies, e.g. one for problem explication, another for requirements definition, and a third for evaluation.

It could be argued, however, that if an artefact is proposed as a solution in an action research project, action research becomes very similar to design science. Clearly, action research is a highly relevant research strategy for many design science projects, and there are also design science methods that are based on action research, e.g. Sein et al. (2011).

4.8   The Scientific Method and the Method Framework for Design Science Research

It has been argued, e.g. by Fischer and Gregor (2011) and Eekels and Roozenburg (1991), that design science research methods are in several respects similar to the scientific method. According to the Oxford English Dictionary, the scientific method is "a method or procedure that has characterized natural science since the seventeenth century, consisting in systematic observation, measurement, and experiment, and the formulation, testing, and modification of hypotheses". One common version of the scientific method is the hypothetico-deductive method, which is typically divided into four steps:

1. *Ask a question.* The researcher observes a phenomenon that is novel, surprising, or interesting for some other reason. She attempts to capture the relevant aspects of the phenomenon by asking a question about it.
2. *Form a hypothesis.* The researcher comes up with and formulates a hypothesis that is able to answer the question. This hypothesis often includes a causal mechanism or a predictive model. The hypothesis may also be made up of a set of smaller, interrelated hypotheses.
3. *Deduce predictions from the hypothesis.* Assuming the hypothesis is true, the researcher identifies some consequences that must then hold, i.e. she makes a number of predictions.
4. *Check the predictions.* The researcher performs observations to determine whether or not the predictions are correct; if correct, the hypothesis is strengthened; otherwise, it is weakened.

The method framework in this chapter has a structure similar to that of the scientific method, as shown in Fig. 4.6. Its first activity, Explicate Problem, is similar to the step "Ask a question" of the scientific method, as both investigate a situation that is experienced as challenging. The key difference is that in the scientific method, a question is asked, while in design science research, a practical problem is examined. Step 2, "Form a hypothesis", is similar to activities 2 and 3 of the design science method framework, which first identify requirements for an artefact and then design and develop it. However, in the scientific method, an answer is formulated in the form of a hypothesis, while design science research produces an artefact (and related knowledge). Steps 3 and 4 of the scientific method correspond to Evaluate Artefact of the method framework, as both intend to show that the results produced are satisfactory. In summary, steps 1 and 2 of the scientific method, as well as activities 1 to 3 of the design science method, are about discovery and invention, i.e. creating a new hypothesis or artefact. Steps 3 and 4 of the scientific method, as well as activities 4 and 5 of the design science method, are about justification, i.e. ensuring that the created hypothesis or artefact is adequate.

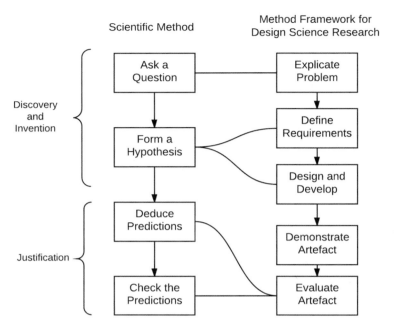

Fig. 4.6 Comparing the scientific method with the method framework for design science research

4.9 How to Write Research Questions and Research Goals

Writing a research question in design science research is about relating two things: an artefact and a practical problem. The idea is that if people use the artefact, it will help them to solve or address the problem. The problem should not be too broad because then it will be impossible, or at least very difficult, to design an artefact that can address it. But neither should the problem be too narrow because then it may be uninteresting or irrelevant. The artefact should be described briefly, indicating its type and some main characteristics. It is too early to provide a detailed artefact description—this is to be done in the artefact design. Here are a couple of examples of good research questions:

- What should the architecture of an EHR system look like to ensure that the system provides a high level of privacy? (artefact: the architecture of an EHR system; problem: privacy can be compromised)
- How should a mobile user interface for book reading be designed in order to be easy to use by visually impaired people? (artefact: mobile user interface for book reading; problem: difficult to use by visually impaired people)

These research questions are perfectly fine, but some people may find them rather awkward and hard to read. If so, one alternative would be to reformulate them as research goals:

- The goal is to design an architecture of an EHR system that ensures a high level of privacy.
- The goal is to design a mobile user interface for book reading that is easy to use by visually impaired people.

Which formulation to choose is not a significant issue; it is often just a matter of taste. Still, the goal formulation can sometimes make it easier to provide more information about the focus of the research, e.g.:

- The goal is to design and evaluate an architecture of an EHR system that ensures a high level of privacy.
- The goal is to define requirements for an architecture of an EHR system that ensures a high level of privacy.

Here is an example of a not-so-good research goal:

- The goal is to design an artefact that will solve global poverty.

Firstly, the goal only refers to an artefact in general without saying anything substantial about it. Even more importantly, the problem is much too big, broad, and wicked—it would indeed be sensational if an artefact could solve global poverty. Obviously, this research goal is unreasonable, but it is sometimes difficult to determine whether or not a particular goal is problematic. Here are some examples of research goals that are successively more precise:

- The goal is to design a system that ensures high quality in health care.
- The goal is to design an information system that can be used to improve patient safety in health care.
- The goal is to design an EHR system that can be used to improve patient safety in diabetes care.

The first of these research goals is probably too broad, and possibly also the second one, while the last goal seems appropriate, depending on the scope and size of the project at hand.

The research problems in focus in design science research are practical problems, i.e. problems experienced by stakeholders that impact them in a non-desirable way in their practice. In empirical sciences, on the other hand, the research problems are typically knowledge problems, i.e. research gaps in a domain. Thus, the focus and justification of such research are about the lack of knowledge in a scientific discipline; it is not about practical problems experienced by stakeholders in a practice. For this reason, research problems in empirical sciences give rise to research questions that ask how some knowledge gap can be filled in, meaning that in most cases there is no good reason to reformulate the research question into a research goal.

4.10   Summary of Chapter

- The proposed method framework for design science research includes five main activities that range from problem investigation and requirements definition, through artefact design and development, to demonstration and evaluation.
- A design science project needs to make use of rigorous research methods. Any research strategy or method can be used to answer questions about artefacts. It is even common to use several research strategies and methods because different design science activities may require different approaches.
- A design science project needs to relate both design science activities and their results to an existing knowledge base, since results from a design science project should be original and well founded.
- A *knowledge base* includes models and theories from different fields of science. A knowledge base also includes information about existing artefacts that are similar to the one under consideration.
- A *kernel theory* is a theory that informs artefact design. In the IT area, kernel theories from natural, social, and behavioural sciences are relevant as well as models from formal sciences.
- A design science project needs to communicate new results to both practitioners and researchers.

4.11   Review Questions

1. What are the activities of the proposed method framework?
2. Can different research strategies be used within the same design science project?
3. How can surveys be used for problem explications?
4. How can experiments be used for evaluations?
5. Why are research strategies and methods less relevant to design and development than to the other activities in the proposed method framework?
6. Which kernel theories could be relevant for a project developing a novel service for virtual patient communities?
7. Which information sources can be used for studying a knowledge base?
8. Is it important that in a design science project, approximately the same amount of effort is spent on each activity?
9. In the IDEF0 representation of the method framework, what is the difference between controls and resources?

4.12 Answers to Selected Review Questions

2. Yes. For example, a survey can be used for problem explication and an experiment for evaluation. However, for a small-scale research project, it may become too expensive and time consuming to use more than one research strategy.
5. Design and development is very much about generating original ideas and inventing creative solutions, and for this purpose research strategies and methods do not provide strong support. Research strategies and methods are more useful when it comes to investigating a problem including its root causes, eliciting requirements from different groups, and empirically evaluating artefacts.
8. No. The amount of effort spent on each activity depends on the goal of the project. Some projects primarily aim to understand the problem context and therefore focus on problem explication, and similar considerations hold for the other activities.
9. Controls provide guidance for how to carry out the activities, while resources consist of the knowledge needed for the activity.

4.13 Further Reading

Several different methods and method frameworks for design science research have been proposed. The method framework introduced in this chapter is similar to the one proposed by Peffers et al. (2007), who put forward a methodology that can serve as a framework for design science research and as a template for presenting design science results. The methodology consists of principles, practices, and procedures. A process model is included, which consists of six steps: problem identification and motivation, definition of the objectives for a solution, design and development, demonstration, evaluation, and communication. The activities in the method framework introduced in this chapter are based on these steps but differ in that the communication step is omitted. Furthermore, the activities in our framework should not be seen as temporally ordered steps but as logically related through input-output relationships, as further discussed in Chap. 11.

Hevner et al. (2004) do not propose any process model for design science research but instead introduce a number of guidelines: design as an artefact, problem relevance, design evaluation, research contributions, research rigour, design as a search process, and communication of research. The purpose of these guidelines is to help researchers, readers, reviewers, and editors to understand the requirements for high-quality design science research. Kuechler and Vaishnavi (2008) discuss a design research cycle, consisting of five steps: awareness of a problem, suggestion, development, evaluation, and conclusion. They also investigate how the process of developing and testing an artefact is related to the testing and refinement of its kernel theory. Alturki et al. (2011, 2013) propose a roadmap for design science research, which synthesises a number of existing methods and approaches. The roadmap differs from other design science research methods in its breadth of coverage of the aspects and activities of design science research.

Sein et al. (2011) argue that design science research methods have focused excessively on building an artefact and have relegated evaluation to a separate phase. In order to address this shortcoming, they propose action design research as an alternative method of design science research, in which building, organisational intervention, and evaluation are intertwined. Similarly to Sein et al. (2011), Rohde et al. (2017) acknowledge the role of social practices and organizational change for the design and use of information system artefacts. They recognize that information systems are not solely representations of social practices but are instead co-designed and appropriated through their use in organizations. Thus, the effects of an information system do not depend only on its functionality but also on how it has been appropriated and put to use in practice.

Gregory (2011) discusses how design science research and grounded theory can be combined, thereby leveraging design science research projects to generate theoretical contributions that go beyond the solution of specific practical problems. Gregory also argues that grounded theory can support the activities of problem explication as well as the definition of requirements. Beck et al. (2013) investigate how design science research can generate novel theory in addition to artefacts, and they show how to integrate methods of grounded theory with the methodology of design science research. Goldkuhl and Lind (2010) investigate design knowledge and its roles in both design science research and design practice. They propose a multi-grounded approach and argue that abstract design knowledge should be grounded empirically (in empirical knowledge), theoretically in other theories (and similar abstract sources), and internally, ensuring that the abstract design knowledge forms a coherent whole.

Nunamaker et al. (2013) discuss the difficulties in producing high-impact results in design science research, in particular for individual researchers and small teams. They argue that high-impact results can be achieved through sustained collaborative research programmes that employ multiple research methods to shepherd concepts from the ideation stage all the way to realised, real-world impact.

Blessing and Chakrabarti (2009) propose a method for design research, called Design Research Methodology (DRM), that has been applied not only in the IT area but also for engineering in general. Educational design research is a research approach that develops solutions to practical and complex educational problems, thereby providing a setting for scientific inquiry (McKenney and Reeves 2014).

Numerous texts describe the scientific method. Gimbel (2011) explains the scientific method but also takes a critical stance, as he introduces a number of case studies from the history of science and evaluates whether the scientific practice actually reflects the prescriptions of the scientific method.

References

Alturki A, Gable GG, Bandara W (2011) A design science research roadmap. In: Jain H, Sinha AP, Vitharana P (eds) Service-oriented perspectives in design science research. Lecture Notes in Computer Science. Springer, Berlin, pp. 107–123

Alturki A, Gable G, Bandara W (2013) The design science research roadmap: in progress evaluation. In: PACIS 2013 proceedings

Beck R, Weber S, Gregory RW (2013) Theory-generating design science research. Inf. Syst. Front. 15(4):637–651

Blessing LTM, Chakrabarti A (2009) DRM, a design research methodology, 2009th edn. Springer, Berlin

Eekels J, Roozenburg NFM (1991) A methodological comparison of the structures of scientific research and engineering design: their similarities and differences. Des Stud 12(4):197–203

Fips (1993) Integration definition for function modeling (IDEF0), Draft federal information processing standards, publication 183. www.idef.com/downloads/pdf/idef0.pdf. Accessed July 3 2014

Fischer C, Gregor S (2011) Forms of reasoning in the design science research process. In: Jain H, Sinha A, Vitharana P (eds) Service-oriented perspectives in design science research, vol. 6629. Lecture Notes in Computer Science. Springer, Berlin, pp 17–31

Gimbel S (2011) Exploring the scientific method: cases and questions. University Of Chicago Press, Chicago

Goldkuhl G, Lind M (2010) A multi-grounded design research process. In: Winter R, Zhao JL, Aier S (eds) Global perspectives on design science research. Lecture Notes in Computer Science. Springer, Berlin, pp. 45–60

Goldkuhl G, Sjöström J (2018) Design science in the field: practice design research. In: Designing for a digital and globalized world. Springer, Berlin, pp 67–81

Gregory RW (2011) Design science research and the grounded theory method: characteristics, differences, and complementary uses. In: A. Heinzl et al (eds) Theory-guided modeling and empiricism in information systems research. Physica-Verlag HD, pp 111–127

Hevner AR et al (2004) Design science in information systems research. MIS Quarterly 28(1):75–105

Kuechler B, Vaishnavi V (2008) On theory development in design science research: anatomy of a research project. Eur J Inf Syst 17(5):489–504

McKenney S, Reeves TC (2014) Educational design research. In: Michael Spector J et al. Handbook of research on educational communications and technology. Springer, New York, pp. 131–140

Nunamaker Jr J, Twyman N, Giboney J (2013) Breaking out of the design science box: high-value impact through multidisciplinary design science programs of research. In: AMCIS 2013 proceedings

Peffers K et al (2007) A design science research methodology for information systems research. J Manag Inf Syst 24(3):45–77

Rohde M et al Grounded design – a praxeological IS research per spective. J. Inf. Technol. Impact 32(2):163–179

Sein M et al (2011) Action design research. Manag Inf Syst Quart 35(1):37–56

Chapter 5
Explicate Problem

The starting point for any design science project is a problem that people experience in a practice. Often, this problem is vague, unclear, and poorly articulated. Therefore, researchers need to analyze, investigate, and reformulate the problem in order to understand it in depth. If they move into design without this understanding, they may develop a solution that is not capable of addressing the problem in an appropriate way.

The first activity of the method framework is Explicate Problem. The goal of this activity is to formulate the initial problem precisely, justify its importance, and investigate its underlying causes. In other words, it addresses the question:

What is the problem experienced by some stakeholders of a practice and why is it important?

The answer to this question consists primarily of descriptive knowledge about the characteristics and the environment of the problem. Sometimes, the answer will also include explanatory knowledge about the causes of the problem.

As discussed in Chap. 1, a problem is an undesirable state of affairs, or more precisely, a gap between a desirable state and the current state. For example, suppose that several customers of a car retailer complain about the long delivery times for cars. The customers expect the time from order placement to product delivery to be less than 1 week (desirable state) instead of the current 3 weeks (current state). This is the gap that constitutes the problem.

The gap between the desirable and the current state is not always made explicit when a problem is discussed. The gap is often so obvious that knowledge of the current state is sufficient to conclude that a problem exists. For example, if many customers of the car retailer complain about the delivery times for cars, the management will realise that customers are dissatisfied and that there is a problem that needs to be addressed. In this case, the desirable state is not explicitly stated but implicitly understood. In other cases, a problem may become apparent only when someone suggests a more desirable state of affairs. For example, suppose

© Springer Nature Switzerland AG 2021
P. Johannesson, E. Perjons, *An Introduction to Design Science*,
https://doi.org/10.1007/978-3-030-78132-3_5

that no customer has complained about the delivery times, but a competitor states in a marketing campaign that its delivery time of cars is only 3 days from order placement. If the management interprets this as a threat, there will be a problem, although the current state was not viewed as undesirable in itself.

Not only threats but also opportunities can be viewed as problems. One example would be an organisation that receives information that mobile devices can be integrated with its internal IT systems. Thereby, the employees can access the systems from anywhere, which could increase their productivity. Therefore, the problem is that currently the organisation does not work as productively as it could because its employees do not benefit from this opportunity of mobile technology.

The two problems above are situated in local practices, and they need to be generalised in order to be treated as problems in design science research. At some stage in the research, the problems need to be transformed into generic problems that are relevant for a global practice, such as "customers often complain about long delivery times among car retailers" and "organisations experience productivity loss because mobile devices are not integrated with their internal IT systems".

The activity Explicate Problem can be structured and visualised as shown in Fig. 5.1. The input is an initial problem that may be vaguely formulated. The output is an explicated problem, which is precisely defined, well justified, and put into a context. The resources used in the activity consist of knowledge from the research literature and other written sources, as well as information from relevant stakeholders. The controls are primarily research strategies and methods but may also include other practice-based approaches to problem elicitation and representation.

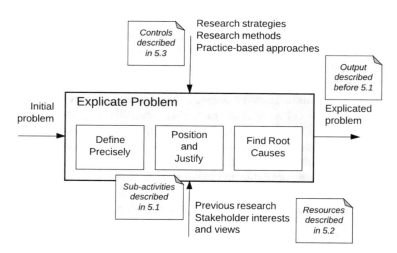

Fig. 5.1 Explicate problem

5.1 Sub-activities of Explicate Problem

When the initial practical problem is obscurely expressed or incompletely under-stood, there is a need to analyse and investigate it in depth. Without a good understanding of the problem, there is a risk that researchers develop solutions that cannot address it appropriately. In many design science projects, problem explication is essential before moving on to requirements definition and design. However, in some cases, the initial problem is already well understood and clearly articulated, meaning that the Explicate Problem activity will be limited. When explicating a problem, researchers engage in three main activities:

- Making the problem definition as precise as possible.
- Positioning and justifying the problem.
- Finding the root causes of the problem.

5.1.1 Define Precisely

A problem is defined precisely if different people understand it in (almost) the same way. Thus, a problem definition is made more precise by reducing the number of ways in which it can be understood and interpreted. For example, a problem definition such as "patient care provided by multiple care providers is often of low quality" is vague and can be interpreted in many ways. The problem can be made more precise by being reformulated as "patient care provided by multiple care providers poses risks for patient safety". This formulation is narrower and has fewer possible interpretations than the original one. There are also other ways of making the original problem more precise, e.g. "patient care provided by multiple care providers is inconvenient for the patients".

In general, precise problem definitions are preferable to less precise ones, as they help people to develop a common view of a problem. Furthermore, a precise problem definition helps to limit the scope of a research project, thereby increasing its chances for success. However, highly precise problem definitions can sometimes be difficult to quickly grasp and understand. There is also a risk that in the process of formulating a more precise problem definition, it becomes too narrow and important aspects are omitted. An overly narrow problem formulation may also exclude potentially innovative solutions.

In order to define a problem more precisely, a researcher can approach different groups of stakeholders, e.g. managers, employees, and customers, as they may have different views and knowledge about various aspects of the problem. By combining contributions from different stakeholder groups, the researcher can achieve a more in-depth and complete explication of the problem.

Different groups of stakeholders often have different views on the problem addressed and therefore have different expectations on the solution to be designed and developed. If the designers do not acknowledge this, there is a risk that a systems development project fails. For example, the system designers may be unaware that powerful groups in the organisation are working behind the scenes to obstruct the implementation of the solution. In order to recognise the needs and interests of different groups, an overall problem definition can preferably be left somewhat vague but complemented with a number of more precise and detailed problem definitions, each related to a certain group's view of the problem.

5.1.2   Position and Justify

When a problem is formulated in isolation, it is often difficult to understand, communicate, and justify. It is therefore helpful to put the problem into a context, which can be done by positioning it in the practice within which it occurs, i.e. describe the purpose, stakeholders, activities, and environment of the practice. The problem introduced in the previous section arises in a healthcare practice, which at a high level of abstraction can be described as follows:

- *Purpose.* To offer effective and safe care to patients.
- *Stakeholders.* Patients, physicians, nurses, other healthcare personnel, managers, family members.
- *Activities.* To diagnose and treat patients.
- *Environment.* Hospitals, care centers, and patients' homes.

A problem should always be well justified so that people can agree that it is worthwhile to address it. This means that the problem should be:

- *Significant.* Viewed as important by the people who experience it in a practice.
- *Of general interest.* Of interest to a global practice, not only to a single local practice.
- *Feasible.* Possible to solve, at least partially.
- *Challenging.* Without a good existing solution.

Sometimes a problem may be original, which is particularly common when technological innovations have created new opportunities. The justification of a problem may also include its ethical and societal consequences. The problem above, about risks for patient safety in care provided by multiple care providers, is significant because it is seen as important by both patients and healthcare personnel; it is of general interest because it exists in almost all healthcare settings; it is feasible to develop solutions; but it is not original because it has been recognized for a long time by many people.

5.1.3   Find Root Causes

At an early stage, a problem is often formulated in an impressionistic way, mainly expressing a feeling that some state of affairs is unsatisfactory. However, in order to do something about the problem, it is usually not sufficient to remain at an impressionistic level; a more detailed understanding is required. In order to arrive at this, a so-called root cause analysis can be performed, in which the underlying causes to the problem are identified, analysed, and represented. By addressing these causes, better results can be achieved than by treating only the symptoms of the problem. For example, an initial problem may be expressed as "patient care provided by multiple care providers poses risks for patient safety". The underlying causes of this problem may be of different kinds, including information deficiencies, lack of competence, inadequate incentives, and unclear responsibility structures. Focusing on information deficiencies, three underlying problem causes are:

- Different care providers lack information about other providers' performed, ongoing, and planned activities.
- Different care providers do not have sufficient knowledge and shared understanding of the patients' problems and conditions.
- Different care providers do not have sufficient knowledge and shared understanding of the patients' care goals.

One widespread tool for representing problem causes is the Ishikawa diagram (also called cause-effect or fishbone diagram) (see Fig. 5.2 for an example). An Ishikawa diagram is a graphical tool that may be used to investigate and represent the potential causes of a problem. It consists of a central horizontal line representing

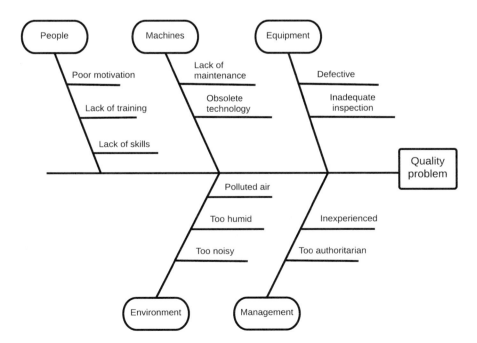

Fig. 5.2 An Ishikawa diagram

the problem and associated slanting lines representing direct problem causes, which in turn may be related to additional lines representing indirect problem causes. These causes can also be classified into different categories, as indicated in Fig. 5.2.

5.2 Resources for Explicate Problem

The results of the activity Explicate Problem should be based on, and compared with, existing related work in order to ensure well-founded and original results. Therefore, researchers need to review previous research that has addressed similar problems and existing solutions. Not only research literature can be used but also other sources, e.g. newspaper articles and white papers.

In some cases, researchers may base the explication of a problem solely on the literature, but usually they also need to directly study the participants and stakeholders of relevant practices. This is often done through interviews, but other research strategies and methods can also be applied, as discussed in the next section.

5.3 Strategies and Methods for Explicate Problem

In principle, any research strategy or research method can be used for the Explicate Problem activity. They all have their own advantages and disadvantages for this purpose, as outlined below.

Surveys—Surveys can be used for eliciting problem statements from a large group of stakeholders. Thereby, they provide an overview of the problems experienced by, for example, managers, employees, end-users, and customers. In many cases, different stakeholders have different views of the problem at hand, and a survey can make these differences explicit. However, a survey is usually an ineffective instrument for eliciting a deep and elaborated analysis of a problem from stakeholders.

Case Studies—Case studies can provide a deep understanding of the practice in which an initial problem emerged. They can help researchers to gain a firm grasp of the root causes of the problem and the stakeholders' views on it. However, case studies are complex undertakings that rely heavily on the skills and experiences of the researchers performing them. This dependency on the individual researchers may be a drawback, as they may have interests and preconceptions that can bias the research work.

Action Research—Action research requires the active engagement of both researchers and practitioners in a practice. The competence and experiences of researchers may offer fresh perspectives on the problem that are not obvious to practitioners. Furthermore, new and more important problems can emerge when researchers investigate opportunities and solutions together with practitioners. However, the dependency on researchers is strong due to their active participation in the practice. Therefore, there is a risk that their interests and preconceptions will have too much of an influence on the problem explication. There is also a risk that practitioners do not have the necessary time to actively participate in the research project or that the collaboration between researchers and practitioners does not work out as expected.

Grounded Theory—Grounded theory is a research strategy in which pure empirical facts have a strong impact on the explication of a problem. Researchers start by gathering facts about the domain under consideration. Based on these facts, they suggest an initial problem explication, which is tested against further empirical facts from the domain, resulting in a refined problem explication. The iterations between fact gathering and problem explication refinement continue until additional empirical facts do not affect the problem explication. An advantage of grounded theory is that it is not restricted by any specific theoretical view that may limit researchers. However, this may also be a disadvantage, as a theoretical lens can support the researchers in finding new perspectives on the problem.

Ethnography—The research strategy ethnography allows researchers to understand the culture of a practice in depth. Thereby, they are able to see a problem not only as outsiders but also from the stakeholders' point of view. Furthermore, based on their competence and experience, researchers may understand the structures behind the stakeholders' views and actions, which they themselves may not recognise. This knowledge can allow researchers to arrive at a deep and rich explication of a problem. However, since ethnographical studies are time consuming, they may only have time to communicate with a limited number of stakeholders. The outcome of this research strategy also relies heavily on the competence and experience of researchers.

Interviews—Interviews allow a researcher to engage in a dialogue with a respondent in order to explicate a problem in an interactive and creative way. This is possible because the researcher, based on the respondent's initial answers, can ask follow-up questions. A drawback of interviews is the dependency on the perspective and interests of the respondent, but this problem can be mitigated by interviewing several respondents. Another disadvantage is that the researcher's personal attributes can affect the outcome of an interview.

Focus Groups—A focus group is a research method in which several respondents in conversations can inspire each other to identify and define problems in a domain. However, there is a risk that dominant individuals in such a group have too great an impact so that other opinions are not voiced. To some extent, this problem can be handled by a skilful moderator.

Questionnaires—A questionnaire is a form that contains predefined written questions. An important benefit of using questionnaires for data collection is that they can easily be distributed to a large number of respondents at low cost. A drawback is that a researcher and a respondent cannot discuss a problem situation informally and creatively, meaning that the respondent's answers may be superficial. Furthermore, the respondent often has little time or inclination to provide detailed answers to the questions. Another drawback is that respondents may interpret the written questions of a questionnaire in different ways. Moreover, if the questionnaire questions are closed (i.e. they have predefined answer options), there is also a risk that the respondents' answers will be biased towards the researchers' views, since they were responsible for selecting the available options.

Observation—In an observation study, researchers can observe the behaviour of people in a practice. A benefit of the method is that researchers, based on their competence and experience, can identify problems and circumstances that are not apparent to the people under observation. A drawback is that the method requires highly skilled researchers to interpret the actions and interactions of the people being observed. There is also a risk that the researchers' interests and preconceptions may influence their interpretations in undesirable ways.

Documents—A document study is a form of observation study, but the focus is on written documents, not actions. Written documents can expose contradictions in a practice and can therefore be a valuable resource for identifying and defining problems. However, the method requires skilled researchers for the interpretation of the documents. There is also a risk that some documents may only represent the official view of a particular stakeholder and may hide existing problems.

5.4   Guidelines for Explicate Problem

The results of the problem explication will govern the rest of the research process. Therefore, a thorough problem explication will be valuable for all the other design science activities. The following guidelines can be used to support problem explication:

- *Position the problem.* Clarify in which practice the problem appears.
- *Formulate the problem precisely.* Describe the problem in a precise but also concise, easily understandable manner.
- *Justify the problem.* Explain why the problem is important and to whom.
- *Ensure the problem is of general interest.* Make it clear that the problem is of interest not only to a local practice.
- *Ensure the problem is solvable.* Define and analyse the problem so that it becomes small enough to be solved, at least partially.
- *Specify the sources of the problem.* Describe the literature and the stakeholders that have previously identified, studied, and experienced the problem.
- *Describe how the problem has been explicated.* Explain what has been done to explicate the problem, in particular how the stakeholders have been involved and how the research literature has been reviewed.

5.5 Summary of Chapter

- The question answered by the Explicate Problem activity is: what is the problem experienced by some stakeholders of a practice and why is it important?
- A problem is a gap between the current state and a desirable state.
- A problem should in most cases be defined as precisely as possible, so that different people understand it in the same way, and to limit the scope of the design science project, thereby making the problem easier to address.
- A problem should always be positioned in some practice.
- A problem should be well justified so that people can agree it is worthwhile to address.
- A problem should be of general interest, i.e. of interest for a global practice.
- A root cause analysis can be performed to identify the underlying causes of a problem.
- A problem explication can be made more comprehensive by involving different kinds of stakeholders, such as managers, employees, and customers.

5.6 Review Questions

1. A company has come to the conclusion that it could improve its business intelligence by analysing social media streams. How can this situation be expressed as a gap between two states?
2. Which are the most important sub-activities of the Explicate Problem activity?
3. How precisely formulated are the following problems?

   - The customers are dissatisfied.
   - The customers are dissatisfied with the customer service.
   - Most customers that shop in the web store are dissatisfied with the customer service.

4. A problem should always be well justified, in particular it should be of general interest, significant, and challenging. Do the following problems satisfy these criteria?

   - The computers in our company are old and we cannot afford to replace them with newer ones.
   - There is no mobile currency converter service tailored to healthcare personnel.
   - Vacuum cleaners do not have a sufficiently long power cord for use in building sites.

5. Can a problem have only one root cause?
6. Are there problems without any root causes?

7. What are the root causes of war and peace? Explain why this question is difficult using the notion of wicked problems.
8. It can be argued that case studies can be problematic to use for problem explication, as their results depend very much on the researchers and their background. Is this an issue also for surveys?
9. Are structured interviews more appropriate for problem explication than unstructured interviews?
10. Why is it important to involve different kinds of stakeholders in problem explication?

5.7 Answers to Selected Review Questions

4. (a) is not of general interest (b) is not significant (c) is not challenging.
5. In principle, it is almost always possible to identify multiple causes of a problem. But in practice, one cause may be so dominating that it is hardly interesting to consider other causes.
6. In principle, it is always possible to drill down indefinitely and keep asking "Why is this the case?". However, in practice, this chain of questions must eventually stop, and in this sense there are problems without root causes.
7. The problem of war and peace is a wicked problem. There is no definitive formulation of it, as the notion of war can be defined in a multitude of ways. The underlying causes of war are, to a large extent, unknown. There is no clear stop condition telling when lasting peace has been achieved.
8. Yes. Analysing the answers from a survey can often be done in an objective way, in particular if the survey is based on closed questions. However, the formulations of the questions are highly dependent on the background of the researcher, and the formulations have a strong influence on the answers. Ask a leading question, and you get the answers you are looking for.
9. Probably not, as the respondent can more easily provide new ideas in an unstructured interview than in a structured one. The interviewer can also more easily probe for more details and feedback.
10. Different stakeholders may have different interests and experiences that result in them having different views of a problem, e.g. about its severity or root causes. All of these views need to be investigated in order to design and build an artefact that offers an inclusive solution.

5.8 Further Reading

A classic text on the formulation, analysis, and solving of problems was written by Polya and Conway (2014). Although this book focuses on mathematical problems, many of its approaches can be transferred to other areas. Similarly, the formulation and analysis of problems can be informed by principles and techniques from critical thinking, which is the process of conceptualising, analysing, and synthesising information to guide belief and action. Haber (2020) offers an introduction to critical thinking, discussing both its history and practice. Several texts on root cause analysis, e.g. Fagerhaug and Andersen (2006), discuss different tools for root cause analysis with applications and examples. The web page Cause and Effect Analysis (2020) provides a brief introduction to root cause analysis and describes the structure and use of Ishikawa diagrams. Ritchey (2011) gives an easily accessible introduction to wicked problems and introduces general morphological analysis as a method for structuring and investigating relationships in multi-dimensional problem complexes. Peters (2017) offers a conceptual analysis of the notion of a wicked problem and applies it in the context of policy design.

References

Cause and Effect Analysis (2020) Cause and effect analysis: identifying the likely causes of problems. http://www.mindtools.com/pages/article/newTMC_03.htm. Accessed Dec 20 2020

Fagerhaug T, Andersen B (2006) Root cause analysis: simplified tools and techniques, 2nd edn, ASQ Quality Press, Milwaukee

Haber J (2020) Critical thinking. The MIT press essential knowledge series, Illustrated edition. MIT Press, Cambridge

Peters BG (2017) What is so wicked about wicked problems? A conceptual analysis and a research program. Policy Soc 36(3):385–396

Polya G, Conway JH (2014) How to solve it: a new aspect of mathematical method. With a foreword by John H. Conway edition. Princeton University Press, Princeton

Ritchey T (2011) Wicked problems – social messes: decision support modelling with morphological analysis. Springer, Berlin

Chapter 6
Define Requirements

Researchers need a clear and deep understanding of the problem being addressed before they can design a solution to it. Sometimes, it is possible to move directly from a problem to a solution, but often this is a large and difficult step. To bridge the gap between problem and solution, researchers can define requirements for a preliminary solution. These requirements can then guide them in further designing and developing the solution. The requirements can also be used to validate the quality of the fully developed artefact; researchers do this by determining whether or not the artefact fulfils the requirements.

The second activity of the method framework is Define Requirements. The goal is to identify and outline an artefact that can address the explicated problem and to elicit requirements for that artefact. In other words, this activity addresses the question:

What artefact can be a solution for the explicated problem and which requirements for this artefact are important to the stakeholders?

Answering this question can be viewed as an extended problem explication. In other words, researchers continue to explicate the problem further, but they do so using the proposed solution outline as a pair of glasses for guiding their examination of the problem. Thus, the question is to be answered by descriptive knowledge that specifies requirements for the artefact.

A *requirement* is a statement, made by a stakeholder of a practice, that a property of an artefact is desirable. We here define requirements in a broad sense, at both high and low levels of abstraction. High-level requirements are about general, sometimes

© Springer Nature Switzerland AG 2021
P. Johannesson, E. Perjons, *An Introduction to Design Science*,
https://doi.org/10.1007/978-3-030-78132-3_6

even vague, properties, while low-level requirements are more specific and concrete. Some examples of requirements are:

- The interface should be user-friendly (high-level requirement).
- The interface should be easy to learn (high-level requirement).
- The interface shall only make use of the colours rgb(34,139,34) and rgb(255,182,193) (low-level requirement).

High-level requirements can be useful for guiding design, though they may be somewhat vague and only provide an overall guidance. However, they are less useful for evaluating an artefact, as it is typically quite subjective to decide whether or not they have been fulfilled. In other words, they are not verifiable. Low-level requirements are better suited for evaluation, as it is easier to determine whether or not they have been fulfilled. The distinction between high-level and low-level requirements is not razor sharp—there is a continuum from very abstract to very concrete ones. (The term "design goal" is sometimes used for denoting high-level requirements.)

A requirement may concern the function, structure, or environment of an artefact as well as the effects of using it. *Functional requirements* refer to the functions of the artefact, and they depend on the problem to be addressed as well as the needs and wants of the stakeholders. Some examples of functional requirements for an Electronic Health Record (EHR) system are as follows:

- The system shall provide storage of X-rays.
- The system shall enable doctors to enter information about investigations and treatments.
- The system shall allow patients to enter information on their self-medication.

As can be seen from these examples, functional requirements are often very specific to the situation at hand, since they are tailored to provide benefits to particular stakeholders when they carry out their activities within a certain practice.

In contrast to functional requirements, *structural requirements* pertaining to structure and *environmental requirements* pertaining to the environment are typically more generic, meaning they are applicable in many situations. Some examples related to the EHR system are as follows:

- The system should have a coherent design (structural requirement).
- The system should not include redundant components (structural requirement).
- The system should be easy to adapt to changes (environmental requirement).
- The system shall be available on mobile devices (environmental requirement).

Non-functional requirements are those requirements that are not functional and encompass both structural and environmental requirements. In addition to the functional and non-functional requirements, it is also possible to formulate goals on the effects of using an artefact—for example, that the use of a new IT system should increase profits by 5%, or that it should make the corporate culture less hierarchic.

The activity Define Requirements can be structured and visualised as shown in Fig. 6.1. The input is an explicated problem provided by the Explicate Problem

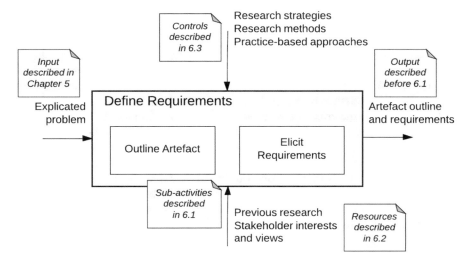

Fig. 6.1 Define requirements

activity, and the output is an artefact outline and a set of requirements. The resources used by the activity include knowledge in the research literature and other written sources, as well as assertions from stakeholders. The controls are primarily research strategies and methods but may also include practice-based approaches to requirements' elicitation and analysis.

In this activity, the explicated problem is transformed into a set of requirements to be used by the designer when designing and developing the artefact. If the problem has been analysed by identifying a set of root causes, these can provide a starting point for defining (some of) the requirements—for each root cause, one or more requirements can be defined. These requirements can then be traced back to the root causes on which they are based.

6.1 Sub-activities of Define Requirements

When defining requirements, researchers need to have a particular artefact in mind for which they can define their requirements. Thus, they first need to outline an artefact that can address the explicated problem. They can then move on to identifying and formulating requirements based on input from stakeholders as well as the literature and other knowledge sources. In other words, when researchers define requirements, they engage in two main activities:

- Outlining an artefact at a relatively high and abstract level
- Eliciting requirements based on stakeholder needs and interests as well as other contextual knowledge

6.1.1 Outline Artefact

The sub-activity Outline Artefact starts by choosing which artefact type should be designed to solve the problem, e.g. deciding whether the solution should be a construct, a model, a method, or an instantiation. This choice is sometimes easy due to the characteristics of the explicated problem. In other cases, it can be more difficult to choose the artefact type to be designed. For example, if IT systems need to be integrated to make a business process more efficient, a solution might be a method for integrating IT systems, a model of an integration architecture, or an instantiation in the form of an integration tool. When the artefact type has been chosen, the artefact is to be described in broad overview, focusing on its overall structure and main functions. This description should be kept brief and include only as much detail as is needed to formulate requirements—adding too much detail may hamper creativity when designing the artefact.

6.1.2 Elicit Requirements

The second sub-activity is to elicit the requirements for the outlined artefact. The requirements to be included depend on the characteristics of the problem, the outlined solution, technological opportunities, previous research including documented solutions to similar problems, and stakeholder interests and opinions. In Chap. 5, the problem "patient care provided by multiple care providers poses risks for patient safety" was analysed, resulting in a set of root causes. If an IT system is chosen and outlined as a solution for the problem, some requirements related to the root causes are as follows:

- Root cause: Different care providers lack information about other providers' performed, ongoing, and planned activities.

  - Requirement: The IT system should facilitate communication among the care providers about performed, ongoing, and planned activities.

- Root cause: Different care providers do not have sufficient knowledge and shared understanding of the patients' care goals.

  - Requirement: The IT system should support care providers in identifying and managing care goals that are conflicting, i.e. goals for a patient that cannot be fulfilled at the same time.

The sub-activity Elicit Requirements can be carried out by gathering requirements from stakeholders, usually including different groups of stakeholders in one or more local practices. The stakeholders may hold differing opinions about the requirements, and these requirements may sometimes even conflict, i.e. they cannot be satisfied at the same time. For example, one requirement for an IT system in health care could be that "The IT system should facilitate communication among the care providers about performed, ongoing, and planned care activities". A conflicting requirement would be that data should only be available based on strict authorization rules to protect patient privacy. The first requirement indicates that care parties should be able to communicate about their care activities in an unrestricted way, while the second requirement indicates that there needs to be strict restrictions on communication about patients. Such conflicting requirements need to be addressed and prioritised. Therefore, it is often worthwhile to ask stakeholders to rank their suggested requirements in order of importance.

6.2   Resources for Define Requirements

The results of the activity should always be based on and related to existing work. The researcher needs to report on previous research that has been carried out to solve similar problems, which artefacts have been designed and developed in that research, and which requirements have been addressed. Even if no other artefact has been designed previously to solve exactly the same problem, the researcher should still specify whether similar solutions exist and in what ways they differ from the proposed solution. Thereby, the requirements will be given a context that supports both researchers and practitioners in assessing the originality and significance of the solution. Another basis for the activity consists of the interests and opinions of stakeholders, as discussed above.

6.3   Research Strategies and Methods for Define Requirements

In principle, any research strategy or research method can be used for the Define Requirements activity. They all have their own strengths and weaknesses, which are discussed briefly below.

Surveys—Surveys can be used to elicit requirements directly from stakeholders. They offer a relatively low-cost approach to identifying requirements, in terms of time and other resources. Therefore, surveys make it possible to investigate the needs and wants of many people and different kinds of stakeholders. This comprehensive coverage increases the likelihood of finding all of the potentially relevant requirements and ensures that all stakeholder groups are included. However, there is a risk that surveys will result in incomplete requirements when stakeholders are not prepared to spend a sufficient amount of time and effort on providing information. Furthermore, the stakeholders may fail to identify requirements because they have limited knowledge or are biased in various ways. In other words, surveys as an instrument for the elicitation of requirements depend on the stakeholders' commitment, knowledge, and interests.

Case Studies—Case studies can overcome some of the limitations of surveys for requirements elicitation. In particular, case studies offer opportunities for investigating stakeholders' needs and requirements as well as their practice in greater depth and over an extended period of time. Furthermore, a researcher can identify requirements even if a stakeholder does not explicitly state them. The deeper understanding provided by a case study and the reduced dependency on stakeholders can help to identify a more complete and relevant set of requirements. However, case studies are time-consuming, their outcomes depend heavily on the competence of the researchers, and they can also be biased by their interests and preconceptions. Furthermore, a case study is always carried out in a single local practice, which may limit the generalisability of the results.

Action Research—The advantages and disadvantages of action research for the elicitation of requirements are similar to those of case studies. However, the dependence on researchers may be even greater in action research than in case studies, as they are actively participating and intervening in a practice. There is a risk that they may impose their own views on the stakeholders and come up with requirements that are not particularly relevant to them. On the other hand, the researchers may be essential for suggesting requirements when their knowledge exceeds that of the stakeholders. This is often the case when a novel artefact is to be designed and introduced in a practice, and its stakeholders only have a limited understanding of the potential of the new artefact. The researchers can then inform and guide the stakeholders to allow them to identify and articulate relevant requirements. Furthermore, the active participation of practitioners as knowledge sources helps to identify relevant requirements.

Interviews—Interviews may be the most common method for gathering requirements. Interviews usually take a direct approach to the elicitation of requirements by asking stakeholders about features that they would like to see included in the outlined artefact and which explicit requirements they would suggest. Interviews can be highly efficient and result in the identification of a large number of requirements in a short time. In addition, by directly asking for requirements, interviews can be used to increase the understanding of the respondents' practices and their attitude to the artefact under consideration. However, interviews may easily become stale and stifle creativity if they are very structured, which is obviously counterproductive. To some extent, this problem can be alleviated by using semi-structured or unstructured interviews, which encourage the respondent to take more initiative. Another issue is that an interview can only be effective if the respondent is knowledgeable and applies sufficient time and effort, which may not always be the case.

Focus Groups—Focus groups can overcome some of the disadvantages of one-to-one interviews for direct requirements elicitation. When people meet, discuss, and brainstorm in groups, more imaginative and creative requirements may be suggested. This is especially true if people with different backgrounds and competences are included in the same group, since they will be able to surprise, inspire, and encourage each other to come up with novel requirements. However, as always in focus groups, there is a risk that one or a few individuals will dominate, which may reduce the willingness of others to offer suggestions for requirements. A moderator who makes sure that everyone gets a chance to contribute can mitigate this to some extent.

Questionnaires—Questionnaires have the same advantages and disadvantages as interviews but often to an even higher degree. Questionnaires are inexpensive to distribute, which makes it possible to gather suggestions for requirements from many stakeholders. However, filling in a questionnaire does not invite much creativity, meaning that innovative requirements can rarely be expected. On the other hand, questionnaires can be effective for ranking the importance of requirements that have already been identified through other methods.

Observation—Observation studies can be used for gaining a better understanding of the practice in which an artefact will be used, which can provide clues for additional requirements. In this way, observation is used as a means for researchers to generate requirements themselves. Observation studies are effective when the stakeholders themselves are not expected to be able to generate all of the relevant requirements, typically because they have a limited understanding of the outlined artefact. The value of the requirements produced through observation studies relies heavily on the competence of the researcher.

Documents—Document studies can complement other methods for requirements elicitation or be an alternative when access to stakeholders is limited. Document studies can improve the understanding of the practice under consideration, which may provide clues for requirements analogously to observation studies.

6.4 Guidelines for Define Requirements

- *Specify what artefact to build.* Specify the type of the artefact (construct, model, method, instantiation) and describe it in broad overview, focusing on its overall structure and main functions.
- *Formulate each requirement clearly.* Describe each requirement in a precise, concise, and easily understandable way.
- *Justify each requirement.* For each requirement, explain why it is needed and relate it to the problem addressed.
- *Be realistic but also original.* Ensure that it is realistic to develop an artefact that fulfils the requirements, but also try to be original.
- *Specify the sources of the requirements.* Identify the literature and the stakeholders that have contributed to defining the requirements.
- *Describe how the requirements have been defined.* Explain what has been done to define the requirements, in particular how the stakeholders were involved and how the research literature was reviewed.

6.5 Generic Requirements and Artefact Qualities

Most requirements for an artefact are situation specific, in particular those concerning its functions. However, there are also a number of non-functional generic requirements that are relevant for almost any artefact, e.g. that it should be easy to use or have a modular design. This section introduces a set of generic artefact qualities that are useful when defining such requirements. Based on the distinction between structure and environment, the qualities are divided into structural qualities that concern the structure of the artefact and environmental qualities that concern the relationship between the artefact and its environment. Furthermore, the environmental qualities are divided into usage qualities, which describe how the artefact works and how it is perceived in use situations; management qualities, which describe how the artefact is managed over time; and generic environmental qualities, which mainly describe how the artefact is structurally related to its environment.

These suggested qualities can be used as inspiration for formulating generic requirements in the early stages of a design science project. They can also be used as a checklist for validation of requirements that have already been formulated. Thereby, important but overlooked requirements may be identified.

6.5.1 Structural Qualities

Structural qualities concern the structure of an artefact:

- *Coherence* is the degree to which the parts of an artefact are logically, orderly, and consistently related; coherence is low if an artefact includes parts that, in some sense, do not fit in with the rest of the artefact.
- *Consistence* (only for models) is the degree to which a model is free from conflicts.
- *Modularity* is the degree to which an artefact is divided into components that can be separated and recombined; common requirements related to modularity are low coupling, i.e. modules are not overly related with each other; high cohesion, i.e. modules are highly related internally; and high composability, i.e. modules can be easily replaced and recombined.
- *Conciseness* is the absence of redundant components in an artefact, i.e. components the functions of which can be provided by other components.

6.5.2 Environmental Qualities

Environmental qualities refer to the relationships between an artefact and its environment, for example, to users or other artefacts.

- *Usage Qualities* describe how an artefact works and is perceived in use situations:

  - *Usability* is the effectiveness, efficiency, and ease with which a user can use an artefact to achieve a particular goal.
  - *Comprehensibility* is the ease with which an artefact can be understood or comprehended by a user (also called understandability).
  - *Learnability* is the ease with which a user can learn to use an artefact.
  - *Customisability* is the degree to which an artefact can be adapted to the specific needs of a local practice or user.
  - *Suitability* is the degree to which an artefact is tailored to a specific practice, focusing only on its essential aspects (also called inherence or precision).
  - *Accessibility* is the degree to which an artefact is accessible by as many users as possible.
  - *Elegance* is the degree to which an artefact is pleasing and graceful in appearance or style (also called aesthetics).
  - *Fun* is the degree to which an artefact is attractive and fun to use.
  - *Traceability* (only for methods) is the ability to verify the history of using a method by means of documentation.

- *Management Qualities* describe how an artefact works and is perceived in management situations:

  - *Maintainability* is the ease with which an artefact can be maintained in order to correct defects, meet new requirements, make future maintenance easier, or cope with a changing environment.
  - *Flexibility* is the ease with which an artefact can be adapted when external changes occur (similar to maintainability; related notions are configurability, evolvability, and extensibility).
  - *Accountability* is the ease with which an actor can be made accountable for the workings of an artefact (a similar notion is auditability).

- *Generic Environmental Qualities* mainly describe how an artefact structurally is related to its environment:

  - *Expressiveness* (only for constructs and models) is the degree to which a set of constructs or a model is capable of representing the entities of interest in a domain.
  - *Correctness* (only for models) is the degree to which a model corresponds to the domain it represents (also called "accurateness").
  - *Generality* is the degree to which an artefact is relevant not only for a local but also for a global practice.
  - *Interoperability* (only for instantiations) is the ability of an artefact to work together with other artefacts, in particular to exchange data (related notions are openness, compatibility, and compliance with standards).
  - *Autonomy* (only for instantiations) is the capacity of the artefact to function without the involvement of another system.

- *Proximity* (only for models) is the degree to which independent aspects of a domain are captured by different constructs and related aspects are represented by related constructs.
- *Completeness* is the degree to which the artefact includes all components required for addressing the problem for which it was created.
- *Effectiveness* is the degree to which an artefact is able to achieve its goals.
- *Efficiency* is the degree to which an artefact is effective without wasting time, effort, or expense.
- *Robustness* (only for instantiations) is the ability of an artefact to withstand environmental change without needing to adapt its construction.
- *Resilience* (only for instantiations) is the ability of an artefact to adapt when faced with major environmental change (related notions are degradability, survivability, and safety).

6.6   The 5Es Framework

While the previous section provided a broad range of artefact qualities, it can also be useful to have access to a short list of such qualities. For this purpose, Checkland and Scholes (1990) propose the 5Es framework, which includes only five high-level qualities: efficacy, efficiency, effectiveness, elegance, and ethicality:

- *Efficacy* is the degree to which an artefact produces desirable effects under ideal circumstances. For example, a weight-loss diet has high efficacy if people who strictly follow it actually lose weight.
- *Efficiency* is the degree to which an artefact is effective without wasting time, effort, or expense. For example, a weight-loss diet is efficient if it is not expensive and does not require too much time to follow it.
- *Effectiveness* is the degree to which an artefact produces desirable effects in practice. For example, a weight-loss diet has low effectiveness if people, due to various situational factors, are not able to follow it in their daily life. However, the diet can still have high efficacy; thus, efficacy and effectiveness are not the same.
- *Elegance* is the degree to which an artefact is pleasing and graceful in appearance or style. For example, a weight-loss diet is elegant if the food tastes good and is visually pleasing.
- *Ethicality* is the degree to which the use of an artefact adheres to ethical norms. For example, a weight-loss diet including the consumption of meat may not be viewed as ethical according to some norms.

6.7   How to Write Requirements

In the following, we provide a number of guidelines that can help in writing clear, concise, and unambiguous requirements.

- *Define one requirement at a time.* Do not combine several requirements into one sentence; each requirement should be atomic. Small is beautiful and easy to understand.
- *Make the requirements as short as possible.* Short requirements are easier to understand than long ones.
- *Use a consistent format.* In most cases, a high-level requirement would be formulated as "The artefact should …". And a low-level requirement would be formulated as "The artefact shall …". This choice of wording may seem a bit arbitrary, but it has become a convention, meaning that many people are familiar with it.
- *Avoid vagueness.* Express the requirements clearly and precisely, avoiding vague words, such as normal, versatile, enhanced, timely, etc. Be as concrete and specific as possible. If a requirement is vaguely formulated, different people will interpret it in different ways.
- *If possible, ensure that the requirements are verifiable.* Try to make sure that it is possible to determine whether or not a requirement has been fulfilled (or to what extent it has been fulfilled). If a requirement is not verifiable, it cannot be used for evaluating the artefact. Although verifiability is usually desirable, it is not always possible to achieve, in particular for high-level requirements.

The following are examples of well-formulated requirements that respect the above guidelines:

- The system should be user-friendly.
- The user interface shall provide screens adapted for visually impaired users.
- The hospital system shall offer single sign-on.

The following are examples of less well-formulated requirements that violate the above guidelines:

- The system shall offer ordinary response time. (The word "ordinary" is vague and means different things to different users.)
- The user interface shall be easy to use for visually impaired users and eliminate all redundant information. (This requirement is not atomic and should be split into two. Furthermore, the vague phrase "easy to use" makes the requirement difficult to verify, although this may be acceptable for a high-level requirement.)
- The hospital system must offer single sign-on. (To stay with the conventions, "shall" is better than "must".)
- Privacy of sensitive information shall be guaranteed. (This formulation does not follow the form "The artefact shall …". Therefore, it is not clear which artefact should guarantee privacy.)

- The system shall support the teacher in correcting exams. (The vague word "support" makes the requirement difficult to verify. This may be fine for a high-level requirement, but then it should be formulated with "should" instead of "shall". The requirement could also be made more concrete, e.g. "The system shall provide a WYSIWYG editor for correcting exams".)

6.8   Summary of Chapter

- The question answered by the Define Requirement activity is: What artefact can be a solution for the explicated problem and which requirements for this artefact are important to the stakeholders?
- Outlining an artefact involves choosing which type of artefact should be designed to solve the problem: a construct, a model, a method, or an instantiation.
- Eliciting requirements means deciding which functional, structural, and environmental requirements an artefact should fulfil:

  – A *functional requirement* concerns the functions of an artefact.
  – A *structural requirement* concerns the structural qualities of an artefact, such as coherence and modularity.
  – An *environmental requirement* concerns the environmental qualities of an artefact, such as usability, comprehensibility, and efficiency.

- Many different groups of stakeholders should be included to determine the requirements, since they may hold differing opinions about the requirements, including their relative importance.
- *Conflicting requirements* are requirements that cannot be satisfied at the same time. These conflicting requirements need to be addressed, for example, by ranking the requirements in order of importance.

6.9   Review Questions

1. Requirements can easily conflict with each other. Give some examples of conflicting requirements for an Internet bank.
2. Which of the following requirements are functional and which are non-functional?

   (a) The calculator service shall be available on both Android and iOS.
   (b) The calculator service shall offer all trigonometric functions.
   (c) The smartphone shall be built from replaceable components.

3. Which are the most important sub-activities of Define Requirements?
4. Give an example of a problem that can be addressed by both a new model and a new method.

5. Which knowledge sources need to be considered when defining requirements?
6. Why are focus groups often more effective than one-to-one interviews for requirements definition?
7. Questionnaires typically do not encourage creativity. Can they still be useful for requirements definition?
8. Why is it important to involve different kinds of stakeholders in requirements definition?
9. Why are high cohesion and low coupling valuable properties of most architectures?
10. Is there a conflict between the requirements of learnability and customisability?
11. Is there a conflict between the requirements of interoperability and autonomy?

6.10   Answers to Selected Review Questions

1. It should be easy for a bank customer to log into the system from any kind of device. It should not be possible for an unauthorised user to access an account.
2. Only (b) is functional.
4. Consider the problem of inadequate query performance in a database management system. One solution is a model for an improved query optimisation component. Another solution is a method that supports database designers in formulating more efficient queries.
6. In a focus group, participants can inspire each other, which can help them to identify interesting and unexpected requirements.
7. Yes. Questionnaires can be efficient when asking stakeholders to rank a set of proposed requirements.
8. Different stakeholders may have different interests and experiences, which result in different requirements. All of these need to be considered and prioritised in order to design and build an artefact that offers an inclusive solution.
9. High cohesion and low coupling typically result in a modularised structure that is easy to understand and maintain.

6.11   Further Reading

Requirements elicitation has been studied in the area of requirements engineering for a long time, with the aim of supporting systems analysts and designers to produce requirements that are complete, consistent, and relevant for customer needs and wants. An established textbook in the area was written by Sommerville and Sawyer (1997), which presents a set of guidelines that reflect the best practice in requirements engineering. A comprehensive textbook on requirements engineering was written by Pohl (2010), which describes principles and techniques for eliciting, negotiating, documenting, validating, and managing requirements for software-intensive systems. Taking a systems engineering perspective, Dick et al. (2017) describe representations used in systems modelling and explains the relationships between requirements and modelling.

Requirements have been studied extensively in software engineering. Glinz (2007) surveys different definitions of the notion of non-functional requirement and proposes a classification of requirements based on the notion of concern, which is a matter of interest in a system. The main categories in the classification are functional requirements, performance requirements, specific quality requirements, and constraints. Chung and Leite (2009) survey several classification schemes for non-functional requirements in software engineering and investigate the extent to which they are consistent with each other. Systems requirements have been investigated in different contexts; one example is the work by Keil and Tiwana (2006), who have studied requirements and evaluation criteria for enterprise systems. Techniques for requirements elicitation need to be adapted to the situation at hand, in particular with respect to the kinds of stakeholders addressed; this topic is investigated by Tuunanen and Peffers (2018) in the context of information systems design.

References

Checkland P, Scholes J (1990) Soft systems methodology in practice. Wiley, Chichester

Chung L, do Prado Leite JCS (2009) On non-functional requirements in software engineering. In: Borgida AT et al. (eds) Conceptual modeling: foundations and applications. Lecture notes in computer science. Springer, Berlin, pp. 363–379

Dick J, Hull E, Jackson K (2017) Requirements engineering, 4th edn. Springer, Berlin

Glinz M (2007) On non-functional requirements. In: Requirements engineering conference, 15th IEEE international, pp. 21–26

Keil M, Tiwana A (2006) Relative importance of evaluation criteria for enterprise systems: a conjoint study. Inf Syst J 16(3):237–262

Pohl K (2010) Requirements engineering: fundamentals, principles, and techniques, 1st edn. Springer, Berlin

Sommerville I, Sawyer P (1997) Requirements engineering: a good practice guide, 1st edn. Wiley, New York

Tuunanen T, Peffers K (2018) Population targeted requirements acquisition. Europ J Inf Syst 27(6):686–711

Chapter 7
Design and Develop Artefact

The major part of many design science projects is the activity Design and Develop Artefact, which can be expressed as follows:

Create an artefact that addresses the explicated problem and fulfils the defined requirements.

The primary result of this activity will be prescriptive knowledge, which can be embedded in the created artefact (see Sect. 2.2). Furthermore, the activity will produce descriptive knowledge about the design decisions taken and their rationale.

The activity Design and Develop Artefact can be structured and visualised as shown in Fig. 7.1. The input is an outline of the artefact and a set of requirements that were provided by the Define Requirements activity. The output is an artefact that fulfils these requirements and knowledge about this artefact. The resources used by the activity consist of knowledge from the research literature and other written sources as well as knowledge embedded in artefacts and assertions from relevant stakeholders. The controls can include research strategies and methods and may also include practice-based development approaches.

7.1 Sub-activities of Design and Develop Artefact

Designing and developing is about moving from initial ideas of a solution all the way to a complete artefact. The activity can be divided into four sub-activities, which are carried out in parallel and iteratively:

- *Imagine and Brainstorm.* The designers brainstorm and generate new ideas or elaborate on existing ones.
- *Assess and Select.* The designers assess the generated ideas in order to select one or more of them as the basis for further design and development.

© Springer Nature Switzerland AG 2021   121
P. Johannesson, E. Perjons, *An Introduction to Design Science*,
https://doi.org/10.1007/978-3-030-78132-3_7

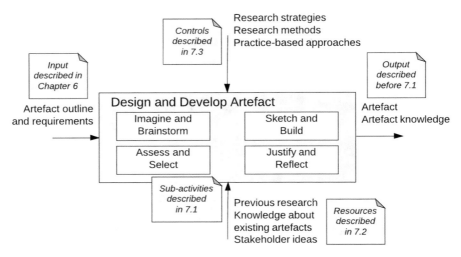

Fig. 7.1 Design and develop artefact

- *Sketch and Build.* The designers outline the artefact and construct it.
- *Justify and Reflect.* The designers both reflect on and justify the design decisions they have made.

The terms "design" and "development" have many different meanings in the literature, and the relationships between them are often blurred. In this chapter, the Sketch part of the sub-activity Sketch and Build can be seen as the design of an artefact, while the Build part can be seen as the development of it. However, it could be argued that the two first sub-activities, Imagine and Brainstorm and Assess and Select, are also part of the design of the artefact. Moreover, many decisions made during development can be seen as design decisions.

In the following sections, a number of tools and techniques for supporting design and development will be briefly introduced without any claim to completeness; there are many other tools and techniques, and more are constantly being developed.

7.1.1 Imagine and Brainstorm

In the sub-activity Imagine and Brainstorm, new ideas are generated or existing ones are further enhanced. One or more of these ideas may later be used as a basis for the design of the artefact.

7.1.1.1 Instruments for the Generation of Ideas

In order to generate as many ideas as possible, so-called *divergent thinking* needs to be applied. This involves generating multiple, alternative ideas or solutions to address a problem—a highly imaginative and innovative activity. While divergent thinking is essential for successful design and development, it needs to be complemented with *convergent thinking*, which evaluates and selects from alternative ideas that have been generated—a more rational and analytical form of thinking. The next sub-section addresses convergent thinking, while this sub-section presents various ways of supporting divergent thinking.

To some extent, generating innovative and useful ideas is always dependent on luck. However, as Louis Pasteur observed in 1854, "Chance only favours the prepared mind". One way to prepare the mind is through exploratory studies of potential users of the artefact in their practices, which may involve the use of action research, ethnography, and participant observation.

There are several practice-based approaches and instruments for the generation of ideas. One of these is *empathetic thinking* (or *empathetic design*), in which a designer tries "to see the world through the eyes of others, understand the world through their experiences, and feel the world through their emotions" (Brown 2019). Undertaking empathetic thinking is similar to working as an anthropologist, who explores a foreign culture to understand, in depth, the values and behaviour of that culture. Empathetic thinking can help to expand the designer's mind, thereby supporting the creation of novel solutions. Sometimes, it may be sufficient to spend some time and observe users in their natural settings. For example, Colgate-Palmolive researchers videotaped people in their homes to see how they used, combined, and made comments about the company's products, so that the company could enhance them and design new ones (Leonard and Swap 1999).

One tool that can support empathetic thinking is *customer journey mapping*, which aims to create a visualisation of the process by which a customer interacts with a service provider in order to achieve a goal. The result of using this tool is a customer journey map that highlights the actions and experiences, joyful as well as painful, in which a customer engages. By analysing this map, designers can identify and understand the problems that customers and users encounter. While a customer journey map focuses on process and interaction, a persona focuses on a typical user. More precisely, a *persona* is a fictitious character that represents an archetypal user, which can support designers in representing and empathising with a certain kind of users.

Another approach for generating solutions is de Bono's *lateral thinking* (Bono 2010), which suggests a non-traditional way of reasoning. Instead of focusing on logical, step-by-step arguments, de Bono suggests a spectrum of techniques for generating fresh ideas. One such technique is *random generation*, in which the thinker chooses a random object and relates it to the area of concern, thereby generating new ideas. Another group of techniques is *provocative generation*, such as wishful thinking, exaggeration, and techniques in which anything can be questioned, especially generally accepted truths. de Bono has also developed a popular technique called *six thinking hats*, which can assist an individual or a group to think in six different directions. Commonly, a group or person trying to generate ideas moves in a non-structured way between specifying the goal of a task, carrying out creative thinking, engaging in critical thinking, etc. By using the technique of six thinking hats, this generation of ideas can be carried out in a more structured and conscious way.

7.1.1.2   Idea Generation by Groups

One well-established instrument for generating ideas in groups is *brainstorming*. The participants attempt to produce as many ideas as possible, encourage new and unusual ideas, discourage criticism, and integrate and improve on the ideas that have been proposed. Brainstorming is a generic instrument for idea generation that has been applied in many areas. First, a group may identify novel ideas by suggesting and documenting as many as possible without any criticism. The next step might be to remove duplicated ideas or to merge smaller ideas into larger ones, thereby reducing the number of ideas. Finally, the group may prioritise the suggested ideas in order to select the most promising ones, thereby moving to the Assess and Select sub-activity described below. Research has shown that brainstorming can be made more effective by preparing and training group members before a brainstorming session and by making use of a trained moderator during the session (Isaksen 1998).

In the area of IT and information systems, a commonly used instrument for the generation of ideas is *participative modelling* (Stirna et al. 2007). To some extent, participative modelling resembles brainstorming, except that it uses specific techniques to express ideas, such as goal, process, and conceptual modelling. It also makes use of certain tools for the visualisation and development of cooperative models, such as whiteboards, plastic sheets, and post-its.

The process of idea generation aims to stimulate the creativity of its participants. Sometimes, the process can be perceived as too time consuming and unproductive, in the sense that it produces results of uncertain value. Therefore, there is always a risk that the participants will strive towards early consensus, which inhibits the generation of ideas. Other factors that can hinder creativity are time pressure, directive leadership, and group norms (Leonard and Swap 2006). Time pressure can force participants to agree on one idea before they have spent sufficient time generating alternative ideas. Directive leadership means that, early in the creative process, a manager presents the ideas that she prefers, which can dampen creativity in a group due to the norm of "do not question your boss". Other group norms that can impede creativity are "conform to the group" and "do not presume to know more than your betters". Therefore, creativity is enhanced by including participants who dare to challenge such norms.

7.1.1.3 Idea Generation by Individuals

It has often been assumed that groups generate more (and more novel) ideas than individuals working by themselves. However, research does not support this assumption, and a combination of individual and group work can be preferable (Diehl and Stroebe 1987; Isaksen 1998). Before a brainstorming session begins, participants should be given the opportunity to generate ideas on their own and suggest these ideas to the group. This will promote divergent thinking in the group, since the participants will have access to many initial ideas before generating new ones.

A method, similar to brainstorming, that emphasises creativity among individuals is *6-3-5 brainwriting* (Heslin 2009), which involves 6 participants who each writes down 3 ideas in 5 min. Each participant's ideas are then passed on to another participant who uses the ideas as inspiration to create further ideas. The method is carried out in six rounds over 30 min.

Approaches such as *user innovation* emphasise that some individuals are more creative than others, and that these can successfully create innovative ideas or improve existing ones (Hippel 2006, 1986). These individuals, called *lead users*, are characterised by their extensive knowledge of a particular domain and a high degree of interest in improving the products within this domain. A reason for this could be that such improvements may support their own activities. This type of individual can be used by an organisation to improve its existing products and services as well as to create new ones. However, this requires that the organisation first identify the lead users, contact and engage them, and then provide them with tools to support their design efforts. It should be noted that these individuals typically carry out their creative actions alone rather than in a group.

One of the first models developed to describe an individual's creative process is Graham Wallas' *Stage model* (Wallas 1926). The model includes the following stages: preparation, in which the individual works on the problem and its various dimensions; incubation, in which the problem is internalised into the individual's unconscious mind; illumination, in which the ideas processed in the unconscious mind will appear in the conscious; and verification, in which the ideas consciously are verified and elaborated. Empirical research has partially confirmed Wallas' ideas that a period of interruption or rest from the problem can help in creative problem solving. Research shows, for example, that an incubation period allows an individual to become less fixated on ineffective strategies to solve a problem (Segal 2004).

7.1.1.4 Classification of Idea Generation Methods

Shah et al. (2000) classify intuitive methods, which aim to stimulate the unconscious thought process of the human mind, into the following categories:

- *Germinal methods*, in which the designer starts with a clean sheet of paper. One example of such a method is brainstorming.

- *Transformational methods*, which are used to generate ideas by modifying existing ideas. One example of such a method is random generation.
- *Progressive methods*, in which ideas are generated progressively by repeating the same steps iteratively. One example of such a method is 6-3-5 brainwriting.
- *Organizational methods*, which can help designers to group together ideas that already have been generated.

7.1.2 Assess and Select

In the sub-activity Assess and Select, the ideas generated in the previous sub-activity are assessed in order to select one or more of them as the basis for the development of the artefact. This activity usually requires convergent thinking, i.e. an analytical approach for selecting among alternative ideas.

The previous sub-activity, Imagine and Brainstorm, can be seen as setting up a solution space consisting of possible ideas or solutions, while this sub-activity can be seen as pruning ideas in this solution space. According to this view, which was introduced by Simon (1996), the designer makes additional design decisions that further narrow the space. The process can be viewed as a systematic exploration of the solution space, which is guided by the requirements defined in the previous activity, Define Requirements.

The design decisions that narrow the solution space may be more or less well founded. To describe and justify how such decisions are taken, various models for organisational decision-making can be used, for example, the rational decision-making, the bounded rationality, and the garbage can model. In the *rational decision-making model*, all relevant ideas are evaluated in depth in order to identify the optimal one. However, in practice, not all relevant ideas are carefully evaluated. Instead, decisions are often based on so-called *bounded rationality*, which means that decision makers stop the decision-making process when they have identified one or more sufficiently good ideas. The reason for doing so is usually that it is not worth exploring more ideas or collecting more information for making a more informed decision—it would be too expensive and time consuming. And sometimes, decisions are made without even considering any alternative solutions at all. This way of making decisions is articulated in the *garbage can model*, which states that decisions are made on an ad hoc basis by matching problems and available solutions without any deeper discussions, often in a meeting but sometimes simply around a coffee machine. Moreover, many times decisions are made in a group. Therefore, the chosen solution is sometimes a compromise to satisfy several individuals in the group. Such compromises may make decisions easier to implement in an organisation since they recognize the needs and interests of many stakeholders in the organisation.

The decision models presented above not only describe different ways of making decisions, but they can also serve as role models for how decisions should be made. In other words, these models can also have a prescriptive function. Often, the rational decision-making model is presented as the preferred model for making decisions, but it could be argued that it is too time consuming for many types of decisions.

During the process of selecting ideas, the decision-maker should be aware of various forms of bias that can give rise to inappropriate decisions, such as the following:

- *Anchor bias.* The tendency of an individual to rely heavily on the first ideas presented in a decision-making situation.
- *Confirmation bias.* The tendency of an individual to favour ideas that confirm her beliefs.
- *Sunk cost bias.* The tendency of individuals to choose ideas that justify earlier decisions, as other decisions would make them look illogical.

Bias can be avoided by supporting a more rational decision-making process or by making decisions in groups where different views can be expressed.

7.1.3 Sketch and Build

In the sub-activity Sketch and Build, a sketch of the artefact is made starting from the ideas selected in the previous sub-activity. Based on this sketch, the artefact can then be developed.

A sketch of an artefact provides an overview of both its core functions and its overall structure. The sketch of the functions typically displays the interface between the artefact and the user, what the artefact offers to the user, and why and how the user will use it. The sketch of the overall structure, i.e. the artefact architecture, provides an overview of the components of the artefact and their relationships. Designers make a sketch of an artefact in order to sharpen their thinking about it, facilitate communication among the stakeholders involved in its construction, and provide guidance for further development.

There are several tools that can be used for sketching the function of an artefact. A *use case diagram* graphically represents the functions of the artefact, as well as the actors in its environment, i.e. the roles of those that use the functions. Use case diagrams are often complemented with *use case descriptions* that describe in text how the users will be interacting with the artefact. Another instrument for sketching functionality is the *user story*, which is less structured than use case diagrams and use case descriptions and typically describes each function of an artefact in only a sentence or two. Yet another instrument is *story-boarding*, which consists of a number of illustrations in sequence, like a cartoon strip, describing how the user will interact with the artefact.

The form of a sketch depends upon the type of artefact at hand. If the artefact is a method, its parts are usually activities or tasks, and the relationships between them represent temporal or logical orderings of the tasks. For a static model or an instantiation, on the other hand, the parts are usually modules or components.

Before developing the final artefact, a prototype may be constructed. There is not much agreement on what should count as a prototype, but it can be seen as an early form of the final artefact, focusing on certain of its aspects. For example, a prototype of an artefact may be a drawing on a paper focusing on the artefact's major components and their relationships, a physical model focusing on the artefact's aesthetic appearance, or a software application focusing on the artefact's user friendliness. By experimenting with the prototype, the designers can learn about the design challenges for developing the final artefact. Users can also more easily provide relevant feedback through inspecting and using the prototype.

Designing and developing an artefact is a process of reusing and adapting parts from existing solutions, inventing new elements, and combining them in an innovative way. In order to clarify how the new solution builds upon and differs from existing ones, a researcher needs to analyse the latter ones by studying previous work, both theoretical and practical. Even if the solution being designed is highly original, the researcher still needs to relate and compare it to existing solutions— there are always similarities worth highlighting.

Modern design and development methods provide different instruments to support the design and development process. One such instrument that has been shown to be effective is *pair design*, based on the agile practice of pair programming, in which two designers work together to simultaneously develop an artefact. Typically, one designer makes a design decision, such as introducing an activity into a method, and the other designer immediately reviews it and suggests possible improvements or potential problems. Another instrument is the *walk-through*, a kind of peer review, in which a designer leads members of a development team and other stakeholders through an artefact. The participants can ask questions, point out problems, suggest alternative solutions, or provide feedback in any other form.

7.1.4 Justify and Reflect

In the sub-activity Justify and Reflect, the designers justify the design decisions that have been made and reflect on them in order to be better prepared for future design and development.

Regardless of the resources used in creating a design, it is valuable to document the *design rationale*, i.e. to make a list of the decisions made during the design process and the argumentation for these decisions. A design rationale should contain the reasons and justifications behind design decisions, alternative decisions that were considered, and the arguments leading to the decisions. A design rationale can not only support communication during a single project, but it is also useful for facilitating reuse between different projects. In fact, a design rationale can be one of the most valuable outcomes of a design science project, as it records the reasoning behind design decisions, including potential pitfalls. This knowledge can be of great value to subsequent projects; in particular, it can help designers to avoid dead ends and other kinds of problems.

The designers and developers should also reflect on the procedures for working on the design and development of the artefact. Such reflections support both individual and organisational learning and are beneficial in future work when a new version of the artefact is planned or when other artefacts are to be built. The reflections can also serve as a basis for deriving design principles that can be applied in new contexts (see Sect. 2.5). Many agile development methods emphasise reflection as a key activity for improving a team's working practices.

7.2   Research Strategies and Methods for Design and Develop Artefact

Design and Develop Artefact differs from the other design science activities in that it does not primarily aim to answer questions by producing descriptive or explanatory knowledge. Instead, its main purpose is to produce prescriptive knowledge by creating an artefact. Therefore, research strategies and methods are less important here than in the other activities. But this does not imply that research methods are without value for developing an artefact; on the contrary, interviews, observation studies, and other data collection methods can be highly effective in producing ideas for design solutions. The point is that it is not essential to use research methods for devising possible solutions—any approach for generating solutions is admissible as long as it works.

7.3   Guidelines for Design and Develop Artefact

- *Clearly describe each component of the artefact.* Describe both the functionality and the structure of each component of the artefact.
- *Justify each component of the artefact.* Explain the purpose of each component of the artefact, in particular which requirements it addresses.
- *Describe the use of the artefact.* Describe how the artefact and its components are to be used in its intended practice.
- *Clarify the originality.* Describe the ways in which the artefact is different from existing ones, with respect to both functionality and structure.
- *Specify the sources of the design of the artefact.* Describe the literature that was consulted and the stakeholders who contributed to the components of the artefact or inspired the design of new components.
- *Describe how the artefact was designed and developed.* Explain what was done to design and develop the artefact, in particular how the stakeholders were involved and how existing solutions and the research literature were reviewed.

7.4   Alternative Conceptualizations and Definitions

There are many ways to skin a cat. And there are also many ways to reason and talk about design. In this book, we have chosen practices, problems, artefacts, and requirements as central notions for conceptualising the design area. But many other notions and terms are being used by other people. This should not come as a surprise, as design is relevant to so many different fields, including Human-Computer Interaction, User Experience Design, Software Engineering, Information Systems, Design Thinking, and the list goes on. People in all of these areas have come up with their own conceptualisations and definitions. The result can feel like the Tower of Babel, where people do not understand each other because they are using different words for the same things, or the same words for different things. Here are a few examples to illustrate the situation:

- *Problem.* A problem is sometimes defined as an undesirable current state. In contrast, we have defined a problem as the gap between the current state and a more desirable state.
- *Need.* A need can be defined as something that is urgently desired. A problem can be seen as an unmet need.
- *Want.* A want is also something desired, but not as urgently as a need. Thus, the borderline between needs and wants is fuzzy.
- *Goal.* A goal can be defined as a desirable state that people want to achieve. Alternatively, a goal is a desirable state that people have decided to try to achieve.
- *Design goal.* High-level requirements are sometimes called design goals.

There is no right or wrong here, only different ways of conceptualising and defining. And if you are familiar with one way of talking, it should not be difficult to switch to another way—they are all about the same design phenomena.

Finally, here is another framework for talking about design with its basis in the area of business models, the *Value Proposition Canvas* (VPC); a strength of this framework is that it offers a nice graphical notation, as described in (Osterwalder 2014). The notions, terms, and definitions of VPC are similar, but not identical, to those of this book. A VPC consists of two parts, a customer profile and a value map:

- A *customer profile* describes a customer, focusing on what she needs to do, what she can benefit from doing this, and what might hinder her. Graphically, a customer profile has three parts:

  - *Customer jobs.* Activities that the customer needs to carry out in a certain context, similar to the activities in a practice.
  - *Pains.* Factors that may hinder the customer to carry out her customer jobs, similar to problems.
  - *Gains.* Outcomes and benefits that the customer will achieve from doing the customer jobs well, similar to the goals of purposive practices (see Sect. 1.1).

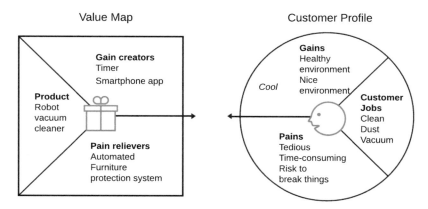

Fig. 7.2 A value proposition canvas

- A *value map* describes a value proposition, i.e. a product or a solution offered to a customer, including the value it can provide. Graphically, a value map has three parts:

  - *Product.* The structure of the offered product or service, similar to an artefact.
  - *Pain relievers.* Functions of the product that can help to alleviate the pains.
  - *Gain creators.* Functions of the product that can create entirely new gains for the customer, i.e. they can help her to achieve new goals.

An example of a VPC is shown in Fig. 7.2. The customer jobs are about cleaning a house, including dusting and vacuuming. If this is done well, the house will be clean, healthy, and pleasant. But cleaning, especially vacuuming, is tedious and time consuming, and there is a risk of breaking things. One solution for addressing these issues is a robot vacuum cleaner. It is fully automated, so vacuuming will not take up a lot of time or be boring anymore, and the risk of breaking things is reduced, thanks to the built-in furniture protection system. For convenient use, the cleaner comes with a timer and a smartphone app, which also creates a new gain of vacuuming—it will feel cool to vacuum, or at least some people may think so. This new gain is italicized in the figure.

In a design science project, the VPC concepts and graphical notation could be used as a complementary way to present the relationships between the problem experienced by a stakeholder in a practice and the suggested artefact, including its structure and function.

7.5 Summary of Chapter

- In the *Design and Development* activity, an artefact is created that addresses the explicated problem and fulfils the defined requirements.

- *Divergent thinking* involves the generation of multiple, alternative ideas or solutions to address a problem.
- *Convergent thinking* involves the evaluation of and selection from alternative ideas that have been generated.
- Divergent thinking can be supported by empathetic thinking, lateral thinking, and brainstorming:
  - *Empathetic thinking* is a type of thinking in which a designer tries to see, understand, and feel the world as others experience it.
  - *Lateral thinking* is a type of thinking in which non-traditional ways of reasoning are used, such as wishful thinking and techniques in which anything can be questioned.
  - *Brainstorming* is an established instrument for generating ideas in groups. The participants attempt to produce as many ideas as possible, encourage new and unusual ideas, discourage criticism, and try to integrate and improve on the ideas that have been proposed.
- A sketch of an artefact can be designed before it is developed. A *sketch* provides an overview of the core functions and the overall structure of the artefact.
- Designing and developing an artefact is a process of reusing and adapting parts from existing solutions, inventing new elements, and combining them in an innovative way. Therefore, related solutions need to be analysed by studying previous work.
- *Design rationale* should be documented. A design rationale contains the reasons and justifications for design decisions, alternative decisions that were considered, and the arguments leading to the decisions.

7.6 Review Questions

1. What roles can the requirements for an artefact play in each of the sub-activities of the design and development activity?
2. How can the ideas of divergent and convergent thinking be useful for the design and development of artefacts?
3. What is the difference between divergent, convergent, and lateral thinking?
4. Why is it important to generate many ideas in the design and development activity?
5. Why can brainstorming sessions in groups hinder the creative generation of ideas and how can this problem be addressed?
6. How can lead users be involved in a design science research project?
7. How can knowledge about decision models and different types of bias support the selection of ideas?
8. Why can it be useful to design a sketch of an artefact before building it?
9. What is the difference between design and development?

10. Why is it important to perform the sub-activity Justify and Reflect?
11. What are the roles of users in design and development?

7.7 Answers to Selected Review Questions

2. According to divergent thinking, a group of people should spend enough time and effort to identify several alternative ideas. Otherwise, there is a risk that no real novel ideas will be created. However, if too much time is spent on divergent thinking, less time can be spent on convergent thinking, that is, selecting and adapting the ideas to fit into the design and development of the artefact. The right mix of divergent and convergent thinking depends on the problem addressed, the requirements defined, and the complexity of the environment in which the artefact will be used. For example, if the problem is well understood and defined and the context is not too complex, less time can be spent on divergent thinking.

4. There is an underlying assumption that many ideas will increase the probability of identifying truly novel ideas. However, this assumption could be questioned.

5. Lead users may be involved in any of the activities in a design science project, but the focus will probably be on the design and development activity, which aims to design novel solutions. If lead users are involved in other activities, such as problem explication and artefact evaluation, the researcher needs to be aware that the lead users may not be representative for a larger group of users.

8. A sketch is a powerful instrument for communication between stakeholders about the artefact to be developed. The sketch is also rather concrete and can therefore help the stakeholders to focus their thinking about the design of the artefact, thereby providing guidance for further development.

10. In a design science project, knowledge about the artefact, such as the design rationale, is a major output, which will be an important contribution to the scientific body of knowledge. Moreover, it is important to have the design rationale documented when new versions of the artefact need to be designed and developed. To contribute to organisational and individual learning, reflections regarding ways of working are valuable.

11. Users may take an active part in the design and development or may focus on giving feedback during the activity. Users can be involved on a daily basis or less often. They may be involved in one sub-activity of the design and development activity or in several sub-activities. And they may focus on functional requirements or non-functional requirements, such as usability. Their participation can be more or less formalised, and their responsibilities may vary.

7.8 Further Reading

There are many good books on the art of designing artefacts, e.g. those written by Brown (2019) and Cross (2011), while Simon (1996) is a classical text. They all describe design-specific activities carried out by designers, sometimes denoted as design thinking, emphasising the cognitive aspects of these activities. However, the term "design thinking" has a different meaning in different discourses. In their literature review, Johansson-Sköldberg et al. (2013) identified eight different design thinking discourses: five major discourses in the theory-based academic area and three discourses in the practice-based management area. For example, one of the academic discourses has its origin with Herbert Simon's book, *The Science of the Artificial* Simon (1996). This discourse is characterised by the systematic study of the design of artefacts and its relation to science. Simon's major concern was science, and he stated, for example, that design science is about creation, while other sciences, such as the natural sciences, social sciences, and humanities, study what already exists. Other academic discourses focus on investigating how design is carried out in practice, including designers' reflections, awareness, and abilities, and their use of different kinds of theories as the theoretical base for their investigations. The management discourses focus mainly on presenting success cases in practical design and design thinking in organisations; they are primarily written for managers, but they can also serve as a basis for the development of theories in management science.

Practice-based design thinking can be seen as both a movement and a way of thinking about cognitive, strategic, and practical processes through which products and services are designed and developed. Design thinking focuses on building empathy for users' needs and experiences, developing solutions in collaboration between designers and users, and working iteratively and in an action-oriented manner. A number of definitions and characterisations of design thinking can be found at the website (IDEO Design Thinking) (Design Thinking Definitions 2018).

Stickdorn et al. (2018) discuss that design thinking can be seen both as an approach and as a process. By way of approach, design thinking includes a number of conceptions and attitudes, in particular to put the user at the center of the design and not a specific service; to emphatically relate to the user instead of looking at her from the outside; to look at the user's overall situation and not just the use of a particular service; and to prioritize practical solutions. As a process, design thinking involves a way of working with design, especially working iteratively in fast cycles with user feedback, experimenting with new ideas, and trying to find unexpected and innovative solutions. Design thinking as a process can be structured using design methods. Within this stream of practice-based design thinking, the company IDEO has been highly influential, and much learning material as well as case studies can be found at its website (IDEO 2020). Muller-Roterberg (2020) offers an introduction to design thinking, and a collection of classical articles can be found in Brown et al. (2020).

Many techniques for divergent thinking can be found in Leonard and Swap (1999), Shah et al. (2000), and Bono (2010). Leonard and Swap (1999) discuss group norms and group thinking, including how these can impede creative thinking. Osborn (1979) introduced the brainstorming technique with a set of guidelines for successful applications. The findings that brainstorming groups generate fewer ideas (and fewer useful ideas) than individual brainstormers (so-called nominal groups) are discussed in, for example, Diehl and Stroebe (1987) and Isaksen (1998), and these are questioned by Rietzschel et al. (2006). Moreover, Simon (1996) reports, interestingly, that people are not very good at recognising their best ideas.

The need for a balance between divergent and convergent thinking was advocated in Leonard and Swap (2006). Different decision models that describe how decisions are made are discussed in Hatch (2018), and different types of bias are described in Hammond et al. (1998) and Lau and Coiera (2009).

The importance of involving users in the design of IT systems is emphasised in many modern methods of design and development. However, the type of user involvement and user participation has impact on the outcome. For example, Lynch and Gregor (2004) investigated the relationship between user participation and the outcome of IT systems in 38 IS development projects found in the literature. Their investigation showed a strong positive relationship between feelings of involvement in the design and development of an IT system and the success of the system but found only a moderate relationship between active user participation in the design and development activities and the success of the systems. To characterise different types of participation, Cavaye (1995) has presented six attributes of user participation, including the type, degree, content, extent, formality, and influence of their participation. The relationships between design, explanation, and exploration are discussed by Gibbons and Bunderson (2005).

References

Bono Ed (2010) Lateral thinking: creativity step by step. English. Harper-Collins e-books, New York

Brown T (2019) Change by design, revised and updated: how design thinking transforms organizations and inspires innovation. Revised, Updated edition. Harper Business, New York

Brown T, et al (2020) HBR's 10 must reads on design thinking (with featured article "Design Thinking" By Tim Brown). Harvard Business Review Press, Brighton

Cavaye ALM (1995) User participation in system development revisited. Inf Manag 28(5):311–323

Cross N (2011) Design thinking: understanding how designers think and work. Bloomsbury Academic, London

Design Thinking Definitions (2018) How do people define design thinking? https://designthinking. ideo.com/faq/how-do-people-define-design-thinking. Accessed 8 Dec 2020

Diehl M, Stroebe W (1987) Productivity loss in brainstorming groups: toward the solution of a riddle. J Pers Soc Psychol 53(3):497–509

Gibbons AS, Bunderson CV (2005) Explore, explain, design. Elsevier, Amsterdam

Hammond JS, Keeney RL, Raiffa H (1998) The hidden traps in decision making. Harv Bus Rev 76(5):47–58

Hatch MJ (2018) Organization theory: modern, symbolic, and postmodern perspectives, 4th edn. Oxford University Press, Oxford

Heslin PA (2009) Better than brainstorming? Potential contextual boundary conditions to brainwriting for idea generation in organizations. J Occup Organ Psychol 82(1):129–145

Hippel EV (2006) Democratizing innovation. English. The MIT Press, Cambridge

Hippel Ev (1986). Lead users: a source of novel product concepts. Manage Sci 32(7):791–805

IDEO (2020) https://www.ideo.com/eu. Accessed: 20 Nov 2020

Isaksen SG (1998) A review of brainstorming research: Six critical issues for inquiry. Creative Research Unit, Creative Problem Solving Group-Buffalo, Buffalo

Johansson-Sköldberg U, Woodilla J, Çetinkaya M (2013) Design thinking: past, present and possible futures. Creativity Innov Manag 22(2):121–146

Lau AYS, Coiera EW (2009) Can cognitive biases during consumer health information searches be reduced to improve decision making? J Am Med Inform Assoc 16(1):54–65

Leonard D, Swap W (1999) When sparks fly: igniting creativity in groups. English. 1st edn. Harvard Business Review Press, Boston

Leonard D, Swap WC (2006) Generating creative options. In: Prusak L, Matson E (eds) Knowledge management and organizational learning: A reader. Oxford University Press, Oxford

Lynch T, Gregor S (2004) User participation in decision support systems development: influencing system outcomes. Eur J Inf Syst 13(4):286–301

Muller-Roterberg C (2020) Design thinking for dummies. For dummies, 1st edn. Wiley, Hoboken

Osborn AF (1979) Applied imagination. English. Scribner, New York

Osterwalder A et al (2014) Value proposition design: How to create products and services customers want (The Strategyzer series), 1st edn. Wiley

Rietzschel EF, Nijstad BA, Stroebe W (2006) Productivity is not enough: A comparison of interactive and nominal brainstorming groups on idea generation and selection. J Exp Soc Psychol 42(2):244–251

Segal E (2004) Incubation in insight problem solving. Creat Res J 16(1):141–148

Shah JJ, Kulkarni SV, Vargas-Hernandez N (2000) Evaluation of idea generation methods for conceptual design: effectiveness metrics and design of experiments. J Mech Des 122(4) :377–384

Simon HA (1996) The sciences of the artificial, 3rd edn. MIT Press, Cambridge

Stickdorn M, et al (2018) This is service design doing: applying service design thinking in the real world, 1st edn. O'Reilly Media, Sebastopol

Stirna J, Persson A, Sandkuhl K (2007) Participative enterprise modeling: experiences and recommendations. In: Krogstie J, Opdahl A, Sindre G (eds) Advanced information systems engineering. Lecture notes in computer science. Springer, Berlin, pp. 546–560

Wallas G (1926) The art of thought, 1st edn. Harcourt, Brace & Company, San Diego

Chapter 8
Demonstrate Artefact

Researchers do not only need to design and develop an artefact; they also need to show that it works well. A bare minimum is to demonstrate that the artefact works in one single case. This may not prove much, but at least it indicates that the artefact can also work in other cases.

The fourth activity of the method framework is Demonstrate Artefact, which illustrates the use of the artefact in a particular case, thereby verifying its feasibility. In other words, the activity addresses the question:

How can the developed artefact be used to address the explicated problem in one case?

The answer to this question will consist primarily of descriptive knowledge describing how the artefact works in one situation, but also explanatory knowledge explaining why the artefact works.

A demonstration shows that the artefact can, in fact, solve some aspects of a problem in one illustrative or real-life case. A demonstration can be seen as a weak form of evaluation—if the artefact can address a problem in one case it might be able to do so in other cases as well. Moreover, a demonstration can also help communicate the idea behind the artefact to an audience in a vivid and convincing way.

The activity Demonstrate Artefact can be structured and visualised, as in Fig. 8.1. The input is an artefact provided by the previous activity, Design and Develop Artefact. The output is a demonstrated artefact including information on the workings of the artefact in a particular case. The resources used by the activity consist of domain-specific knowledge about the artefact and its environment. The controls will vary from case to case.

© Springer Nature Switzerland AG 2021
P. Johannesson, E. Perjons, *An Introduction to Design Science*,
https://doi.org/10.1007/978-3-030-78132-3_8

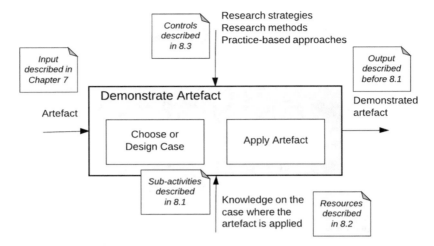

Fig. 8.1 Demonstrate Artefact

8.1   Sub-activities of Demonstrate Artefact

The first sub-activity is to choose or design a case upon which to apply the artefact. This case may be a fictitious one developed by the researchers who designed the artefact, a well-documented case from the literature, a real-life case, or a combination of these. Cases from real-life usually provide better external validity. Still, fictitious cases may sometimes be preferable, as they can be designed to demonstrate the viability of the artefact under extreme conditions. The second sub-activity is to apply the artefact to the chosen case, which includes documenting the outcome of the application.

8.2   Resources for Demonstrate Artefact

The resource needed for this activity is primarily access to and knowledge about the case upon which to apply the artefact.

8.3   Research Strategies and Methods for Demonstrate Artefact

A research strategy is decided upon depending on the case chosen and the characteristics of the artefact. Clearly, action research and case study are natural choices when a real-life case is used. Experiments are useful for fictitious as well as real-life cases.

8.4   Guidelines for Demonstrate Artefact

- *Justify the choice of case.* Explain why the chosen case is representative of the problem and challenging enough to offer an adequate test bed.
- *Make clear how much of the artefact is being tested.* Describe the components of the artefact that are actually used in the demonstration.

8.5   Summary of Chapter

- The question answered by the *Demonstrate Artefact* activity is: How can the developed artefact be used to address the explicated problem in one case?
- A demonstration shows that the artefact can address a problem, or some aspects of it, in one illustrative or real-life case.
- The case may be a fictitious one developed by the researchers who designed the artefact, a well-documented case from the literature, a real-life case, or a combination of these.
- A demonstration can be seen as a weak form of evaluation; if the artefact can address a problem in one case, it might also be able to do so in other cases.
- A demonstration can help to communicate the idea behind the artefact to an audience in a vivid and convincing way.

8.6   Review Questions

1. What is the difference between demonstration and evaluation?
2. Which are the most important sub-activities of Demonstrate Artefact?
3. In what respects can a fictitious case be superior to a real case for a demonstration?

8.7   Answers to Selected Review Questions

1. A demonstration can be seen as a lightweight evaluation. It does not assess how well an artefact works but only shows that it can be used meaningfully in one case.
3. A fictitious case can be designed to include specific features that put the artefact through extreme tests.

Chapter 9
Evaluate Artefact

In order to show that they have designed and developed an appropriate artefact, researchers need to evaluate it. Without an evaluation, they cannot claim that they have produced a valuable contribution.

The fifth activity of the method framework is Evaluate Artefact, in which researchers determine how well the artefact is able to solve the explicated problem and to what extent it fulfils the requirements. In other words, the activity addresses the question:

How well does the artefact solve the explicated problem and fulfil the defined requirements?

The answer to this question will consist primarily of descriptive knowledge but may also include explanatory knowledge explaining why the artefact is able to solve the problem.

9.1 Goals of Artefact Evaluation

An evaluation of an artefact may have several different goals, as discussed by Venable et al. (2012):

- To determine to what extent the artefact is effective for solving the problem for which it was proposed. In other words, the utility of the artefact is tested. This goal is usually the most important one.
- To evaluate to what extent the artefact satisfies the requirements that have been defined, functional as well as non-functional ones.
- To investigate formalised knowledge about the designed artefact and its utility, e.g. concerning its underlying kernel theories and implementation principles. In terms of design theory, this goal is to confirm, disprove, or enhance the design theory.

© Springer Nature Switzerland AG 2021
P. Johannesson, E. Perjons, *An Introduction to Design Science*,
https://doi.org/10.1007/978-3-030-78132-3_9

- To compare and not only evaluate the artefact in isolation, i.e. to study the artefact in comparison to other artefacts that are intended to address the same or a similar problem. The new artefact should offer advantages compared to existing ones.
- To investigate the side effects of using the artefact, i.e. to determine whether there are unintended and harmful effects.
- To evaluate the artefact formatively in order to identify opportunities for improvement through further design.

In a *formative* evaluation, an artefact is evaluated while it is still under design in order to obtain information about how to improve it during subsequent design activities. Thus, a formative evaluation is part of an iterative design process, in which the artefact is designed and evaluated during several iterations. A *summative evaluation*, on the other hand, aims to assess an artefact after its design and development has been completed. The results of a summative evaluation do not feed back into the design process but instead are used to obtain a final assessment of the utility of the artefact.

The evaluation goals can be combined. For example, the goals of an evaluation can be both to investigate the utility of an artefact by comparing it to other existing artefacts and to carry out a summative evaluation.

9.2 Types of Evaluation Strategies

Different strategies can be used to evaluate an artefact. In order to characterise and classify these strategies, a useful distinction is the one between ex ante and ex post evaluations. In an *ex ante evaluation*, the artefact is evaluated without being used or even being fully developed, while an *ex post evaluation* requires the artefact to be employed. For example, an ex ante evaluation of a new collaborative editor could be carried out by interviewing a number of experts on word processing and social software, based on the specifications and an early prototype of the editor. An ex post evaluation could be done by implementing the editor within an organisation and observing its use.

Ex ante evaluations provide several benefits. They can be carried out rapidly and do not require considerable resources or access to users or organisations. They are therefore ideal for formative evaluations when an initial design or prototype needs to be assessed quickly and inexpensively in order to obtain feedback for further improvement. However, ex ante evaluations can easily result in false positives, i.e. an artefact is judged as being better than it actually is, since the ex ante evaluation only investigates a preliminary version of the artefact. Thus, in most situations, ex ante evaluations cannot provide reliable results for summative evaluations.

Ex post evaluations offer advantages and disadvantages that are the mirror images of those of ex ante evaluations. They are less prone than ex ante evaluations to produce false positives, since a completed artefact is being evaluated. However, they consume more resources, take a longer time, and may require access to people or organisations in which the evaluations can take place. Thus, ex post evaluations are often more suitable for summative than formative evaluations.

Another useful distinction is the one between naturalistic and artificial evaluations. An *artificial evaluation* assesses an artefact in a contrived and artificial setting, e.g. in a laboratory. A *naturalistic evaluation* assesses the artefact in the real world, i.e. within the practice for which it is intended. In other words, a naturalistic evaluation involves real users using real systems to solve real problems, as described by Sun and Kantor (2006).

Like ex ante evaluations, artificial evaluations have the advantage of being rapid and inexpensive. From an ethical point of view, another advantage is that they usually expose participants to little or no risk. They can also provide high internal validity, as variables can be controlled in an artificial setting (see Sect. 3.1.1). Consequently, artificial evaluations are appropriate for investigating the efficacy of an artefact, i.e. to determine whether it can produce desired outcomes under ideal circumstances (see Sect. 6.6). However, artificial evaluations may not be suitable for studying the effectiveness of an artefact, i.e. to determine whether it is able to produce desired outcomes in a real-world setting in all its messiness. This implies that there is a considerable risk of false positives.

Naturalistic evaluations often have high external validity because they are carried out in real settings, and their results can, therefore, be generalised or transferred to similar situations. Another strength of naturalistic evaluations is that multiple stakeholders can be involved, thereby ensuring that different perspectives and interests can be taken into account. This is particularly valuable when evaluating socio-technical artefacts, while it may be less important for technical artefacts. Furthermore, naturalistic evaluations are well suited for investigating effectiveness. They are also appropriate for studying the side effects of the use of an artefact. A main weakness, on the other hand, is that internal validity may suffer when an artefact is employed in a complex environment, for example, in an organisation. In such a case, it can be next to impossible to distinguish between the influences of the artefact and those of contingent factors. For example, the alleged effects of introducing a new IT system on power relationships in a workplace may be due to other factors, such as an economic crisis, related change projects, or new employees. Other disadvantages of naturalistic evaluations are that they may be expensive and time consuming.

The choice between an artificial and a naturalistic strategy also depends on the artefact qualities to be evaluated. For some qualities, e.g. structural ones such as modularity and coherence, an artificial evaluation can provide both valid and reliable results. For other qualities, e.g. environmental ones such as usability and effectiveness, the results of an artificial evaluation can be rather speculative. The characteristics of ex ante and ex post and of artificial and naturalistic evaluations are summarised in Table 9.1.

Table 9.1 Characteristics of evaluation strategies (adapted from Venable et al. (2012))

		Ex ante	Ex post
		Formative evaluation Lower cost Faster Evaluate design or prototype Less risk to participants Higher risk of false positive	Summative evaluation Higher cost Slower Evaluate instantiation Higher risk to participants Lower risk of false positive
Naturalistic	Many stakeholders Socio-technical artefact Higher cost Slower Organisational access needed Higher effectiveness Higher external validity Higher risk to participants Lower risk of false positive	Real users, real problem, somewhat unreal artefact Low-medium cost Medium speed Less risk to participants Higher risk of false positives	Real users, real problem, real artefact Highest cost Slowest Identification of side effects Highest risk to participants Lowest risk of false positive
Artificial	Few stakeholders Technical artefact Lower cost Faster Higher efficacy Higher internal validity Less risk to participants Higher risk of false positive	Unreal users, problem, and artefact Lowest cost Fastest Lowest risk to participants Highest risk of false positive regarding effectiveness	Unreal users, unreal problem, and real artefact Medium-high cost Medium speed Low-medium risk to participants

9.3 Sub-activities of Evaluate Artefact

The activity Evaluate Artefact can be structured and visualised as in Fig. 9.1. The
input is an artefact provided by the activity Demonstrate Artefact. The output is
an evaluated artefact, including information on how well the artefact works and
why. The resources used depend on the chosen evaluation strategy and can include
experts as well as sites for case studies or action research. The controls may include
any research strategy or method that is appropriate for evaluation. When researchers
carry out an evaluation, they engage in three main activities:

- *Analyse Evaluation Context.* Researchers analyse and describe the evaluation
  context, which includes the prerequisites for deciding on the goals and strategy
  for the evaluation.
- *Select Evaluation Goals and Strategy.* Researchers do not only decide on the
  goals and the overall strategy for the evaluation but also on which research
  strategies and methods to apply.
- *Design and Carry Out Evaluation.* Researchers design the evaluation study in
  detail and then execute it.

9.3.1 Analyse Evaluation Context

The context of the evaluation needs to be investigated and characterised before
selecting the goals and the strategy for the evaluation. The reason for doing this
is very practical—in any project, you will never have all the resources you would

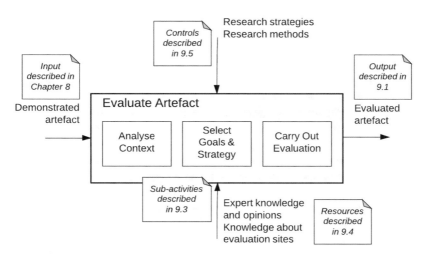

Fig. 9.1 Evaluate Artefact

like to have, and you need to adapt to this fact. The first step is to understand your project's resource constraints, in particular in terms of time, people, competence, budget, and access to users or organisations.

9.3.2   *Select Evaluation Goals and Strategy*

Taking the analysis of the evaluation context into account, the researcher selects the goals and evaluation strategy as well as research strategies and methods for the evaluation.

The goals of the evaluation need to be decided upon by answering the following questions:

- Which are the most important requirements to evaluate? (See Sect. 6.5 for generic artefact qualities.)
- Is it important to investigate knowledge related to the artefact, such as underlying kernel theories?
- Is it important to compare the evaluated artefact with other existing artefacts?
- Should side effects, especially undesired consequences in safety critical systems, be investigated?
- Is the evaluation formative or summative?

The evaluation strategy needs to be decided upon as well. For this purpose, the summary of the evaluation strategies and their characteristics in Table 9.1 can be used as a starting point. There is often no single, best evaluation strategy to choose, meaning that researchers need to strike a balance between the goals they want to achieve. For example, they may want to obtain high effectiveness, for which an ex post and naturalistic evaluation would be the most appropriate. However, time and budget constraints might not allow for this alternative, so they may settle for an ex ante and naturalistic evaluation instead.

Based on the evaluation strategy chosen, the next step is to select appropriate research strategies and methods. For this purpose, Table 9.2 offers a mapping between evaluation strategies and corresponding research strategies and methods.

An ex ante evaluation sometimes consists of arguments provided by the researchers who developed the artefact. In this case, they evaluate it by reasoning and arguing that it fulfils the defined requirements and can solve the explicated problem; this form of evaluation is called *informed argument*. A common line of reasoning is to claim that the artefact fulfils a requirement because it has a certain structure. For example, it could be argued that a new Massive Multiplayer Online Role Playing Game (MMORPG) is easy to learn because its interface is similar to that of World of Warcraft, which is well known to many players. Informed argument is obviously a weak form of evaluation, as it may easily be biased due to the backgrounds and interests of the researchers—there is a high risk of false positives. However, informed argument is inexpensive and is often used when evaluating highly innovative and still immature artefacts. Researchers may also

Table 9.2 Research strategies and methods for different evaluation strategies [adapted from Venable et al. (2012)]

	Ex ante	Ex post
Naturalistic	Action research	Action research
	Focus group	Case study
	Interview	Ethnography
		Phenomenology
		Survey
		Focus group
		Participant observation
Artificial	Mathematical or logical proof	Mathematical or logical proof
	Computer simulation	Computer simulation
	Lab experiment	Role-playing simulation
	Informed argument	Lab experiment
		Field experiment

use informed argument at informal presentations or research workshops. Based on feedback from other researchers, the artefact can then be refined before a stronger form of evaluation is carried out. Thus, informed argument can be very useful for formative evaluations.

9.3.3   Design and Carry Out Evaluation

In this activity, researchers design the evaluation in detail. For example, they will need to set up laboratory environments, design interview questions, book meetings with respondents, or select software for data analysis. These activities should be carried out in accordance with the standard requirements for the selected research strategies and methods, as defined in the literature. Finally, the evaluation is carried out.

9.4   Resources for Evaluate Artefact

The kinds of resources required for an evaluation depend on the chosen evaluation strategy. For naturalistic, ex ante evaluations, the most important resource is a number of experts who have the competence as well as the time and willingness to evaluate the artefact. Obviously, these requirements may involve a trade-off, as the most qualified experts are typically the busiest ones. Naturalistic, ex post evaluations often require one or more sites at which the artefact can be employed. Obtaining access to such sites can be challenging, for example, when a new IT system is to be evaluated within an organisation. Artificial evaluations can require access to specialised laboratory environments or software.

9.5   Research Strategies and Research Methods
for Evaluate Artefact

In principle, any research strategy or research method can be used for the Evaluate Artefact activity. They all have their own advantages and disadvantages, which are discussed briefly in this section.

Surveys—Surveys can be used for gathering feedback on an artefact from a large number of stakeholders and experts. Therefore, the results of a survey have a reasonable chance of being generalisable. However, one drawback of surveys is that they often result in only shallow responses from respondents, who may not be prepared to spend much time and effort on answering survey questions. Thus, surveys are often not very helpful for formative evaluations.

Experiments—Experiments are popular instruments for evaluating an artefact, as they allow a researcher to achieve high internal validity by controlling the conditions under which an experiment is carried out. On the other hand, external validity may suffer since the artificial setting of the experiment may be markedly different from the practice in which the artefact is to be used. These concerns also apply to other forms of artificial evaluations.

Case Studies—Case studies allow a researcher to carry out a deep evaluation of an artefact and understand the reasons for its success or failure, at least in a particular case. However, case studies require a great deal of effort, and their outcomes depend heavily on the competence and experience of researchers. There is also a risk of bias due to the interests and preconceptions of researchers. Furthermore, carrying out a case study on only a single site can limit the generalisability, or the transferability, of the results.

Ethnography—The research strategy ethnography allows a researcher to understand not only how a practice influences the use of an artefact but also how the artefact may change the practice. Therefore, the researcher may identify interplays between artefact and practice that might not be apparent to its participants. The drawbacks of ethnography are that it is time consuming and requires highly qualified researchers to be effective.

Phenomenology—A phenomenological study can be effective for evaluating usage qualities, such as usability, suitability, and accessibility of a new system. This is done by interviewing users in depth about their experiences of using the system. These experiences also include how users perceive the effects of the system on the relationships between people, in particular their own role and empowerment. Thereby, side effects of using the system can be identified.

Interviews—Interviews are effective instruments for gathering stakeholder opinions and perceptions about the use and value of an artefact. Interviews also allow researchers to delve deeper into the stakeholders' views, as they can ask follow-up questions when needed. However, results from interviews are always dependent on the respondents' perspectives, interests, and competences, which needs to be taken into account when interpreting their answers. Furthermore, respondents are usually keen to be pleasant and polite when meeting researchers in person and assessing their results, meaning that they may withhold criticism and express more positive views than they actually hold. Thus, there is a risk of false positives.

Questionnaires—Questionnaires can be highly efficient for gathering the opinions and perceptions of many stakeholders about an artefact. However, the answers are often superficial and do not allow a researcher to gain a deep insight into the views of individual respondents.

Observation—While interviews and questionnaires are effective tools for understanding the subjective views and perceptions of stakeholders, observations offer researchers an instrument for a more objective evaluation. For example, an interview can reveal that some respondents perceive a new information service as easily learnable. However, perceived learnability should not be equated with actual learnability; observations may very well show that the service is not easily learnable, even though the respondents perceive it so, or vice versa.

9.6 Guidelines for Evaluate Artefact

- *Evaluate every requirement.* Each requirement identified in the activity Define Requirements should be evaluated.
- *Evaluate how the artefact can solve the problem.* Investigate not only how well the artefact fulfils the requirements but also to what extent it can address the problem.
- *Describe how the artefact was evaluated.* Explain what was done to evaluate the artefact, in particular how stakeholders were studied while they were using the artefact.

9.7 Summary of Chapter

- The question answered by the *Evaluate Artefact* activity is: How well does the artefact solve the explicated problem and fulfil the defined requirements?
- The *goals of an evaluation* include:
  - To determine to what extent an artefact is effective for solving the explicated problem.
  - To determine to what extent an artefact fulfils the identified requirements.
  - To investigate knowledge about the artefact, for example, about its structure, function, underlying kernel theories, and implementation principles.
  - To compare the artefact with other artefacts.
  - To investigate the side effects of using the artefact.

- An evaluation can be either formative or summative:

    - A *formative evaluation* means that the artefact is evaluated for the purpose of improving the artefact.
    - A *summative evaluation* means that the artefact is evaluated to give a final assessment of its utility.

- An *evaluation strategy* has to be chosen. This choice can be seen as a combination of ex ante or ex post, on the one side, and naturalistic or artificial, on the other.
- An evaluation strategy can be ex ante or ex post:

    - An *ex ante evaluation* means that the artefact is evaluated without being used, or even without being fully developed.
    - An *ex post evaluation* means that the artefact is evaluated after it has been employed.

- An evaluation strategy can be naturalistic or artificial:

    - A *naturalistic evaluation* means that the artefact is evaluated in the real world, i.e. within the practice for which it is intended.
    - An *artificial evaluation* means that the artefact is evaluated in a contrived and artificial setting, e.g. in a laboratory.

- The chosen evaluation strategy will affect the selection of research strategies and research methods to be applied in the evaluation.
- An *informed argument* is an ex ante, artificial evaluation in which researchers provide a line of reasoning to show that an artefact can solve the explicated problem and fulfil the defined requirements.

9.8   Review Questions

1. Why is evaluation not only about determining whether an artefact satisfies the requirements?
2. Which are the most important sub-activities of Evaluate Artefact?
3. What are the main advantages and disadvantages of ex ante evaluations?
4. Why can informed argument be an appropriate strategy for evaluating immature artefacts?
5. Can ex post evaluations be used for immature artefacts?
6. Why is internal validity often low for naturalistic evaluations?
7. Can models be evaluated through experiments?
8. Why can surveys based on questionnaires be problematic for evaluating complex artefacts?
9. Can models be evaluated with naturalistic evaluation strategies?
10. Why are naturalistic evaluations more appropriate than artificial evaluations for socio-technical artefacts?

9.9   Answers to Selected Review Questions

1. Even if an artefact fulfils all requirements that were elicited, it may still fail to address the practical problem for which it was intended. If this is the case, the requirements are probably inadequate or incomplete and need to be reconsidered. Thus, an evaluation also assesses the requirements indirectly.
4. Informed arguments can be carried out with limited resources in a short amount of time. These properties make them useful for evaluating immature artefacts, as it is usually not possible to spend large resources on evaluating artefacts that need a great deal of further development.
5. An ex post evaluation requires that the artefact is actually employed. As it is usually difficult to employ immature artefacts, ex post evaluations are seldom useful.
6. A naturalistic evaluation takes place in the real world, which means that many uncontrollable factors may influence the evaluation. In other words, it is difficult to distinguish the effects of using the artefact from the effects of other factors in the environment.
7. Yes. For example, the comprehensibility of a model can be evaluated by an experiment in which users are asked questions about the model. The number of correct answers can then be seen as an indication of the comprehensibility of the model.
8. For a complex artefact, it is important that a researcher can interact with a respondent in order to ensure that she has a good understanding of the artefact. But in a questionnaire, there is no room for interaction between the respondent and the researcher. Therefore, questionnaires can be problematic for evaluating complex artefacts.
9. Yes. A model can be evaluated by real users in real settings to solve real problems, e.g. using a drawing for building a prototype.
10. A socio-technical artefact involves humans and their social relationships. Simulating this complex social context in a contrived environment is difficult, which sometimes makes artificial evaluations less appropriate than naturalistic ones.

9.10   Further Reading

This chapter builds primarily on the work by Pries-Heje et al. (2008) and Venable et al. (2012). Mettler et al. (2014) propose an evaluation framework that can support researchers in conducting design experiments. Ge and Helfert (2014) propose a framework for guiding experimental evaluation in design science, consisting of three components: artefact, experiment, and data analysis. Tremblay et al. (2010) investigate the use of focus groups for artefact evaluation, making a distinction between exploratory focus groups that study an artefact in order to suggest improvements for further design (formative evaluation), and confirmatory focus groups that aim to establish the utility of an artefact in field use (summative evaluation).

Venable et al. (2016) propose a framework called FEDS (Framework for Evaluation in Design Science) for the evaluation of DSR results. FEDS offers a two-dimensional characterization of DSR evaluations. One dimension is the functional purpose of an evaluation (formative or summative), and the second dimension is the evaluation paradigm (artificial or naturalistic). This characterization helps a designer to develop an appropriate evaluation strategy that consists of several individual evaluation episodes that move from initial formative evaluations to a final summative one. Akoka et al. (2017) propose guidelines for selecting relevant evaluation criteria based on the type of DSR contribution and the role of the evaluator.

There is a great deal of literature on evaluation in various domains. For Human-Computer Interaction, a comprehensive introduction in the form of a presentation is given by Dix (2009). The evaluation of models and methods in information systems is discussed by Moody (2005). Clements et al. (2001) investigate the evaluation of software architectures.

References

Akoka J et al (2017) Evaluating knowledge types in design science research: an integrated framework. In: Designing the digital transformation, May 2017. Springer, Cham, pp 201–217

Clements P, Kazman R, Klein M (2001) Evaluating software architectures: methods and case studies, 1st edn. Addison-Wesley Professional, Boston

Dix A (2009) HCI 3e - Ch 9: Evaluation techniques. http://www.slideshare.net/alanjohndix/hci-3e-ch-9-evaluation-techniques. Accessed 26 June 2014

Ge M, Helfert M (2014). A Design science oriented framework for experimental research in information quality. In: Liu K et al (eds) Service science and knowledge innovation. IFIP advances in information and communication technology. Springer, Berlin, Heidelberg, pp 145–154

Mettler T, Eurich M, Winter R (2014) On the use of experiments in design science research: a proposition of an evaluation framework. In: Communications of the association for information systems, vol 34(10), pp 223–240

Moody DL (2005) Theoretical and practical issues in evaluating the quality of conceptual models: current state and future directions. Data Knowl Eng 55(3):243–276

Pries-Heje J, Baskerville R, Venable J (2008) Strategies for design science research evaluation. In: ECIS 2008 proceedings, January 2008

Sun Y, Kantor PB (2006) Cross-evaluation: a new model for information system evaluation. J Am Soc Inf Sci Technol 57(5):614–628

Tremblay MC, Hevner AR, Berndt DJ (2010) The use of focus groups in design science research. In: Design research in information systems. Integrated series in information systems. Springer US, New York, pp 121–143

Venable J, Pries-Heje J, Baskerville R (2012) A comprehensive framework for evaluation in design science research. In: Peffers K, Rothenberger M, Kuechler B (eds) Design science research in information systems. Advances in theory and practice. Lecture notes in computer science. Springer, Berlin, Heidelberg, pp 423–438

Venable J, Pries-Heje J, Baskerville R (2016) FEDS: a framework for evaluation in design science research. Eur J Inf Syst 25(1):77–89

Chapter 10
Communicate Artefact Knowledge

Within many fields of science, there are mature principles and structures for communicating research results. Many of these can also be applied to design science, but they sometimes need to be adapted, due to the practice-orientation of design science research.

10.1 Communicating with Different Communities

Typically, design science results are communicated to both research and practitioner communities, which may include both technology-oriented and management-oriented audiences. Design science results may sometimes be of such broad interest that it is worthwhile to communicate them to the general public.

Communicating results to researchers requires attention to rigour so that they can evaluate the results and build on them in future work. In particular, the knowledge base should be carefully described as well as its relationship to the results produced. The choice of research strategies and methods should be well justified, and the application of the chosen research strategies and methods should also be described in detail, including discussions on validity and reliability.

These concerns about methodology and related research are less relevant when communicating with practitioners. The focus is then primarily on problems and practice, as well as on concrete outcomes in terms of the structure, functions, and effects of the artefact.

Technology-oriented audiences, such as engineers, benefit from extensive details about the structure of an artefact, i.e. its components and their relationships. This information allows practitioners to construct and implement the artefact in a practice, and researchers to further develop it.

Management-oriented audiences are more interested in the problem the artefact addresses, what benefits it can bring to a practice, how easy it is to use, and its

© Springer Nature Switzerland AG 2021
P. Johannesson, E. Perjons, *An Introduction to Design Science*,
https://doi.org/10.1007/978-3-030-78132-3_10

overall effects, e.g. on efficiency and agility in an organisational setting. Knowledge about these aspects enables managers to determine whether to apply the artefact and how to apply it. The structure of the artefact, on the other hand, is typically less relevant.

When communicating with the public, the main focus is often on the effects of a novel artefact, including its ethical and societal consequences.

When disseminating design science results, the researcher needs to select the right communication channels, which depends on the target audience. For research communities, results are communicated primarily through academic journals, conferences, and workshops. Workshops often accept immature work and provide a forum for feedback and discussion about preliminary results, while journals mainly publish mature work that includes rigorous evaluation. For practitioner communities, research results can be communicated through trade fairs, white papers, magazine articles, blogs, etc. Regardless of the venue and target of the communication, it is valuable to present results in a clear and easily understandable structure, for example, the structure provided by the proposed method framework as depicted by the IDEF0 diagrams and the Design Science Canvas, described in Chap. 4. In many respects, this structure is similar to the IMRAD (Introduction, Methods, Results, and Discussion) structure, which is frequently used for organising empirical research papers.

10.2   The IMRAD Structure

In principle, research results can be presented using many different structures, and it could be argued that the structure chosen for a particular study should be individually tailored to the results presented. However, conventions help, and using a standardised structure for presentation makes it easier for a reader to follow the reasoning of a paper. The IMRAD structure has become an established norm for organising empirical research papers in both the natural and social sciences. IMRAD suggests that a research paper should be organised into four parts:

- *Introduction—why did you start the study?* This part offers a general background to the work presented in the paper. It provides an introduction to the area in which the study is situated, briefly summarises existing research including current knowledge gaps, explains the research problem addressed, formulates research questions or goals, gives an overview of the research strategies and methods that have been used, summarises the results, outlines the significance of these results, and describes the structure of the remainder of the paper.
- *Method—what did you do and how?* This part describes the research strategies as well as the methods of data collection and data analysis that were used, and how they were applied. It offers a justification for the selection of these strategies and methods and discusses research ethics.

- *Results—what did you find?* This part answers the research question of the paper. It presents, explains, and interprets the research findings. This is typically the main part of a research paper.
- *Discussion—what does it mean?* This part provides reflections on the research carried out and its results. It identifies limitations in the study, discusses the generalisability or transferability of the results, compares the results to those of other studies, discusses the practical and theoretical implications of the results, and points out areas requiring future research.

The IMRAD structure has become widespread because it can help readers to quickly browse through and navigate a paper and to identify relevant material. The structure ensures that the material is presented in a clear and logical form so that the reader can easily follow the argumentation of the paper.

10.3 A Structure for Design Science Papers

The IMRAD structure can also, with some modifications, be used to organise design science papers. The beginning (Introduction, Method) and end (Discussion) of IMRAD are unchanged, but the Result part is adapted to correspond to the kinds of contributions produced in design science research. This means that the description of the artefact becomes a fundamental part of the structure. The adapted structure consists of seven parts:

- *Introduction*. This part offers broad background to the work presented in the paper. In particular, it:

  - Provides an introduction to the area in which the study is situated
  - Describes the practical problem addressed and the practice(s) in which it appears
  - Explains the significance of the problem
  - Summarises existing research including current knowledge gaps
  - Formulates research questions or goals
  - Specifies the kind of artefact that is being developed and/or evaluated
  - Describes similar and alternative solutions to the problem
  - Presents kernel theories that have been used as a basis for the artefact design
  - Gives an overview of the research strategies and methods that have been used
  - Summarises the contributions of the paper
  - Outlines the significance of these contributions
  - Describes the structure of the remainder of the paper
  - May include a scenario that illustrates the relevance and significance of the problem addressed

- *Method*. This part offers an overview of the use of research strategies and methods used in the study. In particular, it:

  - Describes the research strategies and the methods of data collection and data analysis that were used
  - Justifies the selection of these strategies and methods
  - Discusses research ethics

- *Problem and requirements*. This part provides an elaborated description and analysis of the practical problem addressed. In particular, it:

  - Positions the problem within a practice
  - Justifies the importance of the problem
  - May include a root cause analysis
  - Defines the requirements for the artefact based on the problem analysis
  - Describes the processes of problem analysis and requirements elicitation, in particular the application of the selected research strategies and methods as well as the use of the knowledge base

- *Artefact*. This part, which is often the main part of a design science paper, describes the artefact. In particular, it:

  - Explains the structure, behaviour, and function of the artefact, preferably with examples
  - Describes how the artefact is to be used in practice
  - Describes the development process, including the design alternatives and design rationale as well as the knowledge base used

- *Evaluation*. This part describes how the artefact was evaluated. In particular, it:

  - Describes the evaluation strategy and the evaluation process, especially how the selected research strategies and methods were applied
  - Describes the findings of the evaluation, focusing on the strengths and weaknesses of the artefact, including its side effects
  - May describe a demonstration of the artefact

- *Discussion*. This part reflects on the research carried out and its contributions. In particular, it:

  - Identifies limitations in the study
  - Discusses the novelty and value of the artefact compared to existing ones
  - Outlines the practical and theoretical significance of the contributions
  - Discusses the ethical and societal aspects of the use of the artefact
  - Suggests areas for future research
  - May reflect on design science and the application of the method framework

- *Conclusion*. This part ties the paper together, showing how the research questions are answered (or how the research goals are achieved).

The structure suggested here will work well for most design science papers, but certain modifications may sometimes be useful. The Introduction part could be split into two (the additional part could be entitled "Extended background" or "Literature review"), for example, when the study builds on a large knowledge base or is situated in a particularly complex or less familiar practice. The Problem and requirements part could be merged into the Artefact part, for example, when the requirements are well known and no process to elicit requirements is needed. Another issue is that the parts Problem and requirements, Artefact, and Evaluation often have fuzzy borders, and how to distribute material over these parts is to some extent arbitrary. This fuzziness is due to the iterative nature of the process of artefact design and development, during which several formative evaluations can be carried out. Chapter 11 discusses these issues in more detail by distinguishing between temporal and logical orderings of activities.

10.4   Summary of Chapter

- The results of a design science project are typically communicated to research as well as to practitioner communities, which may include both technology-oriented and management-oriented audiences.
- Communicating results to researchers requires attention to rigour so that they can evaluate the results and build on them in future work.
- When communicating results to practitioners, the focus should be on problems and practice, as well as on concrete outcomes in terms of the structure, functions, and effects of the artefact.
- The IMRAD structure has become an established norm for organising empirical research papers in both natural and social sciences. The IMRAD structure can also be used, with some modifications, to structure design science papers. A suggested structure is: introduction, method, problem and requirements, artefact, evaluation, discussion, and conclusion.

10.5   Review Questions

1. What are the main types of audiences for design science results and how do their interests differ?
2. What are the main types of publication outlets for reaching academic communities and practitioner communities?
3. What are the components of the IMRAD structure?
4. Does the IMRAD structure reflect the empirical research process?
5. Why has the IMRAD structure become so widespread?
6. What are the main components of a design science paper?

7. Does the suggested structure for a design science paper reflect the process of design science research?
8. The description of the artefact is often the largest part of a design science paper. In what circumstances can it be a minor part?
9. Why should ethics be addressed in both the Method and the Discussion parts of a design science paper?

10.6   Answers to Selected Review Questions

4. No. The IMRAD structure is neat and linear, while the empirical research process typically is messy and iterative. However, this is not an objection to the IMRAD structure, as its purpose is solely to help organise research papers so they become easy to understand for readers.
5. The IMRAD structure helps researchers organise their papers to become easy to read and understand. The IMRAD structure has also become a well-established norm for how to organise papers, which means that readers are familiar with it. Thus, they can easily and quickly navigate in a paper that follows IMRAD.
7. No. See the answer to Question 4, which applies equally well, or even more so, to design science research.
8. If the research was evaluation focused, and the evaluated artefact is well known, the description of the artefact may be a minor part. The same holds for problem-focused and requirements-focused design science research.
9. In the Method section, research ethics is to be addressed (see Sect. 13.1). In the Discussion section, possible ethical consequences of using the investigated artefact are to be discussed (see Sect. 13.2).

10.7   Further Reading

An established and easy-to-read textbook on scientific communication was written by Booth (2008). Sørensen (2002) has written an entertaining paper on how to and how not to write scientific articles. Batmanabane (2018) provides a concise introduction to the IMRAD format. The structure for design science papers in Sect. 10.3 builds on a proposal by Gregor and Hevner (2013).

References

Batmanabane G (2018) The IMRAD structure. In: Sahni P, Aggarwal R (eds) Reporting and publishing research in the biomedical sciences. Springer, Singapore, pp 1–4
Booth WC (2008) The craft of research, 3rd edn. University of Chicago Press, Chicago

Gregor S, Hevner AR (2013) Positioning and presenting design science research for maximum impact. In: MISQ, vol 37(2), June 2013, pp 337–355

Sørensen C (2002) This is not an article. http://stuff.carstensorensen.com/papers/ThisIsStillNotAnArticlePre.pdf. Accessed 8 December 2020

Chapter 11
Systems Development and the Method Framework for Design Science Research

A quick look at the visual representation of the method framework presented in Chaps. 4–9 may suggest that it is nothing more than yet another version of the traditional waterfall model for software development. The *waterfall model* is a sequential design process, in which progress is viewed as a steady flow downwards over a number of consecutive phases (see Fig. 11.1).

The results produced in one phase are handed over as input to the next phase, meaning that a particular phase can only be started if the previous one has been fully completed. The phases in different versions of the waterfall model may vary, but typically include requirements specification, design, construction, testing, installation, and maintenance.

The waterfall model has been heavily criticised for being inadequate for guiding large systems and software projects in unstable environments. In the early stages of the development process, it is often impossible to define precise and complete requirements, meaning that the waterfall model grinds to a halt. As an alternative, rapid prototyping can be used to elicit requirements from stakeholders in an iterative way. By creating and testing prototypes of the software to be developed, stakeholders can improve their understanding and be able to articulate more precise and relevant requirements. Thus, there may be many short iterations between the specification of requirements, design, construction, and testing. For example, based on the requirements initially elicited from stakeholders, the first draft of a prototype is designed, constructed, and tested. The test results will prompt new or refined requirements, which will form the start of a new iteration with a refined design of the prototype, followed by additional tests. The result of these tests will give rise to yet more requirements, which are used to start another iteration, and so on (see Fig. 11.2). Furthermore, the environment may change during the development process, e.g. due to technological developments or government regulations, which implies that there may be a need to iterate all the way back to the requirements specification. The development process therefore becomes highly iterative as there is a need to obtain complex requirements and manage a changing environment.

© Springer Nature Switzerland AG 2021
P. Johannesson, E. Perjons, *An Introduction to Design Science*,
https://doi.org/10.1007/978-3-030-78132-3_11

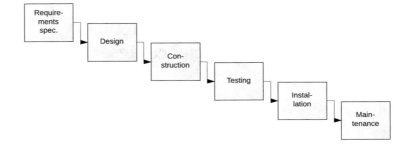

Fig. 11.1 A waterfall model

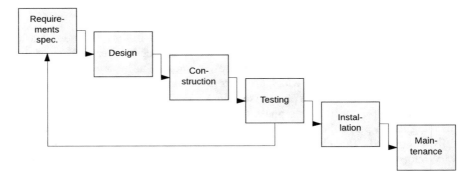

Fig. 11.2 A waterfall model with a simple iteration

11.1   Temporal and Logical Orderings of Work

As the visual representation of the proposed method framework for design science research may look very much like a sequential design process (see Fig. 11.1), it could be argued that the framework suffers from the same weaknesses as those of the waterfall model. In other words, it could be claimed that the method framework does not cater for vague requirements, changing environments, shifting stakeholder interests, unclear problem situations, etc. If this were true, the framework would not be of much interest. However, it does not prescribe a sequential way of working—the arrows in Fig. 4.1 do not indicate a temporal ordering but instead a logical one, expressed through input-output relationships.

In order to understand the difference between logical and temporal ordering, it is helpful to see how it is handled by the Rational Unified Process (RUP) framework. RUP is structured in two dimensions, phases and disciplines, which capture the serial and iterative aspects of software development, respectively (see Fig. 11.3). The phases represent the sequential stages that a project traverses over time, while the disciplines correspond to the logical activities that are carried out during

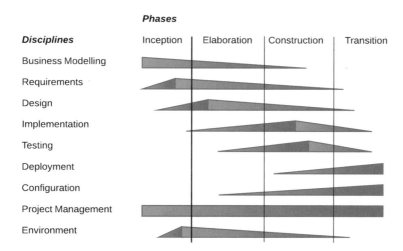

Fig. 11.3 Disciplines and phases in RUP

a project. RUP identifies four phases: inception, elaboration, construction, and transition. The inception phase aims to achieve consensus among the stakeholders about the objectives of the project; the elaboration phase specifies requirements in detail and outlines an architecture for the system to be built; the construction phase focuses on developing the system so that it is ready for deployment; and the transition phase delivers the system into production.

While the phases capture the serial aspects of a project in RUP, the disciplines address the iterative aspects. During each phase, software developers will alternate between (almost) all of the disciplines. For example, during the inception phase, developers will typically address a subset of the requirements, carry out some business modelling, return to the requirements and revise them, suggest an initial design, once again revise the requirements, do some coding and preliminary tests, and then improve the design. Furthermore, the inception phase can be broken down into several iterations, each of which only addresses a small portion of the system to be built, thereby making RUP even more iterative. Similarly, all of the other phases will also include several disciplines.

The relationships between phases and disciplines are shown in Fig. 11.3, which is sometimes called a *hump chart*. The humps for each discipline display how much effort is spent on that discipline in the various phases. For example, the diagram shows that most of the work on requirements is carried out in the inception and elaboration phases, but it continues all the way into the transition phase. The sizes and placements of the humps may vary from project to project and can be tailored as required.

Figure 11.4 shows a version of the hump chart, which is similar to a waterfall model, requiring that, for example, all work on business modelling and requirements be completed before any work on design be started.

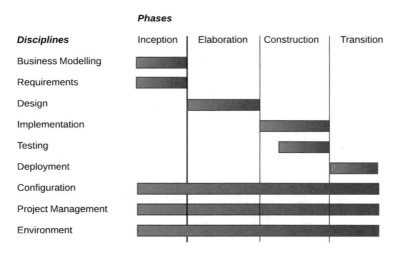

Fig. 11.4 A waterfall version of RUP

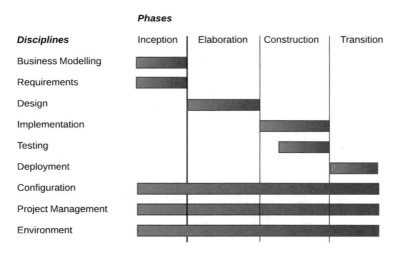

Fig. 11.5 An Agile version of RUP

Another version of the hump chart is given in Fig. 11.5, requiring that all disciplines be given equal attention in all phases. This kind of diagram reflects an extremely agile development process.

In our method framework for design science research, the activities correspond to the disciplines of RUP, not the phases. In other words, the activities are not sequentially ordered in time but can be performed in parallel and in any order. The activities only tell what tasks need to be done in the method, what input they consume, and what output they produce. Hence, the activities are ordered logically, not temporally.

11.2   Differences Between Systems Development and Design Science Research

The activities of the method framework and the disciplines of RUP look quite similar. Explicate Problem is similar to Business Modelling, Define Requirements is similar to Requirements, and so on. This observation holds not only for RUP but also for many other systems development methods. Thus, some new questions arise. Is the method framework redundant? Could it not be replaced by some systems development method? Why introduce a new kind of process when RUP already exists? The answers to these questions depend on the different purposes of design and design science, as introduced in Chap. 1.

The purpose of design is to create an artefact that fulfils the needs and requirements of certain stakeholders, possibly only for a local practice. In contrast, design science research aims to produce and communicate new knowledge that is relevant to a global practice. These differences in purpose give rise to three additional requirements for design science:

Use research methods—The purpose of creating new and generalisable knowledge requires that design science projects make use of rigorous research strategies and methods. These methods are essential in order to produce results that can be critically discussed, evaluated, and validated. One possible objection to this line of reasoning is that many systems development methods already include tools and techniques that are similar to research methods, e.g. techniques for interviews or participative requirements elicitation. Indeed, some of these tools and techniques are closely aligned with established research methods, but this is by no means always the case. Systems development methods only aim to produce effective solutions, not knowledge for global practices or additions to the scientific body of knowledge.

Relate to a knowledge base—The results produced by design science research must be related to an existing knowledge base, thereby ensuring that they are both well founded and original. It is not sufficient to just produce some knowledge; this new knowledge must also be integrated with previous knowledge in the area and must be shown to provide novel insights.

Communicate the results—The new knowledge should be communicated to both practitioners and researchers. This requirement of communication does not exist in most systems development methods, which instead include activities devoted to deployment and maintenance.

In a project for developing an IT system, the method framework can be used in tandem with any systems development method. The following is a typical scenario:

1. A systems development method is chosen.
2. The relevant parts (disciplines, workflows, tasks, or whatever they may be called) of the chosen method are mapped to the activities of the method framework.
3. The tools and techniques used by the method are inspected in order to determine how closely they correspond to adequate research methods.

4. The tools and techniques are adapted or complemented so that sufficiently rigorous research methods are used.
5. The work of the project is carried out according to the chosen systems development method and the selected research methods. In parallel, the project will include work to relate the results to an existing knowledge base.
6. The results are communicated to relevant audiences.

11.3 Design and Appropriation

People often adapt and use artefacts in ways that their designers never intended. For example, email was designed to support communication between people, but nowadays, it is regularly used by people to send reminders to themselves or to store copies of documents for safety. Dix (2007) describes this process of the adaptation of technology as follows. "These improvisations and adaptations around technology are not a sign of failure, things the designer forgot, but show that the technology has been domesticated, that the users understand and are comfortable enough with the technology to use it in their own ways. At this point we know the technology has become the users' own not simply what the designer gave to them. This is appropriation."

Designers should be aware that the artefacts they create may be appropriated in unanticipated ways. They could even try to design in ways that will facilitate appropriation. Dix (2007) suggests a number of guidelines for this, three of which are:

Allow for interpretation—All of the parts of an artefact should not have a fixed meaning. Instead, some elements should be flexible so that users can add their own meanings.

Provide visibility—The functions of an artefact should be made obvious to the users so that they are easy to understand. Users will then be able to make the system do what they would like it to do rather than only what the designer has decided.

Support, not control—An artefact should be designed so as to allow users to carry out many different tasks. This means that it should not be designed to enable users to perform only one or a small number of tasks with high control. Instead, the artefact should provide support for carrying out several tasks, even if the support is incomplete and approximate.

11.4 Summary of Chapter

- The method framework for design science research does not prescribe a sequential way of working. The activities should not be seen as temporally ordered but instead as logically ordered via input-output relationships.

- The main differences between design science and systems development are:

  - Design science research creates new and generalisable knowledge. Therefore, design science projects need to use rigorous research strategies and methods. In systems development, rigorous research strategies and methods could be used, but this is not a requirement.
  - Design science research results should be related to an existing knowledge base, thereby ensuring that they are both well founded and original, which is not a requirement in systems development.
  - Design science research results should be communicated to both practitioners and researchers, which is not a requirement in systems development.

- The method framework can be used in tandem with any systems development method when developing an IT system.

11.5 Review Questions

1. What are the main phases of the waterfall model?
2. Do you need to elicit all requirements before beginning work on design and development in a design science project?
3. Why is the waterfall model inappropriate for both systems development and design science projects?
4. What is the difference between temporal and logical orderings of work activities?
5. What kinds of relationships can exist between logical orderings of work activities?
6. How can the distinction between temporal and logical orderings of work help to model a work process so that it does not become a waterfall model?
7. How important is the use of research strategies and methods in design science projects? Why?
8. How important is the use of research strategies and methods in design projects? Why?
9. How do design work and design science research differ with respect to a knowledge base?
10. How do design work and design science research differ with respect to the use and communication of their results?
11. In what ways have social media been appropriated by different groups?
12. Can companies use design science in their product development?
13. What is the difference between the appropriation and the exaptation of artefacts?

11.6 Answers to Selected Review Questions

4. Temporal orderings interrelate work activities over time in a sequence, i.e. one activity precedes another activity in time. Logical orderings interrelate work activities according to input-output relationships.
5. The main kind of relationship between logical orderings of work activities is input-output, i.e. output from one activity can be used as input for another activity.
6. Temporal orderings are, by definition, relationships over time. However, logically ordered activities do not need to be ordered in time. The main problem of the waterfall model is that it requires logically ordered activities to be ordered in time, thereby putting a straightjacket on designers. By distinguishing between temporal and logical orderings, it can easily be shown how logically ordered activities can overlap with each other temporally.
7. Research strategies and methods are important for design science research to ensure the validity and reliability of the research results, i.e. to ensure scientific rigour.
8. Research strategies and methods are not very important for design work, which only aims to produce useful solutions and not knowledge that builds on and extends an existing knowledge base.
9. Design science research produces results that build on and extend an existing knowledge base, but this is not a requirement for design work.
12. When companies need reliable knowledge about their customers, they can benefit from using design science. For example, if a company wants solid knowledge about the requirements of their customers, it can make use of research methods for requirements collection, including interviews and questionnaires. Likewise, if a company wants to understand how their customers perceive its products, research methods for evaluation may be relevant. However, the goal of companies is not to produce knowledge but to create value for their shareholders and other stakeholders. Thus, scientifically founded knowledge is never an end in itself for a company but only a means to other goals. In many cases, it is still worthwhile to use research methods to obtain reliable knowledge that can be used as a basis for decision-making. But research methods come with a cost, in particular in terms of time. For example, carefully evaluating a product before launching it takes valuable time, which may result in a competitor being first to market. Therefore, companies often deliberately choose to refrain from scientific investigations in order to improve speed and flexibility.

11.7   Further Reading

Dennis et al. (2018) have written a textbook on methodologies for information systems development, which covers the systems development lifecycle, themes of systems development, as well as techniques, tools, and frameworks. Kroll and Kruchten (2003) have written an easily readable introduction to RUP, which introduces the fundamentals of component design and software architecture as well as the proper employment of use cases. The basic principles behind agile development were proposed by Beck and Beedle (2001).

References

Beck K, Beedle M (2001) The Agile manifesto. http://agilemanifesto.org/. Accessed 26 Jun 2014
Dennis A, Wixom BH, Roth RM (2018) Systems analysis and design, 7th edn. Wiley, Hoboken
Dix A (2007) Designing for appropriation. In: Proceedings of the 21st British HCI group annual conference on people and computers: HCI...but not as we know it - volume 2. BCS-HCI '07. British Computer Society, Swinton, pp 27–30
Kroll P, Kruchten P (2003) The rational unified process made easy: a practitioner's guide to the RUP. Addison-Wesley Professional, Boston

Chapter 12
Research Paradigms

A research paradigm consists of commonly held beliefs, assumptions, and norms within a research community about ontological, epistemological, and methodological concerns. Such a paradigm constitutes a mental model that influences and structures how the members of the research community perceive their field of study. A research paradigm answers ontological questions about the nature of reality, what entities exist, and how they relate and interact with each other. A research paradigm also addresses epistemological questions about the ways in which people can know about reality, i.e. how they can gain knowledge about the world. Finally, a research paradigm answers methodological questions about legitimate ways of investigating reality and how to confirm that the knowledge generated is valid. In summary, ontology asks "What is in the world?"; epistemology asks "What can we know about the world and how should we obtain that knowledge?"; and methodology asks "Which procedures can be used to obtain knowledge?".

Two well-established research paradigms are positivism and interpretivism. This chapter introduces these paradigms as well as the alternative paradigms of critical realism and critical theory and discusses their relationship to design science. See also Fig. 12.1, which relates research paradigms to empirical research strategies and methods.

12.1 Positivism

Positivism originated with the nineteenth-century sociologist and philosopher Auguste Comte, who attempted to establish sociology as a science by applying a natural science view on social phenomena. Comte introduced positivism as a reaction to the contemporary theological and metaphysical world views that embraced authority, divine revelation, and tradition as legitimate knowledge

© Springer Nature Switzerland AG 2021
P. Johannesson, E. Perjons, *An Introduction to Design Science*,
https://doi.org/10.1007/978-3-030-78132-3_12

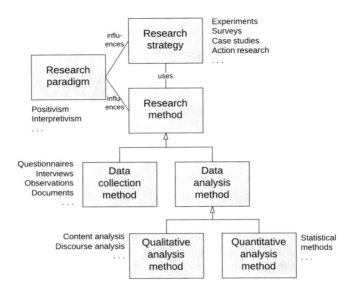

Fig. 12.1 Research paradigms, research strategies, and research methods

sources. In contrast, positivism accepts only knowledge that is based on sense, experience, and positive verification.

Ontologically, positivism assumes a reality that exists independently of human actions and experiences. Just as in natural science, the goal of social science should be to identify regularities among phenomena in the world and to explain them through cause-and-effect relationships. These regularities and explanations can and should preferably be independent of context, i.e. they should be general and should not depend on time, place, or people.

Epistemologically, positivism claims that objective knowledge about the social world is obtainable, but only through observation and experimentation. Social inquiry should be objective, and a researcher should assume the role of a disinterested observer who is separate from the subjects being investigated. In other words, researchers should keep at arm's length from the phenomena they are studying in order to ensure that their background and interests do not bias their findings.

Methodologically, positivist researchers strive for objective and value-free investigations, in which they distance themselves from the entities being studied. Preferred instruments for collecting research evidence are large quantitative studies, including interviews and questionnaires. Experiments are also highly valued research strategies, as they can provide objective knowledge.

Positivism, as described above, may seem natural and commonsensical. However, this is exactly the problem with the positivist paradigm, according to interpretivists. While positivism may be appropriate for natural science, interpretivists argue that it fails to capture essential aspects of the social world, in particular the subjective construction of social phenomena.

12.2 Interpretivism

Interpretivism emerged as a reaction to positivism at the beginning of the twentieth century. One of its forerunners was the German sociologist Max Weber, who claimed that the social world, including social actions, can only be understood through grasping the subjective meanings and purposes that people attach to their actions.

Ontologically, interpretivism argues that in contrast to the natural world, the social world does not exist "out there", independently of human actions and intentions. Instead, the social world is constructed by people who carry out social actions and give meanings to them. For example, housing contracts are created through social actions involving two or more individuals, a national government, and possibly other actors. The meaning of such a contract is not set in advance but is determined by the actors who enter into it. Furthermore, the meaning of the contract may change over its lifetime, as negotiated by the actors involved. It may also be the case that the actors do not fully agree on the meaning of the contract, but interpret it in their own different ways. In extreme cases, such disagreements may result in court trials, in which a third party, the court, decides how the contract is to be interpreted. This example illustrates that even a straightforward social phenomenon such as a housing contract is not part of a stable, objectively existing reality. Instead, it is constructed and continuously modified through the actions and interpretations of the actors who have an interest in it.

Any social phenomenon emerges as a result of the interactions and lived experiences of humans. This holds true for memberships in clubs, employment contracts, marriages, money, debts, holidays, religions, etc. All of these phenomena are created by people, and their meaning depends on the actions, intentions, and understanding of the individuals who participate in them. Thus, the social reality is much more elusive and fluid than the physical one, as it depends on people with all their whims, prejudices, interests, agendas, and other subjectivities.

The ontological differences between the natural and the social worlds have epistemological consequences. As social phenomena are grounded in the actions, experiences, and subjective meanings of people, only superficial knowledge can be obtained by studying people as if they were objects. Instead, a researcher should view people as subjects who are actively creating the social world. Researchers can only achieve a deep understanding of a social phenomenon by actively participating in that phenomenon together with the people who are actually creating it. They should not be detached observers, but instead should try to become members of the culture or group being studied by participating in their daily practices. In short, they need to walk a mile in the other person's shoes. These views and attitudes are in stark contrast to the positivist ideal of separating the researchers from their object of study. Such a separation is self-defeating in an interpretivist view, since subjective knowers are both a part and a source of the social reality they know.

Methodologically, interpretivist researchers prefer case studies, action research, and ethnography, as these research strategies allow them to arrive at an empathetic or participatory understanding of social phenomena. Researchers can get close to the people who are participating in the phenomena being studied and thereby come to understand their views and interpretations. However, this kind of methodology has been criticised for producing subjective research results that are highly dependent upon the skills and experiences of the individual researcher. There is a risk that two researchers with different backgrounds and interests may arrive at very different results. One answer to this criticism is that interpretivist researchers should always acknowledge their subjectivity and explicitly discuss how it may affect the validity of their results.

12.3   Positivism and Interpretivism in the Movies

As the arguments of interpretivism may seem somewhat abstruse in a first encounter, it can be helpful to make them concrete by putting them into a familiar context. One such context is provided by the 1993 stop motion movie *The Nightmare Before Christmas* produced by Tim Burton. This movie illustrates how difficult it is to understand and interpret the habits and symbols of foreign cultures.

The movie's main character is Jack Skellington, the Pumpkin King of Halloween Town, a place inhabited by ghouls, ghosts, vampires, witches, and other monsters. One day Jack stumbles upon a tree that is a portal to Christmas Town. He enters the tree and finds himself teleported to a friendly and joyful world, completely different from his own ghastly Halloween Town. The following video clip shows his impressions: http://goo.gl/yCV88.

The video illustrates how hard it is for Jack to make any sense of the people, activities, and things he discovers in Christmas Town, as they are so unrelated to his own experiences. Still, Jack wants to bring the Christmas spirit to his own people, and he calls for a town meeting when he returns to Halloween Town: http://goo.gl/zkSQt.

In the meeting, Jack presents his findings on Christmas to the Halloween Town residents. They may understand some basic facts about the holiday, but as Jack complains at the end of the scene, "they don't understand that special kind of feeling in Christmasland". The problem is that the town people immediately try to interpret Christmas in their own cultural terms. For Halloween Town residents, a present in a box is a pox. A Christmas sock contains a rotten foot. Toys bite, snap, and explode. Without even thinking about it, the Halloween Town people assume that their own views and experiences can be used to understand the world of Christmas. However, as any interpretivist would be happy to point out to them, this does not work. Gift giving, present wrapping, and other Christmas habits are social phenomena that are created and given meanings by those who participate in them. They cannot be understood by outsiders who are observing them in a casual and disinterested manner. But understanding is what Jack seeks, as he calls out in the next video "What does it mean?": http://goo.gl/r3GcP.

Jack seeks meaning in two ways. He first tries the positivist road with observation and analysis. He puts toys into vials, inspects rag dolls, and learns Christmas rhymes by heart. In some deleted scenes, Jack also dissects a teddy bear with a scalpel, dissolves candy in test tubes, and formulates equations about Christmas notions: goo.gl/j8Xxk. However, he soon realises that these kinds of investigations will not grant him any understanding of Christmas, "something's there I cannot see". So he then switches to an interpretivist mode, summarised in the phrase "Just because I cannot see it doesn't mean I can't believe it". Christmas is not understood by observing Christmas objects. Christmas is understood by believing it. Christmas is understood by making it. And the people of Halloween Town start making Christmas: http://goo.gl/7YVFe.

They become participants of the Christmas tradition by believing it, by making it, and by living it. No longer are they passive observers, but instead active creators. So through their lived experiences, they come to understand Christmas. Or do they? Of course, they do not, and their failure to understand drives the rest of the movie forward to its tragic end. Some may argue that this lack of understanding is a general rule and that people are so caught up in their own culture that they always interpret other cultures in terms of their own. They cannot step outside and truly understand a foreign culture, or at least their understanding is so limited and subjective that it cannot be trusted. Is this a fair conclusion? The movie offers an answer, but it would be a spoiler to give it here . . .

12.4 Positivism and Interpretivism in Design Science

While the differences between positivism and interpretivism may seem deep and substantive, it has been argued that many of the alleged differences are spurious, in particular the ontological ones (Weber 2004). Furthermore, some of the positions ascribed to positivists are outdated and not supported by anyone today. Positivists would nowadays certainly agree that some parts of reality are socially constructed, including most of the research objects in areas such as human-computer interaction, organizational security, and information systems. Historically, however, it has sometimes been assumed that many complex social phenomena are immutable and independent of time, place, and person. For example, phenomena such as childhood, gender, and honour have been treated as stable, well established, and independent of culture and time. Clearly, this is not the case—just compare the gender stereotypes of today's Scandinavia with those of nineteenth-century Prussia. Researchers who have assumed that social phenomena are culturally independent have, in practice, ascribed their own conceptions to people in other cultures, who have actually held widely different views.

Epistemologically, interpretivists do understand, and even appreciate, the positivist ambition for objectivity. However, they contend that objective research results are only attainable if researchers restrict themselves to surface-level phenomena in the social world, such as correlations between income and education level. In order to obtain deeper knowledge, the researcher needs to engage more closely with people to understand their views and interpretations. Obviously, this compromises objectivity, but the interpretivist sees this as a price well worth paying for the insights that can be gained. A positivist may be less inclined to make this trade-off and might argue that many results obtained through interpretivist investigations are so subjective that they are next to useless. Furthermore, the positivist may claim that typically positivist research strategies also can provide a deep knowledge of social phenomena, e.g. ingeniously designed experiments such as versions of the prisoner's dilemma or the ultimatum game.

Another epistemological issue is the social construction of knowledge. Here, positivists would acknowledge that any construct, framework, model, or theory is socially constructed, whether or not its subject matter is socially constructed. Thus, research results are always influenced by the culture, experience, and history of the researcher. This recognition is a cornerstone in Kuhn's account of how researchers develop theories, not only in the social but also in the physical and life sciences (Kuhn 2012). Thus, the ephemeral and culturally dependent nature of knowledge is acknowledged by positivist and interpretivist researchers alike.

As discussed earlier, positivists tend to prefer research strategies, such as experiments, surveys, and field studies, while interpretivists focus on case studies, action research, and ethnographic studies. The pros and cons of these research strategies follow the same line of reasoning as above. Simplifying somewhat, the positivist ones provide reliable but shallow knowledge, while the interpretivist ones offer deep but unreliable knowledge. In order to overcome the weaknesses of the respective research strategies, it has been suggested that they be combined. The interpretivist strategies could then be used to generate and propose research hypotheses, while the positivist ones could be used to verify them.

In design science, just as in empirical research, both the positivist and interpretivist paradigm can be applied. It is even possible, and indeed common, to make use of both paradigms in the same design science project. During problem explication and requirements definition, researchers may choose an interpretivist stance in order to obtain a deep understanding of the needs and wants of stakeholders. This understanding will help them to design and develop an artefact that is highly relevant to the stakeholders of a practice. For evaluation, however, they may value rigour more highly and may therefore decide to use positivist methods, such as extensive surveys and experiments, in order to arrive at objectively valid results. Still, interpretivist methods may also be appropriate for evaluation, especially if there is a need to understand the subjective experiences of users. In summary, a design science project can use and benefit from positivist as well as interpretivist strategies and methods, depending on the goal and context of the project.

12.5 Critical Realism and Design Science

Critical realism offers an alternative to both positivism and interpretivism. In contrast to some positivist views, critical realism argues that science is not only, not even primarily, about formulating laws that express constant relationships among observable events. Science goes beyond the observable by postulating structures, entities, and mechanisms that cause and generate that which can be observed. For example, biology not only records and describes how observable traits are inherited, but it also explains the mechanisms behind heredity through concepts, such as genes and alleles. Thus, science introduces entities and mechanisms that can be used to explain, and sometimes to predict, observable phenomena. However, these entities and mechanisms usually do not completely determine the observable properties and the behaviour of the systems in which they participate. Instead, they have only powers or tendencies that can contribute to certain outcomes, but these may be countervailed by other entities and mechanisms. For example, a person may have genes for tallness, but may still be short due to environmental factors.

Critical realism introduces three layers, or domains, to clarify the relationships between causal mechanisms, what they generate, and what can be observed:

- *The real domain* consists of underlying structures, entities, and mechanisms as well as the objects and events caused by them.
- *The actual domain* consists of events and behaviours caused by structures, entities, and mechanisms in the real domain, which can be experienced.
- *The empirical domain* consists of experienced events, i.e. events that someone has actually observed.

While some strands of positivism would claim that only perceivable entities exist, i.e. those in the empirical domain, critical realism states that all entities that can cause effects exist, i.e. all the entities in the real domain. In other words, existence does not depend upon perceptibility but upon causal power.

The preferred methodological approach in critical realism is retroduction, which is essentially equivalent to abductive reasoning. This kind of reasoning focuses on possible explanations for observed phenomena, and the inference goes from observation to some hypothesis that can account for the observation. As an example of abductive reasoning, consider the observation that the pavement is wet. One possible explanation for this observation is that it has rained—if it has rained, then the pavement is wet. Therefore, abductive reasoning generates the hypothesis that it has rained. Obviously, there may be other explanations for the wet pavement, e.g. that it was cleaned with water. Thus, abductive reasoning only generates explanatory hypotheses that have to be further evaluated and compared to competing hypotheses.

In critical realism, retroduction starts with some unexplained phenomenon in the empirical domain, and moves on to proposing some structure or mechanism in the real domain that can explain the phenomenon. In other words, there is a move from empirical observations to possible causal mechanisms. Since there may be several alternative mechanisms that can explain the same observations, retroduction is not sufficient in itself—it needs to be complemented with additional research that compares and evaluates the alternatives.

The philosophical underpinnings and methodology of critical realism can be valuable in design science research, in particular for evaluation. A positivist approach to evaluation may content itself by inspecting the outcomes of using an artefact in order to determine whether or not the artefact works. Such an investigation may have value, but it produces only shallow knowledge about the artefact use, as it goes no further than observable events. In contrast, critical realism emphasises the need to dig deeper and to study not only the observed outcomes but also the mechanisms that cause them, including the structure and behaviours of the artefact. However, it can be even more important to investigate the environment of the artefact and clarify the mechanisms that cause the outcomes. Researchers should strive to understand why and how an artefact works in its environment, not only that it works. Thus, they need to study the factors in the environment that can support or counteract the effective use of the artefact, and this is particularly true for socio-technical artefacts. These will include technological as well as psychological and social factors, such as power games, resistance to change, and organisation culture. In summary, critical realism encourages evaluations that provide thick descriptions, which include not only phenomena in the empirical domain but also those in the real domain.

12.6 Critical Theories and Design Science

The goal of most social sciences is to explain and understand social and cultural phenomena. *Critical theories*, in contrast, have also added the practical and ethical goal of seeking human emancipation. As expressed by Horkheimer et al. (1975), research should "liberate human beings from the circumstances that enslave them". Critical theories are not only concerned with how things are and why, but also how they might be or should be. Critical theories are critical in the sense that they question hidden assumptions and purposes in academic theories, as well as in political ideologies and cultural practices. By exposing these assumptions, critical theories can make people aware of the oppressing effects of established theories, ideologies, and practices. Such awareness is the first step towards change that can set people free.

As critical theories aim to reduce domination and increase freedom in all their forms, they have been applied in many contexts, including studies on race, gender, ethnicity, and identity. In an analysis of gender within a particular tradition or practice, a critical theory may ask questions about the equal status of women, whether they are demeaned or idealised, and whether they are ignored or patronised. The answers to these questions can help people start to understand if and how women are subordinated in the tradition.

According to critical theories, two of the most common forms of domination in modern society are alienation and reification. *Alienation* is about the psychological effects of exploitation and the division of labour, in which individuals are disconnected from both the tools of production and their fellow workers. In other words, people lose control of their lives and selves by not being able to control their work. *Reification* is about transforming social relationships into things; more precisely, the relationships become mediated and expressed by things, in particular commodities and markets. For example, the patriarchal relationship between a farmer and his farmhand is replaced by an impersonal relationship based on money and market valuations.

Critical theories and design science share the conception that describing and explaining the world is not sufficient—it also needs to be changed. Critical theories bring about this change by raising people's awareness of patterns of domination and subordination, thereby spurring them to action, whereas design science causes changes by developing and introducing new artefacts. However, critical theories and design science differ widely with respect to their goals. While critical theories aim to liberate people from oppressive structures, design science projects have the more limited purpose of satisfying stakeholder needs and wants. In other words, critical theories attempt to realise the universal values of liberty and autonomy, while design science projects are governed by the particular interests of the stakeholders of a practice.

These differences in goals may even give rise to conflicts. One example would be a design science project, in which a new information system is to be designed and introduced into a company. One group of stakeholders, the management, claims that the goal of the new system is to improve efficiency and productivity by eliminating routine work activities. However, a critical theorist could argue that the hidden motive of management is to better monitor, control, and evaluate employees, which would contribute to their alienation and reduce their autonomy. The critical theorist could even claim that the design science researchers are management lackeys who help to strengthen controlling and oppressive structures in the company. This example illustrates that design science researchers need to take a broad outlook during problem explication and requirements definition. They need to acknowledge the viewpoints of multiple stakeholders, and probe into the problem situation using different research methods, in order to gain a rich and unbiased understanding.

12.7   What Design Science Is and Is Not

Design science is still young, and some might say immature. In order to better characterise it, Baskerville (2008) discusses what design science is not:

Design science is not design—The purposes of design and design science differ with respect to generalisability and knowledge contribution, as pointed out in Sect. 1.6.

Design science is not a research strategy—Instead, different research strategies can be used in design science projects, as pointed out in Sect. 4.2.

Design science is not action research—Design science always creates or positions an artefact, which is not required in action research (see Sect. 4.7).

Design science is not a research paradigm—A design science project can benefit from both positivist and interpretivist approaches, as discussed in Sect. 12.4, as well as from critical realism and critical theory.

So, what is design science? The definition given in Sect. 1.5 states that design science is the scientific study and creation of artefacts as they are developed and used by people with the goal of solving practical problems. Thus, design science is one approach to investigating artefacts. Design science takes a problem-solving stance, starting from problems experienced by people in practices and then trying to solve them. It does so by creating, positioning, and repurposing artefacts that can function as solutions to the problems. In this work, design science includes empirical studies, in particular for problem explication and evaluation. Thus, by building and studying artefacts, design science creates knowledge.

12.8   Summary of Chapter

- A *research paradigm* is a set of commonly held beliefs and assumptions within a research community about ontological, epistemological, and methodological concerns:

  – *Ontological questions* are about the nature of reality, what entities exist, and how these are related and interact with each other.
  – *Epistemological questions* are about the ways in which people can know about reality, i.e. how they can gain knowledge about the world.
  – *Methodological questions* are about legitimate ways of investigating reality and how to confirm that the knowledge generated is valid.

- Two well-established research paradigms are positivism and interpretivism.
- *Positivism* is a research paradigm that:

  – Assumes that reality exists, independently of human actions and experiences
  – Claims that objective knowledge about both the natural and social world is obtainable, primarily through observation and experimentation
  – Prefers experiments and surveys as research strategies

- *Interpretivism* is a research paradigm that:

  – Assumes that the social world does not exist "out there", independently of human actions and intentions, but instead is constructed by people who carry out social actions and give meanings to them
  – Claims that researchers can achieve a deep understanding of a social phenomenon by actively participating in that phenomenon together with the people who actually create it
  – Prefers case studies, action research, and ethnography as research strategies

- *Critical realism* is a research paradigm that:

  - Assumes that science goes beyond the observable by postulating structures, entities, and causal mechanisms that are not observable and which generate events and behaviours which can be observed
  - Prefers the methodological approach of retroduction, which is a kind of reasoning that starts from an unexplained phenomenon and then moves on to proposing different structures or mechanisms that are able to explain the phenomenon

- *Critical theory* is a research paradigm that:

  - Claims that research should not only explain and understand social and cultural phenomena, but also strive for human emancipation
  - Claims that hidden assumptions and purposes in academic theories, political ideologies, and cultural practices should be exposed, thereby making people aware of their oppressive effects

12.9 Review Questions

1. What kinds of questions are addressed by a research paradigm?
2. How does a positivist researcher attempt to achieve objectivity?
3. Which research strategies and data collection methods are preferred by a positivist researcher? Why?
4. Which research strategies and data collection methods are preferred by an interpretivist researcher? Why?
5. Determine which of the following objects are socially constructed: a tree, a marriage, a gender role, Darwin's theory of natural selection, a vacuum cleaner.
6. Is it possible to achieve objectivity in the social sciences? How do positivists and interpretivists differ in answering this question?
7. Should researchers try to distance themselves from the people they investigate in a social science study? How do positivists and interpretivists differ in answering this question?
8. Why may interpretivist research be strong in proposing research hypotheses but weak in verifying them?
9. What are the main goals of critical theory?
10. How can modern Information and Communication Technology (ICT) solutions contribute to alienation and reification?
11. Why may both positivist and interpretivist research be relevant to design science?

12.10   Answers to Selected Review Questions

2. Positivist researchers try to achieve objectivity by keeping a distance to the phenomena they investigate. The researchers are disinterested observers who do not engage with the people they study.
3. To keep a distance, a positivist researcher can use large surveys with questionnaires and experiments that she strictly controls.
4. To attain a deep understanding of a social context, interpretivist researchers can use action research, case studies, and ethnography. These research strategies will allow them to arrive at an empathetic and participatory understanding.
5. A marriage and a gender role are socially constructed objects, as they are constructed, upheld, and continuously reinterpreted by people in a social context. The same is the case for Darwin's theory of natural selection. A vacuum cleaner is constructed by people, but as a physical object, it has an existence that is independent of people. Still, its function in a practice is determined by the people in that practice. Whether or not it is to be viewed as a socially constructed object depends on how you choose to define "socially constructed".
7. If researchers distance themselves from the people they study, they can be more objective, and the results may become less dependent on their interests and background. However, by staying at a distance, researchers may not be able to study people and their social interactions in depth, meaning that the research results may become shallow and fragmented. A positivist may emphasise the first argument, while an interpretivist may stress the second one.
8. Research strategies, such as action research, ethnography, and case studies allow for the study of social phenomena in depth, which can help a researcher to discover new and unexpected relationships and patterns. However, these research strategies are seldom strong in testing the validity of the proposed discoveries.
10. ICT solutions can be used to divide work tasks into small and isolated components, so that workers cannot see the larger context in which they are involved, thereby increasing alienation. ICT solutions can also be used to facilitate the use of mediating instruments, thereby increasing reification. However, ICT can also be used to counteract both alienation and reification.

12.11   Further Reading

Oates (2005) discusses research paradigms in the context of information systems and computing. An introduction to interpretivism is given by Burr (2003), who covers key debates on the nature and status of knowledge, truth, reality, and the self. Avenier (2010) investigates how constructivist epistemology and organisational design science can be combined to form a constructivism-founded scientific paradigm for organisation research. Bronner (2011) provides an overview of critical theory, discussing concepts such as method and agency, alienation and reification, repressive tolerance, non-identity, and utopia. Collier (1994) expounds and defends the main concepts of critical realism, including the stratification of nature and explanatory critique. Carlsson (2006) proposes a framework for design science research based on critical realism and applies it to artefact evaluation, as discussed in Sect. 12.5. Aljafari and Khazanchi (2013) investigate the veridicality of knowledge claims in design science research and propose scientific realism as an underlying philosophical stance. Vaishnavi and Kuechler (2004) discuss research paradigms and their relevance to design science. Baskerville (2008) discusses what design science is not.

References

Aljafari R, Khazanchi D (2013) On the veridicality of claims in design science research. In: 2013 46th Hawaii international conference on system sciences (HICSS), January 2013, pp 3747–3756

Avenier M-J (2010) Shaping a constructivist view of organizational design science. In: Organization studies, September 2010, vol 31(9–10), pp. 1229–1255

Baskerville R (2008) What design science is not. Eur J Inf Syst 17(5):441–443

Bronner SE (2011) Critical theory: a very short introduction. 1st edn. Oxford University Press, Oxford.

Burr V (2003) Social constructionism, 2nd edn. Routledge, New York

Carlsson SA (2006) Towards an information systems design research framework: a critical realist perspective. In: Proceedings of the first international conference on design science research in information systems and technology (DESRIST 2006), Claremont, CA, 2006, pp 192–212

Collier A (1994) Critical realism: an introduction to Roy Bhaskar's philosophy. Verso, London/New York

Horkheimer M et al. (1975) Critical theory: selected essays. 1st edn. Continuum Publishing Corporation, New York

Kuhn TS (2012). The structure of scientific revolutions: 50th anniversary edition, 4th edn. University of Chicago Press, Chicago

Oates BJ (2005) Researching information systems and computing. 1st edn. SAGE Publications Ltd, Thousand Oaks, CA

Vaishnavi V, Kuechler W (2004) Design research in information systems. http://www.desrist.org/desrist/. Accessed 26 June 2014

Weber R (2004) Editor's comments: the rhetoric of positivism versus interpretivism: a personal view. MIS Q 28(1), iii–xii

Chapter 13
Ethics and Design Science

As in any other kind of research, design science researchers need to address ethical issues. These relate not only to the work carried out in a research project, but also to the possible ethical and societal consequences that can follow from the use of a created artefact. This chapter starts by introducing a number of general principles for research ethics and then goes on to discuss ethical issues related to the information society. We conclude by a set of ethical principles for design science research.

13.1 Principles for Research Ethics

The overarching principle for research ethics is that the ends do not justify the means in the pursuit of knowledge. One way to operationalise this principle is to identify more concrete sub-principles that put constraints on research work, and four such principles are introduced below. These are not to be viewed as absolute rules always to be followed; instead, researchers need to balance these principles with the potential benefits of their research project.

Principle 1: Protect the interests of participants—This principle states that the participants of a research study should not come to harm. This implies that the researcher should take precautions to eliminate or minimise any risk of harm. In this context, harm may come in different forms: physical, psychological, and social harm.

The researcher should ensure that the physical safety of participants is not compromised. While this is an obvious concern for certain kinds of research, such as medical research, it can also be an issue for other kinds of research studies, e.g. those involving travels to and meetings in unsafe environments.

The researcher should also make sure that the participants do not suffer psychological harm. There is a risk of upsetting or embarrassing them if the researcher collects information about painful experiences or disturbing events. In extreme

© Springer Nature Switzerland AG 2021
P. Johannesson, E. Perjons, *An Introduction to Design Science*,
https://doi.org/10.1007/978-3-030-78132-3_13

cases, participants may even lose self-confidence or become depressed. To a large extent, the risk of harm depends on the capacity of the participants, which means that special care must be taken when vulnerable individuals, such as children, are involved in a study.

The researcher is required not to disclose information about the participants, as this could affect their social standing. In some cases, disclosure of information could even cause legal or economic harm, e.g. information on diseases could influence an individual's job opportunities or possibilities to obtain insurance. Thus, researchers should treat all information disclosed to them as confidential and not disclose it to others. They should also guarantee that the participants can remain anonymous, unless they have explicitly agreed that their names can be disclosed.

Principle 2: Ensure that participation is voluntary and based on informed consent—This principle states that no one should be coerced or fooled into participating in a research study. People should not be viewed as passive objects but as individuals with the right to decide for themselves whether or not to participate. Participation should not only be voluntary but should also be based on sufficient information, i.e. people should be informed about the purpose and design of the study so they can make a rational judgement about their participation. Only when people have this information will they be able to give informed consent to participate in a research study.

Participants can provide informed consent in different ways. They may sign a written consent form, which usually includes the following items:

* Name and contact information of the researcher, including her affiliation.
* The purpose of the study.
* The design of the study.
* Potential benefits of the research.
* Specification of the commitment made by the participant.
* Information on how the researcher will ensure the confidentiality of data collected.
* Information on how anonymity will be guaranteed.
* Information on how to withdraw from the study.

The general rule is to obtain written consent for any research study. Still, sometimes this is not possible or appropriate, e.g. when asking people at a bus stop about their travel habits. In such a situation, no sensitive data are collected, and tacit consent can be viewed as having been given if a person is prepared to answer questions. However, even in such situations, it is advisable to inform the participants orally about the study and their rights.

One of the most important rights of participants is the right to withdraw from a study. Even if participants have signed a consent form, it does not mean that they are obliged to take part in the research. If they change their minds and do not want to participate, they should be free to do so, and this right should be made explicit on the consent form.

Principle 3: Operate openly and honestly—This principle means that researchers should perform their work openly and honestly with regard to both participants and other researchers. Researchers should clearly inform other people about their study and work according to the standards of the scientific community. In particular, the researcher should:

- Refrain from deceiving participants about the purpose and design of the study, and instead provide full and clear information about it.
- Communicate the results of the study honestly, without being biased by personal preferences or demands from sponsors and other vested interests.
- Refrain from plagiarising the work of other researchers and instead give due credit to all sources that have been used for the study.
- Inform participants and others about the potential benefits that may arise from the study.

Participants should always be aware of the purpose of the study, which means that the data collected should not be used for other purposes. For example, data on shopping behaviour that have been collected in a research study may not be used by a company for advertising purposes. Another example is that social authorities providing compulsory care may not use data on an individual's drug abuse from a research study.

There are situations in which a researcher cannot be completely open with the participants, since certain studies require that participants are not fully informed, e.g. psychological experiments. Ethnographical studies may also require that researchers work in disguise, as participants may be unduly influenced if the researchers reveal their real intentions. Situations like these are problematic from an ethical point of view, and the researchers need to balance the requirements for openness and honesty with the possible benefits that can emerge from the study. One way to mitigate this ethical dilemma is to debrief the participants after the study has been completed and tell them why they were not correctly informed.

Principle 4: Comply with laws—This principle states that researchers should comply with the laws of the country in which their research is being carried out. The principle reflects the idea that researchers do not stand above the law but should abide by it as any other citizen. When collecting data, researchers need to pay special attention to laws on data privacy and intellectual property.

13.2 Ethics in the Information Society

In today's information society, new ethical challenges concerning individual and social life have emerged due to the development of Information and Communication Technology (ICT). This section offers an overview of recent discussions on these challenges.

13.2.1 Social Issues

Many ethical challenges in the information society pertain to social issues. What is common to these social issues is that they concern conflicting interests between social groups, and they can often be understood as struggles over the distribution of resources, e.g. between copyright holders and music listeners.

13.2.1.1 Intellectual Property

An ethically controversial issue relates to *intellectual property*. Property can be seen as a bundle of rights, in which owners have various rights on their property, in particular the use or exchange of it. For example, car owners have the right to drive their cars or to sell them. To protect property rights, modern societies provide advanced legal structures and instruments. For intellectual property, these instruments include the following:

- A *Copyright* is the right to make, use, and distribute copies of an original work.
- A *Patent* is the right a creator has on the use of an invention.
- A *Trademark* involves rights related to a sign that represents products or services from a particular source.

A natural question that arises is why societies spend so much ingenuity and resources on protecting property. Arguments for doing so can be based on natural law, essentially stating that because people own themselves and their labour, the results of their labour should also be their property. However, utilitarian considerations are more commonly used to defend property rights. It is argued that property rights are beneficial for the society as a whole because they provide incentives for individuals and organisations to innovate, create, and take responsibility.

Utilitarian arguments for property rights also extend to intellectual property. For example, if the property rights on works by writers, artists, musicians, and filmmakers were not protected, they might, in no small extent, cease to produce books, art, music, and movies, thereby reducing the cultural richness of their society. However, intellectual property has certain properties that distinguish it from goods and that make the protection of rights problematic. First, intellectual property is easy to reproduce, and in many cases ICT has brought the reproduction cost down to almost nothing. Secondly, the use of intellectual property is not, in itself, exclusive, i.e. if one person uses some intellectual property, this does not prevent another person from using (a copy of) it. Therefore, some would argue that society would be more prosperous if intellectual property were freely available, as this would allow everyone to benefit from it. Thus, there are valid utilitarian arguments both for and against the protection of intellectual property rights.

13.2.1.2   The Digital Divide

ICT has the potential not only to make societies richer but also to offer opportunities for more equality. However, there is currently a huge divide between people who have access to new information and communication tools, such as the Internet, and people who have no or only limited access to such tools. This situation is commonly called the *digital divide*. In addition to unequal access to ICT, the digital divide is also about the differences between those who have the skills and knowledge to use the technologies and those who do not. The digital divide is often seen as a threat to realising the opportunities that ICT offers. Therefore, governments around the world, as well as companies and non-government organisations, have launched initiatives to reduce the digital divide. Many of these initiatives have focused on providing Internet access, but education has also been an important component. While such initiatives are largely uncontroversial, there has been some criticism of their underlying assumptions. Walsham (2001) argues that the attention paid to the digital divide may have created a mindset in which people and lifestyles with low use of ICT are viewed as problematic. Such views can encourage policies that impose ICT solutions onto environments for which they are not suitable.

13.2.1.3   Work and Employment

Since their beginnings in the 1960s, ICT applications have substantially changed the kind of work people do. Much routine work, both manual and clerical, has been more or less automated. Other kinds of work have been radically transformed through personal and mobile computing, and also by the Internet. While ICT so far has reduced employment levels primarily for unskilled work, an open question is how it will affect the employment of knowledge workers in the future.

Brynjolfsson and McAfee (2014) argue that the global economy is entering a period of dramatic growth, driven by intelligent machines that make use of advances in computer processing, artificial intelligence, networked communication, and access to huge amounts of digital data. The networked machines will enable new kinds of ICT applications, such as self-driving cars and language translation based on pattern recognition of existing texts. These developments may create unprecedented wealth such as immediate access to vast cultural resources, but they also have a flip side. The new economy may lead to both higher unemployment and rising inequality due to the characteristics of digital production, as the marginal costs of producing ICT services often are close to zero. Furthermore, new ICT applications may replace not only unskilled workers, but also knowledge workers, such as doctors, lawyers, and teachers.

In addition to affecting the kinds and levels of employment, ICT may also change the relationships between employers and employees. It can provide employees with new sources of information, thereby empowering them and making them more independent. At the same time, ICT can also be used to monitor and control employees on a minute level, e.g. by recording keystrokes and tracking physical movements.

13.2.2   Individual Rights

The use of ICT has created new ethical challenges in balancing individual rights with public concerns, in particular with regard to freedom of speech and surveillance.

13.2.2.1   Freedom of Speech

Freedom of speech is a key human right in Western countries, and the Internet has created new opportunities for people to exercise this right. Social media now empower ordinary citizens to participate in dialogues that earlier were restricted to the elites of societies. Overall, this is viewed as a principal benefit of ICT, as it increases individual freedom and enriches societal discourses. However, these new opportunities can not only be used but also abused:

Hate speech—Hate speech is speech that attacks or offends a person or group based on race, religion, ethnicity, gender, sexual orientation, or other factors. The Web offers online spaces for spreading hate speech, and there are now a number of so-called hate sites.

Child pornography—Before the birth of the Internet, child pornography was difficult to obtain, but today it is easily available on the Internet.

Cyberbullying—Cyberbullying is the use of ICT to harm, harass, or threaten someone. On the Internet, bullies can hide their true identities, which makes it difficult to trace them and also encourages them to behave more aggressively than in a face-to-face interaction.

The line between use and abuse is undoubtedly blurred and varies between cultures and countries. What is viewed as a nuisance in one country can count as a severe offence in another. Government regulations also vary widely, but nowhere is the freedom of speech unrestricted.

13.2.2.2   Surveillance and Privacy

Surveillance is about monitoring people in order to control, direct, influence, or protect them. The word "surveillance" is based on the French words "sur", which means "from above", and "veiller", which means "to watch", indicating that surveillance is carried out by governments and other large organisations that observe individuals and groups. Surveillance can be of the Orwellian kind, where an oppressive and all-knowing government clandestinely monitors every aspect of the lives of its subjects. However, it can also be more mundane, for example, in the forms of web cookies, bonus programmes for loyal customers, and financial records.

Surveillance is becoming so central to the workings of everyday life in modern societies that some scholars have coined the term "surveillance society", arguing that in all aspects of life, people are the subjects of surveillance. At work, their performance is monitored by their employers. As consumers, their transactions are recorded by sellers and financial institutions. As computer and mobile device users, their information, interactions, and physical movements are recorded. Many people even contribute voluntarily to providing information about themselves and their environment, particularly through social media (Surveillance Studies Network 2012).

A recent related phenomenon is that of sousveillance, in which a participant of an activity records that activity by means of wearable or portable personal technologies. Simplifying somewhat, surveillance is about the elite watching the masses, while sousveillance is about the masses watching the elite (and themselves).

Surveillance has traditionally been carried out using low-technology methods, such as human intelligence agents and postal interception. Today, ICT offers numerous other information sources and methods, including social media, aerial vehicles, cameras, biometrics, satellite imagery, geolocation devices, and RFID tagging. Vast amounts of data are generated and analysed through big data techniques. Thus, ICT can be seen as the main enabler of the surveillance society.

The surveillance society brings substantial benefits, including increased security, more efficient markets, and improved personalisation for consumers. As stated by Jeff Jonas, "A surveillance society is not only inevitable, it's worse. It's irresistible" (Computerworld 2011). However, the surveillance society also poses serious privacy threats. Since governments and companies can record every phone call, every web search, and every financial transaction, they are now able to map out the lives of ordinary people in full detail, thereby making privacy an illusion.

13.2.3   Warfare and Terrorism

Throughout history, people have always used new technology for armed conflict, from knives and stones to predator drones. Today, ICT is becoming essential for both traditional warfare and terrorism.

13.2.3.1   ICT in Warfare

ICT has become a key technology in modern warfare between states with major effects in three areas. Firstly, ICT has brought about entirely new forms of communication, which have made novel types of field operations possible in conventional military conflict. Secondly, the analysis of big data collected by sensors has enabled the military to act ever more swiftly and accurately. Thirdly, as societies become more and more dependent on ICT systems and networks, digital or cyberspace attacks can have dramatic effects on the functioning of a society. Such attacks may be carried out not only by states but also by terrorist groups or even individuals.

An example of an ICT-enabled military technology is drone warfare. A drone is an unmanned aerial vehicle, i.e. an aircraft without a human pilot aboard. The drone is controlled either autonomously by onboard ICT systems or by the remote control of a human pilot. In warfare, drones offer the possibility of highly targeted attacks against military goals, which can limit the number of civilian casualties. While this can be seen as an advantage from an ethical point of view, there is also a risk that the limited harm done by drones can lower the threshold for military attacks. In some sense, war becomes more ethically acceptable when less harm is done.

13.2.3.2 Cyberterrorism

Terrorism is the systematic use of violence and threats to achieve some goal, often of a political or religious nature. The word "terrorism" has taken on strong negative connotations and is not used by those who carry out terrorist acts; instead, they prefer to call themselves freedom fighters, revolutionaries, patriots, etc. Terrorism and terrorists have received a bad reputation, primarily because their acts often inflict massive harm, often lethal, on innocent people. However, this situation may change with the advent of cyberterrorism.

Cyberterrorism is the combination of terrorism with cyberspace. Cyberterrorist attacks are intended to cause large-scale disruptions of computers, networks, and the information stored therein. As the Internet continues to expand and computers become ever more networked, the opportunities for cyberterrorism constantly increase. From an ethical point of view, cyberterrorist attacks may seem preferable to those of traditional terrorism, as they are less lethal. However, similar to drone warfare, cyberterrorism may lower the threshold for initiating hostile acts and thereby start processes that escalate into deadly violence.

In summary, the introduction of ICT into warfare and terrorism has made it easier to go to war, but the immediate lethal effects may be more limited than before. The ethical implications of this state of affairs are still an open question.

13.2.4 Personal Values

The information society may also have consequences for the personal values of people, especially regarding identity and inclusion.

13.2.4.1 Identity and Virtual Communities

In psychology and social science, *identity* is about an individual's conception and expression of her individuality or group membership, e.g. national identity or gender identity. Sometimes, people may perceive their identity as something valuable that provides meaning to their life. Still, they can also experience it as something degrading that others have forced upon them, such as being a slave or an outcast. Identities are neither singular nor fixed, i.e. a person may have multiple identities, which can also vary over time, such as being a mother, an Italian, or a lawyer. Furthermore, identity is not inherent in people but is shaped by how they perceive themselves, how others perceive them, and how others treat them. In other words, identity is socially constructed.

The identities of a person are constructed through social interactions, which can be carried out face-to-face or mediated through ICT. Thus, identities can be created and maintained through *virtual communities*, i.e. networks of people who use social media to pursue mutual interests or goals. Such communities may be essential for establishing identity when groups of people are scattered over large geographical areas and have difficulties in meeting each other physically, e.g. individuals with rare diseases. In such cases, a virtual community can be the only option for interacting with like-minded people. While virtual communities offer much promise for enabling new identities to be constructed, they also have a more sinister side. Virtual communities may be highly exclusive and accept only people with very similar and special beliefs and inclinations. In this way, they may reinforce prejudices and support narrow-minded identities in small and closed groups in which people become insulated from the broader society.

13.2.4.2   Inclusion and Technology

ICT offers new opportunities for *inclusion*, i.e. for including socially disadvantaged people in society. ICT solutions can make it easier to provide employment, healthcare, democratic participation, and other resources to individuals who otherwise would have had difficulties in obtaining them. One example is that ICT can offer disabled people alternative forms of communication that are adapted to their needs and requirements. At the same time, there is a risk that some ways of designing ICT solutions may exclude many people with disabilities. Inadequate ICT solutions may then be seen as creating disability, in the sense that people who could work well with older forms of communication may be more or less unable to use the new solutions.

One issue related to both identity and inclusion is the limited number of women in ICT jobs. Although ICT in the 1950s and 1960s was a new technology that could have attracted both men and women, it soon turned out that jobs in the ICT sector were primarily taken by men. The limited inclusion of women in the ICT job market, in particular as entrepreneurs, can be seen as an ethical issue as it reflects inequality between the genders.

13.3   Ethical Principles for Design Science Research

Just as in any other kind of research project, design science projects should adhere to the research ethics principles set out in Sect. 13.1. Design science projects should also consider the potential ethical and societal consequences of using the artefacts they produce. To capture these requirements, Myers and Venable (2014) have suggested a number of ethical principles for design science research, which are given below with some minor modifications and extensions.

Principle 1: The Public Interest—Design science researchers should explicitly identify all stakeholders who may be affected by the artefacts once they are placed into use. They should critically consider the benefits or harms that may result from using the artefacts. Generally, principles of safety, health, democracy, empowerment, and emancipation for all, especially the public, should dominate when choosing the features and capabilities that an artefact should or should not have. Social issues, as well as consequences for individual rights and personal values, should be addressed explicitly.

Principle 2: Informed Consent—Researchers in a design science project should obtain informed consent from any person who is in some way involved with the research project.

Principle 3: Privacy—Researchers in a design science project should ensure that there are adequate safeguards in place to protect privacy, not just for those people who are directly involved with the current project but also for those who might use or be affected by any developed software, system, or method in the future.

Principle 4: Honesty and Accuracy—Design science researchers should not plagiarise ideas but should acknowledge inspiration from other sources. They should also honestly report their research findings about the artefacts they create.

Principle 5: Property—Researchers in a design science project should ensure that there is an agreement about the ownership of the intellectual property (IP) right at the start of the project. There should also be an agreement on the ownership of any information that is collected during the project and what rights the researchers have to publish the findings.

Principle 6: Quality of the Artefact—Every attempt should be made to ensure the quality of the artefact(s) produced in a design science project. Where risks are potentially high, for example, in safety critical situations, design should account for and address such risks. Evaluation and testing should be sufficiently rigorous to ensure safety in use.

The above principles should not be seen as a recipe to be strictly followed, but rather as guidelines that can help researchers to reflect on ethical issues in their work. Conflicts between the principles may occur, which can be solved only by the careful consideration of researchers.

13.4 Summary of Chapter

- From an ethical standpoint, researchers in a design science project should:

  - Critically consider what benefits or harms an artefact may have on all possible stakeholders.
  - Obtain informed consent from any person who is in some way involved with the research project.

- Ensure that privacy is protected, not just for those people who are directly involved with the current project but also those who might use or be affected by any developed software, system, or method in the future.
- Refrain from plagiarising ideas and instead acknowledge inspiration from other sources.
- Ensure that there is an agreement on the ownership of the intellectual property (IP) right at the start of the project.
- Ensure that if the risks of using a created artefact are potentially high, the design should account for and address such risks and that evaluation and testing are sufficiently rigorous to ensure safety in use.

• Due to the development of information and communication technology, new ethical challenges concerning individual and social life have emerged in many areas, such as intellectual property, the digital divide, unemployment and inequality, relationships between employers and employees, freedom of speech, surveillance and privacy, warfare and cyberterrorism, and inclusion and exclusion.

13.5 Review Questions

1. One of the main principles behind research ethics is that the ends do not justify the means. Are there situations where this principle does not apply?
2. What kinds of physical, psychological, or social harm can be caused by a study on:

   (a) The use of photo sharing on social networks.
   (b) Responses to early childhood trauma.
   (c) The use of drones for civilian applications.

3. Should a researcher always obtain informed consent before involving a participant in a study?
4. The German journalist Günter Wallraff has become well known for his style of research, in which he covertly became part of the group he studied. Is this acceptable from the point of view of research ethics?
5. Are there situations in which researchers are allowed to break the laws of the country in which they carry out their studies?
6. Is it as important to uphold intellectual property rights in developing countries as in developed countries?
7. How can the digital divide be overcome?
8. Eric Schmidt, the former CEO of Google, has said that robots will ultimately eliminate all jobs that are not related to creativity or caring. Could ICT solutions also eliminate these jobs? (Ferenstein 2014)
9. Can smart speakers be used for sousveillance?
10. Why can both drone technology and cyberterrorism increase the risk of escalating violent processes?

11. What are the dangers of virtual communities?
12. How can ICT solutions support or hinder inclusion?
13. Are there any additional ethical principles for guiding design science research than those of empirical research?

13.6   Answers to Selected Review Questions

3. In principle yes, but in some cases the nature of the study may prohibit obtaining informed consent in advance.
4. "Wallraffing" is clearly problematic from an ethical point of view. One defence for the method is that it can reveal the ills of society that would have been difficult to discover through other methods.
10. In the initial phases of a conflict, drone technology and cyberterrorism often result in a small number of casualties. Therefore, the conflict may not be perceived as alarming, and people may allow it to continue until it escalates.
13. Yes, design science research produces artefacts, and researchers need to reflect on the possible ethical consequences of using them.

13.7   Further Reading

Most introductory books on research methodology include a chapter on research ethics. The principles of research ethics introduced in Sect. 13.1 build on those suggested by Denscombe (2017). Shamoo and Resnik (2014) offer a comprehensive introduction to ethical and legal issues facing researchers today. Section 13.2 on ethics in the information society is, to a large extent, based on Floridi (2010). This text addresses not only information and computer ethics in a societal context but also addresses the ethics of IT artefacts and foundational approaches, such as information ethics. Menell et al. (2020) address legal protections for intellectual property focusing on media issues, including computer software. Gilliom and Monahan (2012) explore surveillance and its relationships with issues of law, power, privacy, and inequality. Zuboff (2019) explores how the threat of surveillance has shifted from a totalitarian state to a digital architecture that enables companies to use surveillance data to predict and modify the behaviour of consumers. She argues that this behaviour modification will change not only the economic but also the social order and usher in an era of surveillance capitalism.

The ethical principles for design science research in Sect. 13.3 are based on the work by Myers and Venable (2014). Lee (2020) argues that ethical principles for designers and researchers are important but still have only a limited effect, as many of the most detrimental effects of introducing new artefacts in complex systems depend on factors that cannot be anticipated by the designers.

References

Brynjolfsson E, McAfee A (2014) The second machine age: work, progress, and prosperity in a time of brilliant technologies, 1st edn. W. W. Norton, New York

Computerworld (2011) Big data to drive a surveillance society. http://www.computerworld.com/s/article/9215033/Big_data_to_drive_a_surveillance_society?pageNumber=1. Accessed 31 May 2014

Denscombe (2017) The good research guide. 6th edn. Open University Press, Maidenhead

Ferenstein G (2014) Google's schmidt says inequality will be number one issue for democracies. http://techcrunch.com/2014/03/07/googles-schmidt-says-inequality-will-be-number-one-issue-for-democracies/. Accessed 22 June 2014

Floridi L (2010) The Cambridge handbook of information and computer ethics. Cambridge University Press, Cambridge

Gilliom J, Monahan T (2012) SuperVision: an introduction to the surveillance society. University of Chicago Press, Chicago

Lee EA (2020) The coevolution: the entwined futures of humans and machines. Illustrated edition. MIT Press, Cambridge

Menell PS et al (2020) Intellectual property in the new technological age 2020 vol. ii copyrights, trademarks and state ip protections: vol. ii copyrights, trademarks and state ip protections. Clause 8 Publishing. https://papers.ssrn.com/sol3/papers.cfm?abstract_id=3884159

Myers MD, Venable J (2014) A set of ethical principles for design science research in information systems. Inf Manag 51(6):801–809

Shamoo AE, Resnik DB (2014) Responsible conduct of research, 3rd edn. Oxford University Press, Oxford

Surveillance Studies Network (2012) An introduction to the surveillance society. http://www.surveillance-studies.net/?page_id=119. Accessed 16 Mar 2014

Walsham G (2001) Making a world of difference: IT in a global context. John Wiley Series in Information System, 1st ed. Wiley, Hoboken

Zuboff S (2019) The age of surveillance capitalism: the fight for a human future at the new frontier of power, 1st ed. PublicAffairs, New York

Chapter 14
Digital Consultations: A Case Study

Online medical consultations offer a convenient alternative for patients to communicate with physicians and possibly other health-care practitioners. They are especially valuable for people who live in rural areas, find it difficult to travel, or have busy schedules. Online consultations are enabled by video conferencing platforms and smartphone apps, through which physicians can interact with patients, diagnose them, and prescribe treatments. Many health-care providers offer online consultations, and some even specialise in them, providing no other forms of consultation.

The case in this chapter introduces a fictitious company, called DIGCON, that specialises in digital consultations. The company employs more than 500 physicians who carry out about 10,000 consultations daily. In general, patients are satisfied with the company's services, but lately there have been indications that the communication between patients and physicians is sometimes less than satisfactory. In order to address this issue, DIGCON has, together with a number of university researchers, initiated a design science project called DICOS (DIgital COnsultation Support). The activities of the project, which follow the method framework introduced in Chap. 4, are described in the following sections.

14.1 Explicate Problem

The first activity for the DICOS project is to explicate the problem. There are three sub-activities to be addressed: defining the problem precisely, positioning and justifying the problem, and finding its root causes.

© Springer Nature Switzerland AG 2021
P. Johannesson, E. Perjons, *An Introduction to Design Science*,
https://doi.org/10.1007/978-3-030-78132-3_14

The first sub-activity involves defining the problem precisely to reduce the number of ways in which it might be understood and interpreted. The initial problem was formulated as "Patients and physicians often miscommunicate", which is a vague formulation that is open to many interpretations. Addressing such a vague and broad problem is difficult, maybe even infeasible, and the problem therefore needs to be narrowed down to something more manageable. A document study is carried out, in which the logs of 2000 contacts between patients and the company are read and analysed with the aim of identifying a narrower problem. Based on this analysis and interviews with physicians at the company, a new problem is formulated: "Patients have difficulties in communicating their symptoms and medical history".

The second sub-activity involves positioning and justifying the problem so that the stakeholders can agree that it is worthwhile to address. The problem is clearly significant to the patients, as they may get inadequate care if the physicians do not correctly understand their health problems. The problem is significant to the company as it may reduce the quality of their services and hence alienate customers. The problem is also of general interest, as it occurs not only in DIGCON but also in other companies engaged in digital consultations.

The third sub-activity is to find the root causes of the problem so that these can be addressed rather than its symptoms. As a basis, academic literature in the area of health care is consulted, and two topics are found to be of particular relevance. Firstly, consultation models offer a patient-centred view of the interactions between patients and practitioners, taking into account both biomedical and psychosocial aspects, as discussed by Pawlikowska et al. (2007) and King and Hoppe (2013). Secondly, work on gaps and barriers to communication between patients and physicians investigates the feasibility and desirability of the patient-physician partnership, as discussed by Ting et al. (2016). In addition to this literature study, deep interviews with ten patients are carried out, and the answers are analyzed using thematic analysis. The following root causes of the problem are identified:

- Patients feel hurried and anxious during consultations.
- Patients are afraid of reporting symptoms that may indicate serious diseases.
- Patients forget what they wanted to say to the physician.
- Patients feel they do not possess the right vocabulary to express their concerns.
- Patients are often unable to relate their present concerns to previous health issues.

The Explicate Problem activity is summarised in Fig. 14.1.

14.2   Define Requirements

The second activity of the DICOS project is to define the requirements. There are two sub-activities to be addressed: outlining the artefact and eliciting requirements.

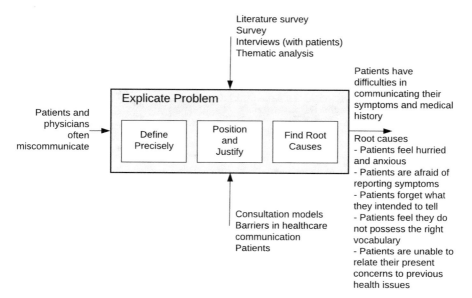

Fig. 14.1 Explicate problem for the case

First, the artefact is outlined. This means to decide on the type of artefact to be designed and its basic characteristics. The project concludes that one solution to the problem is a web-based service through which patients can list their symptoms and concerns before their consultation with a physician. Thus, the artefact is an instantiation in the form of a service that enables patients to provide detailed information about their situation before communicating with a physician.

To elicit the requirements, the relevant academic literature is consulted, including that used for problem explication. In addition, documentation on health informatics standards is studied to identify what types of knowledge exist in EHR (Electronic Health Record) systems. Furthermore, a number of patients and physicians at the company participate in semi-structured interviews, and the answers are analysed through thematic analysis. The most highly prioritised requirements for the service include the following:

- Patients shall be able to provide information about their symptoms, concerns, self-medication, family history, and risk factors.
- Patients shall be able to state the questions they want to ask the physician during the consultation.
- Patients shall be offered guidance, meaning that they are given follow-up questions when they report certain symptoms.

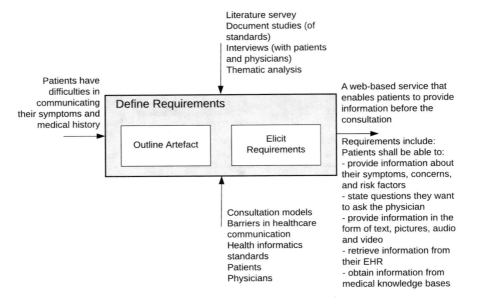

Fig. 14.2 Define requirements for the case

- Patients shall be able to provide information in the form of text, pictures, audio, and video.
- Patients shall be able to provide information both in a structured format and as free text.
- Patients shall be able to retrieve information from their EHR via the service.
- Patients shall be able to obtain information from medical knowledge bases through the service.
- The service should provide good usability.

The Define Requirements activity is summarised in Fig. 14.2.

14.3   Design and Develop

The third activity of the DICOS project is to design and develop the outlined artefact: a service that enables patients to state relevant information before the consultation. The activity is divided into four sub-activities, which are carried out iteratively and in parallel.

The first sub-activity, Imagine and Brainstorm, aims to generate a number of ideas for the service. This is achieved by carrying out a number of brainstorming sessions together with different stakeholders, including physicians at the company and representatives of patient associations. The brainstorming sessions are led by a trained facilitator, who encourages the participants to generate ideas on their own and to suggest them to the group before all participants start to generate ideas together.

The second sub-activity, Assess and Select, aims to decide which of the generated ideas should be used in the design and development of the artefact. Again, this is achieved in sessions including a group of stakeholders. The ideas generated from the brainstorming sessions are assessed based on their feasibility and the requirements defined.

The third sub-activity, Sketch and Build, aims to design and develop a set of service functions, their user interface (UI) representations in the form of UI components, and the overall architecture of the service. This is carried out by a small group of health informatics specialists, software engineers, and usability experts, who often work in pair design. The knowledge base for this sub-activity includes health informatics standards, such as FHIR and HL7, software engineering techniques, principles for service-oriented architectures, and UX design. Furthermore, techniques from expert systems are used to provide guidance to patients. The work in this sub-activity is closely intertwined with that in the Define Requirements activity. The group uses peer reviews in the form of walk-throughs during the design work to obtain feedback from different kinds of stakeholders. Finally, the group decides to design a layered architecture for the service. The reason for this choice is improved flexibility and maintainability, even though performance could suffer as a result.

The fourth sub-activity, Justify and Reflect, aims to specify the justification for the designed functionality and the structure of the artefact and its components, including a listing of and argumentation about the decisions made during the design process. Researchers also reflect on the entire design process and how it could be improved.

The Design and Develop activity is summarised in Fig. 14.3.

14.4 Evaluate Artefact

The final activity of the DICOS project is to evaluate the service. The first sub-activity is Analyse the Evaluation Context. The main constraint in the evaluation environment is that time is short before the launch of the service, meaning that it is not possible to conduct a time-consuming evaluation.

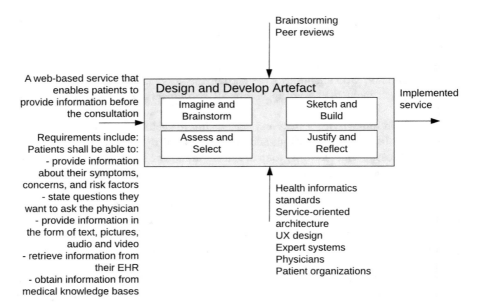

Fig. 14.3 Design and develop for the case

The second sub-activity is Select Evaluation Goals and Strategy, based on the evaluation context. The goals selected are about evaluating the utility of the artefact and the fulfilment of the defined requirements. It is decided that there is a need for two formative evaluations that can help to guide the design work, as well as a summative evaluation to ensure that the final service is ready for launch. For the formative evaluations, an artificial and ex ante evaluation strategy is selected, meaning that the artefact is evaluated without being used. For the summative evaluation, in contrast, the evaluation strategy is artificial and ex post. The goals and strategy are decided based on the short time available before the launch of the service—a naturalistic strategy would have been valuable but the time constraints did not allow for this.

The third sub-activity is Design and Carry Out the Evaluation. The formative evaluations make use of semi-structured interviews with physicians as well as specialists in usability and software engineering, who are provided with interface mockups, data structures, and a diagram of the software architecture. The summative evaluation consists of an experiment that introduces a prototype of the service for a group of patients. The patients are instructed to use the prototype to provide information about their situation for a fictitious consultation. Afterwards, the

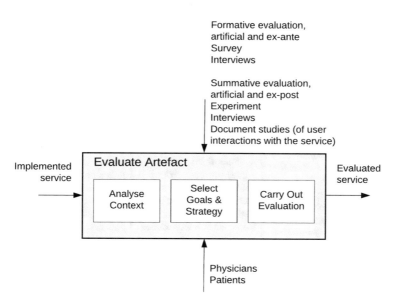

Fig. 14.4 Evaluate artefact for the case

patients are interviewed about their experiences. The interviews, as well as the patient interaction with the prototype, are video recorded and then independently analysed by two members of the research team.

The main conclusion is that the functionality offered by the service is adequate, but there are some concerns about its usability.

The Evaluate Artefact activity is summarised in Fig. 14.4.

14.5 Design Science Canvas Representation

A representation of the DICOS project in the form of a design science canvas is shown in Fig. 14.5.

Practice The practice is digital consultations within health care. The purpose of a consultation is for a physician to learn about the situation of a patient, including the patient's symptoms and medical history. The primary stakeholders are the patients and the physicians, but also other health care professionals, relatives and friends of the patient, and health care organizations. A consultation consists mainly of questions, which can be asked by both the patient and the physician, and answers to the questions.

	Research Process	**Artefact**
Problem The explicated problem was that patients have difficulties in communicating their symptoms and medical history. This problem may result in physicians not understanding the situation of the patients and, therefore, making incorrect diagnoses and ordering inadequate treatments.	For problem explication and requirements definition, a literature survey was carried out and health informatics standards were studied. Patients and physicians were also interviewed. For design and development, brainstorming and peer reviews were two important forms of activity. Both patients and physicians participated as well as IT specialists. Two formative evaluations, both artificial and ex-ante, were carried out in which physicians and IT specialists reviewed mockups and specifications. For the summative evaluation, which was artificial and ex-post, an experiment was carried out in which a group of patients used a prototype of the service and were interviewed about their experiences.	The artefact is a web-based service that allows a patient to provide information about their situation in advance of the consultation. The service asks both closed and open questions and allows the patient to complement textual answers with audio, photos and video. The information provided by the patient will be read by the physician before the consultation.
Requirements Patients shall be able to: - provide information about their symptoms, concerns, and risk factors - state questions they want to ask the physician - provide information in the form of text, pictures, audio and video - retrieve information from their EHR - obtain information from medical knowledge bases - . . .		**Quality and Effects** It was concluded from the evaluation that the service provided adequate functionality but that the usability was not fully satisfactory.

Knowledge Base
Academic knowledge about consultation models and barriers in health care information was used for problem explication and requirements definition. Health informatics standards were used for both requirements definition and design and development. The design and development activity also used knowledge about expert systems, SOA and UX.

Fig. 14.5 A design science canvas for the case

References

King A, Hoppe RB (2013) "Best Practice" for patient-centered communication: a narrative review. J Grad Med Educ 5(3):385–393

Pawlikowska T et al (2007) Consultation models. In: Learning to consult. Radcliffe Publishing, Abingdon, pp 178–215

Ting X et al (2016) Patient perception and the barriers to practicing patient-centered communication: a survey and in-depth interview of Chinese patients and physicians. Patient Educ Couns 99(3):364–369

Index